i puT a SpeLL on YoU

THE BIZARRE LIFE OF SCREAMIN' JAY HAWKINS

BY STEVE BERGSMAN

INTRODUCTION BY EUGENE ROBINSON

Feral House
1240 W Sims Way #124
Port Townsend WA 98368
www.feralhouse.com
10 9 8 7 6 5 4 3 2 1

Designed by designSimple

INTRODUCTION

SpeLLboUNd

It rankles. In the murk of America's wholly dishonest relationship with the confusion and our obsession with the confusion attending race relations, faking it until you make it has been deemed necessary by both greater and lesser personages. Martin Luther King Jr., I imagine, could have found half a dozen better ways to spend his weekends without getting his head kicked in, but compelled by higher ideals and a lot more than animal needs for cash and succor he took one for the team. Where it gets hazier is when we lose sight of what both "taking one" and "the team" are.

He stood off to the side of a stage in Portland, Maine. The usual receiving line for performers at the conclusion of a performance. I had, in a departure from my usual time on stage with OXBOW, performed with local greats Conifer in a special one-off encore. One song appended to a show that had seen me sing acoustic OXBOW songs. Lack of volume and electrification slowed none of the burn, and by show end the stage had been slathered with slobber, sweat and bile.

But there he stood. I had grabbed my suit in a sweaty bolus of clothing that would never come clean, before he spoke.

"I just watched your show." He was a light-skinned Black cat. Possibly biracial. Definitely shaking. Shaking badly enough that I noticed and I noticed enough to put my sweat-stinking clothing to the side. If I had to fight it always pays to be ready to fight.

"OK."

"Yeah. And I think it's going to take me some time to figure out why I'm so angry with you....It...it felt like....when I looked out at the audience....and then you on stage...I don't know. Like I was at some kind of SLAVE AUCTION."

In Portland, Maine the audience for an OXBOW show is mostly White. Not just Portland, Maine. Portland, Oregon, Berlin, Madrid, Helsinki, Rome or wherever else we've played in the 30 years we've been playing, excepting Japan. Me? I'm mostly Black, as I have consistently been since 1962.

So then from me to the twisted rictus of a face truly trying to figure "it" out, I laughed and then added right afterward, "As light-skinned as you are that maybe made you feel right at home?"

We stared at each other. Glared at each other. He shook his head. He walked away.

But you know Paul Robeson, Bill "Bojangles" Robinson and dozens up and down a long timeline of Black artists understood both the calculus of going along to get along *and* the need to rock your muse. Doesn't mean they liked it. Also, doesn't mean that they *didn't* like it. Sort of like how most of us manage life where we don't call the shots.

So when genius and payola-encrusted DJ Alan Freed decided to have Screamin' Jay Hawkins—a name Hawkins hated that he had been glossed with by his record label—climb out of a coffin in the mid-1950s, right after Hawkins broke big with the song that would end up defining his career, and to a certain degree his character, "I Put a Spell On You" Hawkins declined.

"No black dude gets in a coffin alive..." Hawkins reportedly said. Three hundred dollars later Hawkins climbed out of the coffin, sporting some variation of what would be a lifelong outfit of gold and leopard print, sharkskin suits festooned with voodoo accoutrements, up to and including a smoking skull on a stick that he called Henry.

Like the Kafka scribble about the children that had been given the choice of being kings or couriers of kings, it became pretty clear early on that Hawkins would have preferred to have given up his miserable game, but after stints in the military and an expanding base of both inside and outside children, well, a man's got to eat.

What Hawkins lacked as a father he more than made up for as a force on stage. As long as he was on the stage, which was nonstop from the 1956 release of his signature song to his death at 70 from an aneurysm on February 12, 2000.

And what he was on stage, the physically imposing former boxer, was a man who wholly occupied what he had created and, embodied by both his role as a creator and the creation itself: a player of a game that he was, beyond a shadow of a doubt, winning. This is the curse of the clown and the cure of the clown. Because while the bones through the nose and the drunken ooga-booga act were dangerously close to the kind of pop culture niggerisms that fundamentally drove comedian Dave Chappelle off of his feed when he walked away from his show and the $60 million paycheck for said show, Hawkins owned that shit. Every bit of it.

So while being vocal about how much he hated the prison it had afforded him creatively, he still managed to be creative within that prison. Well beyond competitors (a steady list of everyone covered by The Cramps over their wonderful career) and whole branches of rock that he could be credited with creating. From The Cramps to The Damned to maybe even the whole damn goth rock deal, the most significant lesson they had gathered even if not directly influenced was Hawkins' refusal to let there be any daylight between Jalacy Hawkins, his birth name, and Screamin' Jay Hawkins.

In other words, he didn't feel a need to laugh with you if you were laughing at him. He didn't feel any need to validate that this was "just" an act. He didn't exhibit any need to embrace "serious" arts to take what he had done and who he was as the person who had done it, seriously.

He was as he was. Like other great American icons and here Popeye comes most quickly to mind with his "I yam what I yam."

And beyond that with his hair conked to the high heavens and the gun-brandishing, drinking, philandering, tall tale telling, personal reinvention, TV, movies, later songs of note like "Constipation Blues," "Feast of the Mau Mau" and "Frenzy," Hawkins rode life hard and clearly put it away wet. Regardless of how out of step he might have been in the '50s, '60s and, well, pretty much any time.

Yeah, it was that kind of edge-riding that made Hawkins as a ride so well worth taking. He made everyone uncomfortable and uncomfortable for as many ways and reasons as there were. Black folks for his jive-y primitivism, White folks for his unmistakable sexuality, men for the threats to their physical safety represented by a Negro with cash and a gun, and women lest they fall under the spell that got him 33 kids.

There was no corollary that did it as long and as well. Ol' Dirty Bastard recalls him but Ol' Dirty Bastard is dead while Screamin' Jay lives on. In about 43 recorded pieces of history, eight films and several hundred cover versions of a song he had written but was so drunk when he recorded it that he had to re-learn it later when it became a hit.

Not just a hit but name a song covered by Nick Cave, Nina Simone, Bryan Ferry, Marilyn Manson, a disco version by Sonique, Grammy noms, Billboard charts, the Rock and Roll Hall of Fame's 500 Songs That Shaped Rock and Roll, and a Rolling Stone magazine nod for being one of the 500 greatest songs of all time.

And standing on stage in England on an OXBOW tour, well lubricated, wearing nothing but shoes and underwear, bottles exploding around my head on the wall behind me because I had just choked an audience member into unconsciousness for having totally misunderstood what's going through the mind of a well-lubricated, near-naked man on stage, I bust loose with a little doggerel before trailing off with "because you're mine."

Screamin' Jay Hawkins is dead. But digging deep, deep, *DEEP* into the writhing guts of all of that libidinal heat that marked his magnificent place in the not always hospitable space of modern music and culture, he lives on and on and on. Now, most significantly, in this giant of a book you're about to read. It marks, with great certainty, that voodoo, hoodoo and magic happen all the time for those whose grasp of it is unapologetically long, hard and hot.

And for Hawkins—broke, flush, stoned or stone cold sober—it always was. As it most definitely should be, and sometimes even is.

—Eugene S. Robinson,
author of *Fight: Everything You Ever Wanted to Know About Ass Kicking But Were Afraid You'd Get Your Ass Kicked for Asking* (Harper Collins), *A Long Slow Screw* (Robotic Boot), and *The Inimitable Sounds of Love: A Threesome in Four Acts* (Southern), also sings for OXBOW when not whiling away his time as editor-at-large for OZY.com.

PREFACE

kARma

"We went to Chicago to do a gig; actually it was just outside the city. The venue was a bar/club, and the owner was this old Irish guy by the name of Flaherty," remembers recording artist and record producer Robert Cutarella, who early in his career played in Screamin' Jay Hawkins' backup band.

"I called him old man Flaherty because he looked like he was in his seventies. He looked old but you could tell he had been a real force when he was young; a tough guy from Ireland who had made his way in America. Now, Screamin' Jay Hawkins, when we traveled, always carried a gun. So, we arrived at the club, and Flaherty had Jay's name spelled wrong on the marquee. He spelled it Harkins instead of Hawkins. We looked at the sign and turned toward Jay. You could see steam coming out of his ears. We said, 'Oh shit, this is not going to be good.'

"Meanwhile, the old man was just happy to meet Jay. He comes out of the club saying, 'Hi, Mr. Harkins, how are you?' Jay scowls.

"'The name is Hawkins,' he says menacingly, and he pulls his gun and points it at the man's face. 'You better fix my name right now.'

"The old man was stunned and more than a little shaken. He exclaimed, 'No problem, we'll fix it right away.' And the next thing you saw was Flaherty with his crew out there. They're on the ladder fixing the name. We all felt terrible."

Robert continues, "The interesting part was that night they had a stage with a curtain that closed. Jay decided to start the set with 'I Put a Spell on You.' Jay jumps in the coffin, which was lifted, and set in the middle of the stage. As the curtain opens, the smoke machine went off with colored smoke blowing everywhere. The band starts playing. This was the signal for Jay to pop out of the coffin. Nothing was happening. Then, we see the coffin starting to shake, and we hear from inside all these expletives. None of us wanted to open the coffin, because we felt it was karma for the old man who had been trying to be nice and do the right thing. Jay had been in there two minutes and finally he pops out, whiter than me. He's so distraught, he forgets the words to the song. Ginny goes on stage and gives him some pills. Karma is a bitch."

Over a lifetime, Jay generated good karma, but that was nothing compared to all the bad karma that piled up around him.

A personable guy who made friends quickly, Jay could charm a snake out of its rattles, or a friend out of his last $10 bill. Women loved him, and he loved them back in his own eerie way. He slipped engagement rings on many a dainty finger, only to end up marrying someone else with a daintier hand. Those who did marry him had to be all things, from nursemaid to stagehand, and sometimes even procurer. He abandoned one wife, married one without divorcing a prior, and is said to have beat another wife. His musical talents were immense, but once he found a groove, he could not let go of it. He became stuck in time, expecting the large audiences that once propelled him to success, and the payout that came with such performances. As his star faded, Jay refused to adapt, or to work for rates that were in line with his new reality. After decades of similar vocal stunts and shows, he was trapped in his own tonal coffin, suffering unnecessarily due to his own larger-than-life obstinacy. When he wasn't charming—which was often—he was dangerous, argumentative and unscrupulous. He burned a path through agents, venues, promoters and even friends. However, through the wreckage, he always took care of his musicians.

CHAPTER

1

**in** Nicholas Triandafyllidis' wonderfully entertaining documentary *Screamin' Jay Hawkins: I Put a Spell on Me*, we first see Jay sitting in the back of a limousine where he is being interviewed. The year is 1999, and Jay was 70 years old, but he looks like a man 20 years younger. The camera finds him in a semiclose-up, from about mid-chest upward. He wears glasses, which oddly reflect the outdoors. He sports a thin strip of a mustache, a quarter-inch wide over the top lip. A large brownish hat covers his hair; otherwise he is dressed in a well-coordinated black jacket shirt with white adornments, and a bolo tie with a black core.

Hawkins is relaxed in front of the documentary camera. He has spent most his life on stage, and this is just another extension of reaching an audience, which he does here, not through singing but storytelling. Hawkins is an off-kilter songwriter, but with the spoken word, when it comes to recounting stories of his life dating back more than 50 years, he is either a fabulist extraordinaire or a performance artist, forever trapped in a role that he created for himself, like an insect in amber.

The story Jay tells Nicholas and the cameraman is about his World War II years. It's a yarn that he has told forever—to girl-friends, bandmates, Hollywood folk and now to this documentarian. Jay has been telling this story for more than a half-decade. To him, it wasn't a story, but a pronounced truth, something that he had viscerally experienced, even if it only existed inside his head. The story shows his character, his bravery, his perseverance and his ability to survive. The story also shows his penchant for lying, and creating grandiose fabrications.

The version of this story that he tells the camera is longer, more elaborate and with a few life-affirming axioms—he's 70 years old, and lessons have been learned over the years. The camera rolls and so does Jay. Like a good storyteller, he eases into it, riffing evenly, and without hesitation.

"In the Second World War, my outfit got run over by a battalion of Japanese, and I was isolated for eight months in one of these Japanese internment camps. I was a sergeant. I did a lot of killing. I didn't have no [sense of] danger. I figured they were going to kill me, so I killed as many as I can. And it was beautiful to me to take a life, knowing that I didn't have to go to jail; but he's the enemy and if I don't kill him, he'll kill me.

"They overran our camp; we were asleep. So this guy says he's a sergeant. He saw my stripes. He says, 'We want to know the strength, how many people, how many mechanized.' I said, 'Let me tell you something, you can ask me—I was raised in America, I went to Yale, and you know asking me questions ... will get no answers because I am black in America, and they don't even tell me what time the chickens wake up. They put me over here and told me to fight, or they would kill me. So, you got me, do what you want. You want to torture me. Kill me, because I don't know nothing because all I want to do is scream you to death. I'm going to make enough noise to drive you crazy. But you might as well kill me. I'm over here killing you, so you might as well kill me.'

"They turned around and beat me for about three months. Every morning they stuck knives in my butt, in my thighs. I got knife marks here and here [he points to spots above his eyebrows and neck]. The doctors said I have more scars than a crossword puzzle. I became a joke. They said, 'don't bother him, he don't know nothing.' When they caught the American white boys, they were mad because I wasn't tortured. I said, 'I was tortured before you got here, but I don't expect you to believe it.' They said, 'Why don't they ask you questions? We don't know nothing.' I said, 'You're white you gotta be right; I'm black so I gotta get back.' They didn't like me making jokes, but it's the only way—to laugh when you are facing death. You got to find something to live and be happy about or you are dead anyhow.

"When they did save us, the 82nd Airborne came through there and they liberated us from that camp; so I told them, 'Give me a gun and in one hand a grenade and leave me alone for about one hour.' They said, 'What are you going to do?' I said, 'I want the [unintelligible].' I busted in and shot three of his guards before I got to him. And then, I tied him up, and put him in a chair. He said, 'What's your problem? We stopped bugging you.' I said, 'But what you done to me, I gotta get even.' I forced the hand grenade into his mouth, and taped it around his head. I looked at the door, yanked the pin, and ran and leaped out the door. On the ground, I watched his whole head disappear. Then I gave the guy back his gun, and I said, 'OK, we can go now.'"

Jay told so many versions of this story that it ended up being a part of his mythology. Liner notes to an anthology of his songs wrote it this way: "At the age of 14, Jay joined the army. He saw plenty of fighting in the Pacific: '13 combat missions,' he says." The story becomes more confusing when the liner notes change direction later on. "He helped to clean up Okinawa, where the Japanese were still fighting even when the war was over. He also saw duty in Germany and Korea."

Military records show that Jay was honorably discharged in June 1952; but he sometimes claimed to have been invalided out of the Armed Forces earlier, having sustained an injury from a hand grenade in a Korean foxhole. That version almost jibes with the tale he relayed in the early 1980s to writer Gerri Hirshey, who was informed that Jay sustained vast "war injuries incurred when a grenade blew him clean out of his South Pacific foxhole."

Mike Armando, who played in Jay's backup band during the 1970s, said Jay told him he was in the service in Korea and it "felt so good when he was in the service because he could kill legally." It didn't make any difference how close you were to Jay, or what kind of break you might have given him, you got the same bullshit as everyone else.

In Nicholas Triandafyllidis' documentary there is a lengthy interview with movie director Jim Jarmusch, who cast Jay in his 1989 film *Mystery Train*. Jim, who clearly had a warm relationship with Jay, retells the tale: "When he was captured by the Japanese, he was tortured." As a result, Jay had a big problem interacting with Asians; but in the film he had to work with two young Japanese actors. Jim had to help Jay through a reacclimation process.

Having to overcome his apprehensions about interacting with Asians because of the horrors suffered during his war years is an interesting embellishment, especially because Jay had been married to a Filipino American woman for nearly two decades.

Writer Nick Tosches spent time with Jay in 1973, writing about their time together in his book *Unsung Heroes of Rock 'n' Roll*. Tosches gets very close to the truth. "He [Jay] quit high school in 1945 and went to work in the Special Services division of the U.S. Army-Air Force, performing at service clubs throughout America, Germany, Japan and Korea."

Nick could have been referring to the United Service Organization's (USO) camp shows program, which was initiated by President Franklin Roosevelt during World War II. It recruited, and fielded, live professional entertainment for military shows. As all units of U.S. Armed Services boast military bands that perform a variety of events, it is likely that someone with Jay's musical talents would have been welcomed into this select group of musicians.

Performing in the Special Services Division was not quite like being on the front lines dodging hand grenades, or being tortured in a prison camp, yet Jay always returned to the grimmer but much more interesting tales of derring-do. Eighteen years after his interviews with Nick Tosches, Jay sat for an interview with Karen Schoemer of the *New York Times*. Jay told her that he went to fight in World War II in 1944: "I got caught on the island of Saipan when I found out that our drop zone was right in the middle of the enemy compound. Before we could get the straps of the parachutes off, we were in the enemy's hands. We never got a chance to fire a shot. They had a field day on us—those who survived. Those who didn't survive I felt were lucky. It was 18 months before we got rescued."

Schoemer, based on her interview, wrote: "Mr. Hawkins stayed in the armed forces until 1952, and also fought in Korea."

To other interviewers, the incidences of being captured, starved, tortured and, later, wreaking vengeance, happened during the Korean War. Jay sometimes forgot what war he was fighting. Was it World War II? Or was it the Korean War?

According to the U.S. National Archives and Records Administration, the term of Jay's enlistment was six years, and he enlisted in December of 1945. World War II officially ended in September 1945. He had missed that war. He was honorably discharged in June 1952. The Korean War started in the middle of 1950. The Army would have had to ship Jay overseas very quickly for him to see action, get captured, rescued and returned home. So far, no record of Jay having combat service in Korea has turned up.

When Jay began telling this story he probably assumed no one would check—or could check—his military enrollment records, so he had carte blanche to tell whatever story he wanted. As wonderful as his tales of heroism on the battlefield and as a prisoner of war were, none of them were true. Jay was simply a talented performer in the Special Services Division of the Army. Combat would always be a thousand miles away, no matter how much effort he spent trying to convince the public otherwise.

There is a germ of truth to Jay's stories, but he preferred to craft his life history into a series of grand fairy tales—which is odd because he was such a larger-than-life character to begin with. His real-life history was more colorful and bizarre than anyone else who ever stood behind a microphone. Through it all, he wailed a song that captured the audience's imagination in the 1950s, beyond his death and up to this very day.

CHAPTER 2

Jalacy J. Hawkins'

father is unknown, but his mother was Marie Hawkins. According to his daughter, Lee Anna "Sookie" Hawkins, Jay had three sisters, Ireeta (Rita), Clara and Avine, although, at various times in his life, he would declare he was one of seven children.

After interviewing Jay, a British reporter wrote this brief biography: "His mother had six other children, each by different fathers. 'My mother didn't want me,' he [Jay] says. 'She just wanted a good … what's that word … orgasm. Before I was born, they ran her out of Washington and she went to Cleveland, where she put me in an orphan home.' He says he knows nothing of his father except that he was Sudanese. 'And that he was no good. That's all my mother ever told me.'"

The American version of that story, which Jay told Nick Tosches, went like this: "There were seven of us with one mother and different daddies," he explained. "My sister once told me that as long as my mother didn't mess with no black people, she had it made. She had babies by a Chinese man, and a baby by a white man. My father was from Arabia. I understand my mother was pregnant with me in Washington; they stoned, beat and kicked her and forced her to get on a bus and go to Cleveland. The bus arrived in Cleveland just in time for her to have me, and drop me at the nearest welfare center."

In either story, there is a strong undercurrent of anger at his mother.

What's interesting is that when Jay released his first album, *At Home With Screamin' Jay Hawkins*, in 1958, the liner notes played it straight: "Screamin' Jay Hawkins was born in Cleveland, Ohio, in 1929, the youngest of four children."

After that, Jay's history gets a bit blurry although there is definitely a reason for his anger at his mother.

According to Jay, after he was born, he was sent to an orphanage before being adopted by a family (sometimes it was a tribe) of Blackfoot Indians.

In one interview, the reporter wrote, "he says he was born … to a prostitute who left him at an orphanage. He says he was adopted by a wealthy Blackfoot family that taught him Indian culture." To Nick Tosches, he said, "Then she talked a tribe of Blackfoot Indians who were very wealthy into taking me out of that welfare home when I was 18 months old."

Here's what we know about Blackfoot (Blackfeet) Indians. The name "Blackfoot Confederacy" applies to four Native North American bands that spoke a similar language and mostly lived in the Canadian provinces of Saskatchewan, Alberta and British Columbia. They were an aggressive tribe, and were among the fiercest of the warriors who inhabited the northern plains of the North American continent. Horses originally came to this loose grouping of related tribes through trading with another tribe called Kutenais. This latter conglomeration of families were then driven across the Canadian Rockies by the Blackfeet who not only had horses, but guns as well, exchanging furs for weapons with the white traders exploring in what today is Canada. The Shoshones, who roamed across the American Great Plains, thought they could raid with impunity into the more northern stretches of North America, but the Blackfeet, who over the decades became very adept with the white man's weapons, drove them back out of the Canadian provinces.

There is only one band that remained in the United States, in Montana. There the Blackfeet Indian Reservation, sometimes called the Blackfeet Nation, sits east of Glacier National Park and encompasses about 1.5 million acres. Other than farming, there's not a lot of employment in isolated Montana, so a Blackfeet family could have migrated to Cleveland for work.

In an early interview, he referred to the woman who raised him by saying, "I *called* her my Blackfoot Indian." The woman who raised Jay had the un-Indian name of Edith Randolph. Jay's oldest daughter, Sookie, remembers Edith Randolph well and she believes the woman she called Mrs. Randolph was a Native American. "I could tell by the food she cooked. The things she did. She didn't cook like my mom. Everything was natural, came from the ground. I learned a lot from her ... to make everything from scratch."

What we do know for sure about Edith Randolph was that she ran a boarding house at 2268 East 49th Street in Cleveland, and was a foster parent. As Sookie says, "one of those foster kids was Jay."

In one of the most extensive and in-depth liner notes to a Screamin' Jay Hawkins compilation album, the producer Bear Family Records in Germany noted, "official records confirm Jay's natural father was unknown and that he was raised in a foster home with a foster mother, Mrs. Edith Robinson [sic]."

Sookie was born in 1950. At the time, Jay and his wife Anna Mae were living in Mrs. Randolph's boarding house. In fact, all Jay's children by Anna Mae were born in the house where Jay lived as a child. "It was fun," says Sookie. "Even though there were three different families in the house, we were all one big family. When Mrs. Randolph cooked, she didn't just cook for herself, she cooked for everyone. She acted like the mother of everyone." Sookie knew Mrs. Randolph well. "She was a kind woman. She helped my own mother take care of us [Jay's three children, Sookie, Irene and Jalacy Jay Jr. by his wife, Anna Mae] even though she was an elderly woman. She told my mother what to do with us because my mother was like a baby who had babies."

In 1991, Jay was interviewed by the *New York Times* and recalled, "My mama said that out of all the men, my father was the hardest, the meanest and the rottenest. She would look at me and say, 'You're no good, you're gonna be just like your father.' I said, 'I'm gonna fool you. I'm gonna make something of myself.'" What is interesting about this story is that Jay claims he was in communication with his mother, which means he knew who she was and had some kind of relationship with her. That part of the story is definitely true.

Marie Hawkins lived nearby to Edith Randolph in an African American neighborhood, walking distance to downtown Cleveland. Anna Mae's sister, Helen Vernon Branner, when growing up, lived on East 40th Street in Cleveland. "It was an old neighborhood, but not bad. It was a village to us. Everybody knew everybody. We played on the streets, outside all the time, without fear. It was an African American neighborhood with the stores owned by Jewish and Italian shopkeepers. There was a community swimming pool, movies and bowling alleys. Then they tore it all down when I was in junior high school and built a community college."

Even Helen knew Marie Hawkins. "We used to see her all the time. She used to come by to visit. She was a nice person as far as I knew. She would come over to see Jay's children and then come by our house as well when she was in the area."

Marie Hawkins was a compassionate, tearful woman, says Sookie. "She would come and see us when we were little and she would come during the holidays, bring us gifts, and later on, would read us letters from my father when he was in prison because my mother would have him put in jail when he wouldn't pay child support."

From what Sookie could understand, Marie Hawkins suffered much remorse for not being able to raise Jay. When visiting her grandchildren, she would hold them tight, rock back and forth, crying "Jay, Jay, Jay."

The reason that Marie Hawkins decided not to raise Jay, and put him into foster care instead, remains a family puzzle that not even her grandchildren can solve. One thing everyone knows for sure is that Jay resented her for it. "Jay didn't have a good relationship with his real mother," says Sookie. "When his mother gave him away, it really messed him up. He always talked about it, lamenting, 'Why did she give me away? Why did she keep the other kids? Why me?'"

When Marie Hawkins died, Jay didn't even attend the funeral. Decades later, he told Alex Kalofolias "a very moving story" about going to his mother's grave with one of his siblings, who told him that his mother was so poor, she could not afford to be buried in the grave. Jay was so emotional when telling this story, Kalofolias succumbed to the performance, commenting, "Jay had an almost a biblical quality about him."

For a time, the real love story of Jay's life was Anna Mae Vernon, whom he married in 1949. The two met at Rutherford B. Hayes Elementary School, stayed friends through Kennard Junior High School and went to East Technical High School, where they both dropped out of school. They were best friends as children and then high school sweethearts.

Anna Mae was one of eight children. Her father worked for the city of Cleveland and her mother was a homemaker. She was about five-feet-six, slim, and by all accounts "gorgeous," with a happy-go-lucky personality.

Helen Vernon Branner was 13 years younger than her sister Anna Mae, and mostly remembers Jay before her sister got married. "He came over to our house a lot. He would eat over or just snack. He was just fun to be around, and spent a lot of time with us kids. Everybody laughed when he was around. Usually, they went skating. That was their main activity, and I remember that more than anything because he always had his skate pads hung from his shoulder when he came to pick her up. He always dressed neatly and he was always loud. He hollered a lot, and in a crowd, he was the loudest one. He was so tall; we just admired him at that time."

Helen attended their wedding. "They got married in 1949. Jay was still in the service and got married in his uniform. The marriage was at his sister Clara's house. It was just a small family gathering. I was just six years old at the time."

Helen saw her sister less and less afterward as Anna Mae gave birth to her first child, Sookie. Jay was still in the service, and when he would come home, he would tell stories about such exotic places as Alaska and Korea, places Helen couldn't even imagine.

In 1950, Jay and Anna Mae were a happy couple with one child. Two more children would follow: Irene in 1951, and Jalacy Jr. in 1956.

"My father and my mother were like best friends," says Sookie. "They partied together and danced together. My father used to flip my mother over the top of his head and through his legs. Boy, they knew how to dance. And she loved his music. My mother played the piano, wrote music and helped my father when he was starting his career. My mother once told me she was the one who wrote 'I Put a Spell on You' but let Jay take all the credit. She loved her husband."

Helen put it this way about Anna Mae: she was naïve and in love with Jay.

Jay once said that his raucous voice developed during childhood, when Mrs. Randolph whipped him with a barber's leather strop. In an even more bizarre story, he told musician/actor Robert "Smokey" Miles that he learned to sing from a Jewish cantor. Jay also said that he studied opera at the Ohio Conservatory of Music. Jay could have been referring to the Cleveland Institute of Music, or he could have just made up the whole thing on the spur of the moment. According to Jay's fanciful accounts, either Mrs. Randolph was very cruel or benevolent, but the one thing she wasn't was wealthy, so it is doubtful that Jay went to something called the "Ohio Conservatory." There is a College-Conservatory of Music at the University of Cincinnati, downstate, a long way from Cleveland. As a foster kid from upstate Cleveland, it is unlikely that Jay even visited Cincinnati.

In one interview, Jay claimed his "Blackfoot family" bought him expensive clothes, had him tutored in classical music and that his greatest love was opera, which inspired his stage act.

Mike Armando, who was in Jay's backup band during the 1970s, said Jay loved opera and used to sing it.

In 1999, when Jay was in Greece to film the documentary about himself, Demetra Madzouka, one of the producers for the film, spent the day with Jay, driving him around Athens. Then, as a surprise, she took him to the Athens Opera House, because, she says, "I knew his dream was to perform opera." They walked and talked while touring the opera house. Jay, who wasn't in good health, had to sit. Afterward, Demetra and director Nicholas Triandafyllidis came up with the idea to have Jay perform at the opera house.

Liner notes to one of his albums state that Jay studied piano, listened to Paul Robeson and that he was besotted by opera. Apparently, Jay had a talent for music and began to play at an early age. Although Edith Randolph wasn't "wealthy," she could have easily paid for music lessons. Jay would have first learned classical music when beginning his lessons, and would have listened to people like Paul Robeson. In Cleveland, he would have also heard the barrelhouse blues players coming up from the South.

Jay told writer Gerri Hirshey that at 12 years old, he quit taking lessons from the piano teacher his mother hired for him because he wanted to play like the blues-jazz pianists he heard on the radio like Big Bill Broonzy. Jay was getting an extracurricular lesson in music theory.

Starting about 85 years ago, a section of Cleveland known as Doan's Corners was a hotbed of jazz music and fun. In the 1950s, this part of town boasted several movie houses (at the Keith, you could watch two features and a vaudeville show); a huge, indoor ice rink (remember Jay and Anna Mae skating); shops and delis—all of which drew throngs. Cleveland, then the sixth largest city in the country, was so vibrant that Doan's Corners became a second downtown. All the major jazz musicians—Billie Holiday, Louis Armstrong, Art Tatum, Miles Davis among many, many others—would play Doan's Corners venues such as Tia Juana, Loop Lounge, Club Rendezvous, Gleason's, and the legendary Lindsay's Sky Bar.

From the moment it opened its doors in 1936 behind the Fenway Hall Hotel, Lindsay's Sky Bar on Euclid Avenue became "Grand

Central Station" for jazz on Doan's Corners. When owners Phil and wife Rickie Bash hired a boogie-woogie pianist to liven things up, the local folks flocked to the tavern and the Bashes decided to move to grander quarters just down the street. The music room, according to the *Cleveland Plain Dealer*, was decorated in blue and striking red—the decor was heavy on the crimson including the tufted bar seats. The ceiling was adorned with twinkling stars. The feeling inside was electric in every way. By the early 1940s, Phil and Rickie began booking major jazz acts such as Coleman Hawkins and the Nat King Cole Trio. The entertainment columnist for the *Plain Dealer* wrote, "Lindsay's Sky Bar continues to fly high as the town's most profitable temple of feverish jazz music." The club closed in 1952 and one of its last star billings was the jazz-bluesman Tiny Grimes—the man who would later give Jay his first chance to shine in the music business.

Jay was musically inclined, and so was his girlfriend, and eventual wife, Anna Mae. In Cleveland they would have received universal exposure to some of the most groundbreaking acts in music.

Talented, uninterested in school and with World War II still fresh in everyone's mind, Jay lied about his birthday and enlisted at the age of 16. In the Special Services Division of the military, Jay learned how to play the saxophone, which was becoming a staple of the smaller bands and combos who were belting out the blues in the Cleveland clubs. Whenever home, while on leave from the service, he could see and hear the new music at the local clubs, especially those on Doan's Corners, which began to showcase some rougher, but often jovial music from the likes of Bull Moose Jackson, Eddie "Cleanhead" Vinson and Peppermint Harris. There was a lot of fun stuff out there—all one had to do was listen and learn. Jay listened with attentive ears. He applied the sounds, rhythms and rule-breaking performances he saw at the packed Cleveland venues to his very own stage show once his time was ready.

Besides music, Jay had one other outlet: boxing.

In Gerri Hirshey's wonderful 1984 book *Nowhere To Run: The Story of Soul Music*, the first chapter, "Sympathy for the Devil," is all about Screamin' Jay Hawkins. The chapter is introduced with a quote from Jay, "I wish I could be who I was before I was me." Even Jay knew that his artfully crafted history and larger-than-life persona were too much to bear.

By the 1980s, Jay had told so many stories about his life that he had lost track of whatever grain of truth there might have been to start. Gerri, a great writer, unfortunately caught Jay in his high point of confabulation. In the 1980s, every Jay story was suspect. Gerri wrote, "at 55, Jay is a tall, robust man, with square shoulders and a long, tensile reach that helped him snare the Golden Gloves middleweight crown in 1947."

The Golden Gloves champ story has a lengthy beginning, going back at least to 1957 when a magazine reported: "He [Jay] earned a reputation as a solid left-hooker in the fight ring, winning the 1947 Golden Gloves and two years later beating the middleweight champ of Alaska, Billy McGinty [actually, McCann]." Eventually Jay went on record saying he beat Billy McCann to become the middleweight champ of Alaska. Billy McCann, a nice guy, and well-respected Alaskan, somehow got caught up in the mythology of Screamin' Jay Hawkins.

In further exploration of Jay's Golden Gloves tale, we must first address the title itself. In 1947, the Golden Gloves middleweight champ was Nick Ranieri of Chicago. To find a Clevelander who was a middleweight champ, one has to go back to 1943 when Samson Powell won the belt. There was a Clevelander who won the Golden Gloves welterweight championship in 1947. His name was John "Jackie" Keough.

The liner notes to Jay's first album read "he won the Golden Gloves Diamond Amateur Contest in 1947." That could be true, although in 2009, reporter Joe Maxse of the *Cleveland Plain*

Dealer compiled a list of all Cleveland Golden Gloves amateur boxing champions from 1929 to 2009. In 1947, there were eight "novice division" champs and eight "open division" champs. None of them was named Jalacy J. Hawkins. The same holds true for 1943.

That brings us to Billy McCann.

Billy McCann was not a middleweight, but a welterweight, and he fought his first professional bout in 1934 when he was 18 years of age. He knocked out Woody Clark in a fight in Bremerton, Washington. Things went well until October 1935 when McCann suffered his first loss. From then on his boxing career was essentially a split decision with 13 wins, 10 losses, and 14 decisions on points. He retired from boxing in June 1944 at the age of 28 and never fought professionally again—three years before he was supposedly said to have fought Jay for the middleweight title of Alaska. No record of a fight between McCann and Hawkins exists in the public record, or in Billy's obituary. As it stands now, the McCann vs. Hawkins bout is yet another liner note in the tall tales of Screamin' Jay Hawkins.

In some accounts, Jay got his start as a civilian performer at Gleason's Musical Bar in 1951, although Sookie maintains it was another location right near where he lived at a place called the Majestic Hotel. Built in 1907 on the corner of East 55th Street and Central Avenues, for most of the twentieth century it served as Cleveland's primary African American hotel. Although it was listed as an apartment building, it was perennially listed as the largest Cleveland accommodation in *The Negro Motorist Green Book*, a guide for black motorists in America (hotels were not integrated through the first 60 years of the twentieth century). Starting in 1931, the hotel also provided a venue for African American entertainers, changing names frequently over the years, ending in the 1950s as the Rose Room Cocktail Lounge where it attracted an integrated crowd of hipsters.

The Majestic, and the Log Cabin across the street, were fixtures in the "black and tan" scene in Cleveland's version of Harlem. The big attraction was the local jazz scene, which featured "Blue Monday" jam sessions. Through the 1950s, these storied gigs kept Central Avenue hopping until the wee hours of the morning. Talented but raw, Jay wouldn't be featured in these coveted performances.

The Majestic was a good venue for a young musician to get a start, and for a while, very convenient, as Anna Mae Hawkins worked across the street as a waitress at a diner called Rosie's. Soon afterward, Jay found steady work on the road with famed musician Tiny Grimes and was away from home a lot. Anna Mae was still very much in love with Jay and made the marriage work even with the long absences.

Into her elementary school years, Sookie says her parents got along well and Jay often called to have the family stay with him on the road, especially when he played in Atlantic City. "It was fun. We traveled by train and stayed at a hotel. If he was singing on stage, sometimes he would sit me on top of the piano and then tell me to dance, which I would do on top of the piano. When I was about six or seven, we were in Atlantic City a lot."

Then the love story ended.

"Eventually it got to the point where he stopped taking us because he was moving farther and farther away from the family," Sookie remembers.

The final break came when Sookie was about seven or eight years of age. She was sitting on the porch with her sister when her dad walked by, and told them that was going to the store. He didn't come back for two years. When she was 10, Jay rambled up the street in a pink Cadillac. When she saw that it was her father in that pink car, Sookie ran into the house to tell her mother.

Suddenly the day turned into a holiday. It was like a party, and Jay bought all the kids on the block popsicles. Afterward, he got in his car and drove away. Sookie didn't see him again for almost two decades.

In 1993, Jay told *The Observer Sunday* his first wife "left him for a woman," which was a complete fabrication. With Jay gone, Anna Mae's father took care of the family. Anna Mae went on welfare. Sometimes when food was short, Sookie and the kids would go to their grandfather's house. It was, says Sookie, "a difficult childhood." Says Helen Vernon Branner, "when he first left around 1955 or 1956, we didn't even know he was gone. Anna Mae never said anything. She would talk about him as if he still was around."

For Anna Mae, the love story ended up to be a love/hate story. Since Jay wasn't paying child support, every time she found out that he came back to Cleveland, she would call the police and have him put in jail. Years later, he complained to Sookie, "I stopped coming to Cleveland because every time I did your mom put me in jail." Sookie didn't suffer fools. "I said, 'well, pay the money you're supposed to pay.'"

Around the beginning of the 1960s, the family started reading in popular black magazines like *Jet* that Jay was engaged to Pat Newborn, and then, that he had gotten married to Virginia "Ginny" Sabellona. They found this odd, because he had never officially divorced from Anna Mae. "I don't think either of those women even knew he was still married," says Sookie.

Anna Mae Hawkins was finally granted a divorce on February 2, 1970 on the grounds of extreme cruelty. "She had to do the divorce all by herself, Jay didn't do it," says Helen Vernon Branner.

Despite all the animosity, Anna Mae was a forgiving person. When Jay would come to Cleveland for a performance, she would always go to see him, and often allowed him to stay in the basement apartment of the house she lived in. "I don't care how many times he came back to Cleveland with another woman, she always went to see him," says Sookie. "One time she let Jay and his woman stay in the basement apartment." In later years, he would stay with his daughter Irene.

One time he brought his third wife, an African American woman named Cassie, whom he married in the mid-1980s, with him to Cleveland. According to Audrey Sherbourne—an exotic dancer with the stage name of Lee Angel who was a friend and lover of Jay since the mid-1950s—Jay took Cassie to Cleveland and left her there.

Jay married three more times. Right after the two-year marriage to Cassie ended, he married a Japanese woman who, says Audrey, "was in and out of his life real fast." Again, in *The Observer Sunday* interview in 1993, he told the reporter that his marriage lasted three months and ended in divorce in 1991, which was probably true, but in complete fantasyland mode, he added, the woman was 40 years his senior. That last part wasn't true because Audrey says after that disastrous, short-lived marriage ended, the Japanese bride's parents came to the United States and brought the delusional young lady back home. He married her because he was planning to tour Australia and Japan and considered living overseas, she says.

Robert "Smokey" Miles, who met the woman, says Jay would take her around with him but wouldn't let her talk to anyone because he didn't want her to become Americanized.

In the 1990s, Jay moved to Europe where he married a French woman named Colette. After that divorce, he was married for a sixth and final time to an African woman living in Paris named Monique. He was still married to her when he died.

As for Anna Mae, she managed to get her life on the right track by eventually going to community college and getting a diploma in food service. However, her personal life continued on a downward spiral as she fell for more men just like Jay. She ended up having four more children, with four different men.

Sookie saw very little of her father over the years. However, two incidents stand out in her memory.

In one instance, she was reading the local newspaper when she saw that Screamin' Jay Hawkins was going to appear at a Cleveland club called Peabody's Downunder. Sookie, her sister, and her mom went to the show without telling Jay. Sookie and Irene went upstairs to meet Jay but a bouncer was threatening to throw them out. Jay recognized his daughters, whom he hadn't seen in years, and told the bouncer to get his hands off the girls. The bouncer argued, urging Jay to realize that they have no business up here, and that's when Jay said, "Those are my daughters." The bouncer looked at the ladies and then turned to Jay, asking, "You have daughters this age?" Sookie realized the horrible truth: Jay never told anyone he had daughters.

A second incident was even weirder. Sookie and her husband were in Washington, D.C. Her marriage was in disarray as she suffered constant physical abuse from her husband. Somehow Jay found out and made his way to D.C. Confronting Sookie's husband, Jay put in his son-in-law's face what Sookie initially thought to be an ink pen, but soon discovered was actually a gun! What was just as interesting and a lot less dramatic was that Jay arrived with Ginny, which was the first time Sookie had met the new "wife."

"All Jay did was make it worse," says Sookie. "My husband got more physical with me but then he passed away about a year later because he was an alcoholic."

CHAPTER

3

SoMe

musicologists give credit to Ike Turner for the first rock 'n' roll song, "Rocket 88," which rocketed to the Number 1 slot on the rhythm and blues charts in early June 1951. For the rest of his life, Ike's biggest lament wasn't the breakup of his marriage to Tina Turner, but the fact that the song "Rocket 88" was mislabeled. Ike's band Kings of Rhythm recorded the song with Jackie Brenston doing the vocals. Much to Ike's surprise, when the record came out, it was attributed to Jackie Brenston and his Delta Cats. Ike would remain an angry "cat" all his life.

In some regards, "Rocket 88" was a jump blues-infused update of such prior songs as "Rocket 88 Boogie" Parts 1 and 2 by Pete Johnson in 1949 and "Cadillac Boogie" by Jimmy Liggins in 1947. So, could either of those been the first rock 'n' roll records? Milton

Russ, a longtime session drummer and the original percussionist for the group The Undisputed Truth, which had a big hit with "Smiling Faces Sometimes" (Number 3 in 1971), says no. The inventor of rock 'n' roll, he claims, was Tiny Grimes, a close friend of the Russ family in the early 1950s and the man who gave a young Jalacy J. Hawkins his first break in the music world.

"There's always been a dispute about who started rock 'n' roll, was it guys like Little Richard and Jerry Lee Lewis?" says Russ. "They didn't start nothing. Tiny Grimes wrote the first rock 'n' roll tune, called 'Tiny's Boogie,' which was recorded in 1946."

If Jalacy J. Hawkins was looking for someone in the music industry to give him a break, he could not have picked a better person than Tiny, a generous man and an accomplished musician who could fluidly shift music styles with the times, whether recording jazz, rhythm and blues, popular or even rock 'n' roll. Perhaps more importantly, Tiny understood what it was like to take a band to the very edge of what would be accepted by a contemporary audience and the music-buying public. Jay absorbed a lot from Tiny.

Having Tiny Grimes as a mentor was significant because by the early 1950s Tiny had already traveled a long, winding road in the music business.

Lloyd Grimes was born in 1916 in Newport News, Virginia. After teaching himself to play the piano, he began appearing in amateur shows around Washington, D.C. Two years later he was in New York playing at the Rhythm Club. By 1938, he began using "Tiny," an old nickname, as his stage name while playing in a group called The Four Dots. About this time, he bought himself a banged-up four-string guitar, which he taught himself to play. In 1940, he joined a harmony group called The Cats and the Fiddle, which hit the recording studios a year later.

By 1943, Grimes fell in with jazz pianist Art Tatum to form the Art Tatum Trio. That gig lasted two years. In New York, Grimes recorded steadily, shifting between his own groups and many top blues and jazz musicians including Billie Holiday, Ike Quebec, Cozy Cole and Leonard Feather. As the jazz world was sliding into the bebop era, Tiny made four recordings with Charlie Parker. Although by this time Tiny was a steady jazz guitarist, on two of the Charlie Parker recordings, "Romance Without Finance" and "I'll Always Love You," he was the lead singer.

It's hard to say whether Tiny trusted his voice or that he preferred the instrumental harmonies of pure jazz, because his best records and cuts from the 1940s through the early 1950s were either jazz instrumentals or cuts where he made those weird turns into the jump blues origins of rock 'n' roll such as his tasty recording "Juicy Fruit" on the Red Robin label in 1952.

Tiny had a true survivor mentality, trying to keep pace with the music curve and staying as busy as possible in the highly competitive New York music shuffle. Although he started out as pianist and drummer, he shifted to the guitar. He played behind fronted bands and he fronted his own bands. Gregarious and skillful, he was a team player when necessary and progenitor when the creative spirit was upon him. As one writer noted about him, he "performs with passion, skill and down-home joy."

Always at the fringes of greatness, Tiny was the selkie of jazz musicianship, continually shifting with the times and circumstances. After his jazzed-up version of the classic Scottish folk song "Loch Lomond" proved popular, he went way out there. He billed his band as Tiny "Mac" Grimes and His Rocking Highlanders, appearing in kilts and tam o'shanters. Since no one seemed to be offended by the joke—five black dudes decked out in full Scottish regalia—Tiny maintained the Rocking Highlanders concept into the 1950s. "The kilts really did it for us, they were the best threads on the scene," Tiny said.

This was no group of goofballs. Among the stalwart players was tenor sax great Red Prysock.

In the early 1950s, Milton Russ was still in elementary school when he first met Tiny, and it was because the Russ family was knee-deep in the jazz world. His grandfather William Russ played drums and guitar at the legendary Harlem nightclub Smalls Paradise. His uncle, Sonny Greer, was Duke Ellington's drummer, and his cousin, Jimmy Lewis, played bass for Count Basie and also worked with Art Tatum. Sammy Davis Jr. was another cousin. Milton began playing drums when he was four years old.

Jimmy Lewis had opened up a club called The Doll House between 133rd and 135th Streets and Lenox Avenue in Harlem. Everyone in the jazz scene played there at one time or another. Milton was even employed as a water boy, dressing in white shirts and a western bowtie. Tiny played The Doll House often and because Tiny and Jimmy were close, Milton would see and hear him play at his cousin's house as well. Jazz singer Billy Eckstine also used to pop over to Jimmy's house to chat, eat and jam with friends.

"Tiny was a gentleman's gentleman," says Milton. "He and Jimmy were pioneers with Art Tatum. When he would come to a place for a show, they would say, 'God's in the house.' He was like a hero to me. You felt his presence. When Billy Eckstine and Tiny would come to Jimmy's house, they were so sharply dressed they were like GQ or Superfly. Everything they wore was what everybody else wanted to wear. When my father came back from World War II he played some clarinet but he didn't pursue it. Instead he opened a dry cleaners, and Tiny and Jimmy would bring their clothes to him. They were sharp as a tack."

Milton only remembers Tiny playing the four-string guitar. When Tiny died, he left the four-string to Milton, who still has it.

Milton met Jay only once in New Orleans during the 1970s. He didn't know too much about him even though Jay had joined Tiny's band in the early 1950s. "When Tiny and Jimmy and others got together, they only talked about the great ones," says

Milton. "Screamin' Jay was just someone they took under their wings at one time."

Since Tiny was based in New York, how did Screamin' Jay hook up with him? That had something to do with Alan Freed.

Starting in the later 1940s, Freed was a successful, hard-drinking, troublemaking disc jockey working his way up the career ladder, moving from one Midwest market to the next, ending up at station WJW in Cleveland. According to legend, Freed was introduced to a fellow named Leo Mintz, who owned one of the biggest record stores in Cleveland. Mintz had noticed that white teenagers were coming into his store by the dozens and buying up rhythm and blues records recorded by black musicians. He suggested to Freed that he should do a late-night show that played nothing but black music. In June 1951, Freed debuted *The Moondog Show*, which for its time was the Wild Wild West of radio shows. Freed howled and jowled in hipster slang as he played the latest hits of rhythm and blues. WJW, with Freed at the helm, was 50,000 watts of musical revolution, beaming into the eardrums of Cleveland teenagers far and wide.

Jay mustered out of the Armed Services around the end of 1951 and headed back to Cleveland where he encountered this crazy show one late night on WJW radio. His curiosity running wild, Jay tells a couple of versions of going to meet Freed. This would have been very early in 1952.

Here's how writer Gerri Hirshey reports the tale:

> *"This cat was stone wild," Jay Hawkins remembers. He first heard Freed's show when he returned to his native Cleveland on leave from his third military stint.*
>
> *"I went to the station," he says. "I went to find out who we had in Cleveland that would dare, I*

mean, how could a black cat get away with such shit. So, I go there, and I say, 'I want to talk to this Alan Freed.'"

He gaped at the short, stocky white man who came at the receptionist's call.

"I says, 'Oh, no, you're playing black music on a white station?' and he says, 'That's me.' So I shook his hand, and I said, 'well, thank you, you're doing us very good.'"

This is one Hawkins story that seems to ring true. As he told another interviewer, "We could not believe that a black man got on a white radio station. I find out it was this white guy and come to find out this was a white guy with a black soul. He said, 'Any records you make you bring them to me. No matter where I'm at I'll play them.' That man kept this word."

When Hawkins came back to Cleveland after serving in the military, he knew one thing for sure: that he wanted to pursue a career as a musician. If author Nick Tosches is correct, and he probably is, Hawkins' military career was spent in front of audiences, where he played piano or saxophone in a military band. Hawkins was a good musician and felt the adrenaline of performing live in front of a crowd. When he went to see Freed, who was now a much talked-about character in Cleveland's music firmament, he was curious as to what a guy like Freed could do for him. The surprise was that Freed was white, not black. As many who knew Freed pointed out, he was not a saintly character; but he went out there in public, when the United States was a deeply segregated country, and promoted not only "Negro music" but the Negro musicians as well. In that first year as the pilot of the crazy *Moondog* radio show, Freed would have been most encouraging to a young, local, African American musician trying to find his way.

It appears Freed took to the handsome young man, because a few years later, when it really counted, Freed would do everything possible to make Jay a star.

From 1951 to 1952 there was a passing of the torch in the world of rhythm and blues. Whereas the top R&B songs from 1951 still included some older singers who came to fame late in the 1940s such as Amos Milburn and Charles Brown, by 1952 a bunch of young, new R&B shouters and crooners were topping the charts: B.B. King with "3 O'Clock Blues," Lloyd Price with "Lawdy Miss Clawdy," and Johnny Ace with "My Song."

Tiny had begun the new era dusting off old standards like "Begin the Beguine" and "Frankie & Johnny," reinterpreting in the way any good jazz stylist would do, but that sound was not cutting it anymore on the R&B stations in 1952. His boogie would have to get harder and he might have to bring in a singer for the Rocking Highlanders. He accomplished the first part in '52 by introducing an instrumental that boasted a very modern beat. The song was called "Juicy Fruit."

Freed, who used African American slang in his show, began calling his radio show mix of rhythm and blues and country music "rock 'n' roll." "Juicy Fruit" certainly fit the new mix.

Freed so popularized the phrase rock 'n' roll that he is often given credit for coining the term, although it had been around the African American music world in one form or another since the early 1920s when blues singer Trixie Smith recorded "My Daddy Rocks Me (With One Steady Roll)." Freed is given less credit, but is on more solid ground, as being the father of the rock 'n' roll concert. As part of his ongoing effort to promote the new rock 'n' roll music he was evangelizing, Freed organized a monster concert called the Moondog Coronation Ball that was to be held on Friday, March 21, 1952.

The venue, Cleveland Arena, could hold about 10,000 people, but on the night of the concert an estimated 20,000 to 25,000 young people showed up, all trying to crowd into the hall. Fearing a riot, the fire authorities shut down the concert after the first song by the opening act. Among the acts that were supposed to play that night were the Dominoes, Danny Cobb and Varetta Dillard. The headliners for the show were Paul Williams and His Hucklebuckers and Tiny Grimes and His Rocking Highlanders.

Jay never said whether Freed facilitated a meeting between him and Tiny. According to Jay, he just walked up to Tiny and asked for a job. Maybe security was much more lax in that era, or perhaps Freed tipped Tiny off about Jay. Nevertheless, soon after the concert, Jay joined the Rocking Highlanders, partly as a valet and chauffeur, and also as a performer. In Jay's words, he was hired "as Tiny's valet, bodyguard, dog walker, piano player and blues singer and all this for $30 a week." Jay always knew the value of a dollar because he never felt he was paid his true worth. Money would be a big bone of contention for the rest of his life.

No doubt Tiny got a lot for a little money with Jay. He could play the piano and saxophone, sing the blues and he was willing to present himself as audacious as the Rocking Highlanders could get. "I'd come out in a Scottish kilt," he told an interviewer. "And I'd have these small Carnation milk cans hanging off my chest, like tits. I sang 'Mama He Treats Your Daughter Mean' and the cans would be jiggling all over the place. Ruth Brown came to see me. She said, 'This is the only bitch that who can sing my song better than me.'"

Ruth Brown's "Mama He Treats Your Daughter Mean" was not only a Number 1 record on the R&B charts in 1952, it also crossed over to the popular charts and was a Top 25 hit. Tiny was apparently trying to remain au courant with his Rocking Highlanders. For Jay, it was an invaluable lesson that he would carry with him throughout his musical career: outrageousness on stage always attracts attention.

Tiny was generous to Jay. Toward the end of 1952, Tiny took his band into the recording studio to record a couple of tunes, including "Coronation Jump" and "Why Did You Waste My Time?" The latter song had a solid boogie beat not unlike a Big Joe Turner tune. To carry that kind of rhythm and blues lead, Tiny turned to the young man Jalacy J. Hawkins, who opted to be called "Screamin' Jay Hawkins" for the record. If there is a Big Joe Turner, why not a Screamin' Jay Hawkins? The record was released the following year.

Jay also has a colorful story for why he took on the nickname "Screamin'" Jay Hawkins.

Here's a version of the story he told Stuart Colman of Radio London:

> I started out as a piano player—no singing—then I wound up singing and I couldn't sing that well until I went to a place called Nitro, West Virginia, and this was in 1950. And there was a big, big, huge fat lady ... Just allow your mind to roam free. When I say fat ... Glutton! Beast! O-bese! The woman made the average elephant look like a pencil, that's how fat she was! And she was so happy. She was downing Black & White scotch and Jack Daniels at the same time, and she kept looking at me and she said, "Scream baby, scream, Jay!" And I kept saying to myself, you wanted a name, there it is—Screamin' Jay Hawkins! And that's how that name was born, before I got with any big-name bands. So when I went with these big-name bands, I used the title Screamin' Jay Hawkins.

It's 266 miles due south from Cleveland to the town of Nitro, West Virginia, and back in 1950, it was probably about a six-hour journey if not more—on only local roads. It's doubtful that Jay was doing much barnstorming that year as he was still in the military. Even if he was at home on leave, gigging around Cleveland, it would have been a major commitment to go to Nitro, which in 1950 had a population of 3,300.

In the *I Put a Spell on Me* documentary, Jay offered a more introspective version of how he decided on his moniker: "I said, how can you be different and still be right at the same time? I can't sing, I can holler. I can scream. You want a name, Screamin' Jay Hawkins, and I'm going to scream on everything. That means you are never going to be a good singer. You can't sing anyhow. So, I began to scream."

He was still tentative about the nickname early in his career, because when he began recording outside of the Rocking Highlanders, he did so as Jalacy Hawkins or Jay Hawkins. No matter Jay's early apprehensions about the name, or the veracity of its origins, the name Screamin' Jay Hawkins would soon find its rightful place in rock 'n' roll history.

One reason why teenagers were turning to R&B was due to the numbness of the popular charts. The year 1953 was truly one of the most lackluster, if not boring, for popular records. One might take an interest in the guitar work of "Vaya Con Dios" with Les Paul and Mary Ford, but of the Top 10 records that year, the other performers were white, non-jazz, non-blues, non-interesting bandleaders and singers including Percy Faith, Patti Page, Eddie Fisher, The Ames Brothers, Teresa Brewer, Les Baxter and Perry Como. Not a stalwart in the group. In comparison, the top R&B songs of 1953 showed some real spunk and originality including "Hound Dog" by Big Mama Thornton, "Crying in the Chapel" by The Orioles, "Money Honey" by Clyde McPhatter and "The Drifters" and "Honey Hush" by Big Joe Turner.

In January 1953, Atlantic Records scheduled a recording session for Tiny Grimes and his band. Jay wrote some songs for himself, and Tiny agreed to let his protégé sing a couple of his own tunes as a solo if there was time at the end of the session. When they arrive at Atlantic's office on West 56th Street in

Manhattan, Jay is introduced to Ahmet Ertegun who cofounded the record label in 1947. Ahmet was a Turkish American whose father had been a diplomat in Washington, D.C. He also had an abiding interest in R&B. Starting in 1949, after a major hit with Stick McGhee's "Drinkin' Wine Spo-Dee-O-Dee," the label had a continuous, strong run focusing almost totally on R&B. Ahmet boasted a good ear for what might make the charts, and with Big Joe Turner's success he was not going to turn away a good blues shouter. So with Tiny's studio work concluded, Jay would get to record two songs, the first of which was "Screamin' Blues." The song is pretty raucous and Ahmet does not like what he's hearing. Depending on which version of this tale Jay tells, he begins the song four or five times and is stopped midway through by Ahmet each time. The atmosphere in the recording studio turns unstable, only to get worse.

Ahmet calmly suggests that maybe Jay can tone the song down a bit, perhaps like Fats Domino. That's when Jay loses it.

Hirshey writes the incident with Jay screaming, "What the fuck you have me here for? Why don't you go and get Fats Domino? I wrote the song. I wrote the song. I'm just now breakin' into the business. And this is the kind of act I want to have. I want to be known as the Screamer."

Ahmet again tries to calm Jay down but Jay continues his torrent. "You go to hell!" And as Hirshey writes, "And here Jay commits one of the great mistakes of his career. He tries to belt Ahmet Ertegun."

Time would alter the telling of this tale, with the violence aspect getting amped up. Later versions that Jay would relate ended this way, "He [Ahmet] started up again and pow! I just punched him in the mouth."

Another version states: "Our unrepentant boxing champ is said to have punched out Ahmet Ertegun when the company boss asked him to sing like Fats Domino."

Ahmet was a small, balding, bookish-looking man with glasses. Jay was a former boxer. One good punch by Jay would have done some serious damage to Ahmet's face.

While the recording session clearly didn't go well, it's doubtful that Jay actually hit Ahmet. There has never been any reportage of Ahmet being punched out, other than from Jay. In any case, "Screamin' Blues" was never released.

Jay was a strong, intimidating man who stood well over six feet tall, and his altercations or "near-altercations," of which there were many, would in Jay's retelling often end with him punching someone's lights out.

Rudi Protrudi, whose punk band The Fuzztones backed Jay in the 1980s, says when he met Jay, one of the first stories he was told was about Jay collectively kicking the shit out of the singing group The Drifters. Around the same time, James Marshall, who was writing for the *Village Voice* in New York, interviewed Jay. He got a similar story. "Jay used to stick some kind of shim on the coffin latch so it wouldn't lock him in. One of the Drifters stole the shim so he got stuck in the coffin. He didn't know which one of the Drifters stole the shim so he beat them all up," Marshall recalls.

As Rudi remembered the tale: "One night Jay was on the same bill as the Drifters. They were all sitting around backstage drinking his 'rider,' according to him. They all got drunk. Meanwhile, he had to go onstage and he asked the Drifters to put him in the coffin. One of the Drifters locked it. When he got onstage and realized he couldn't get out, he also realized he had just a short amount of time in there, so he freaked out, messed in his pants, and with a last bit of adrenaline shook the coffin off a chair. It broke in a million pieces. He is standing there in a white suit with brown stains. When he ran off the stage, he found the Drifters and kicked all of their asses."

In 1959, after the Ben E. King-led Crowns became The Drifters and before Ben E. wrote "There Goes My Baby," the new Drifters sometimes appeared with Screamin' Jay Hawkins, who asked them to serve as his pallbearers on the stage. They would leave the coffin before Jay's band and then watch. At some point Jay would pop out to sing "I Put a Spell on You."

The two leaders of the ex-Crowns, now the new Drifters, were Ben E. King and Charlie Thomas. They were the ones who put Screamin' Jay at risk. The story begins with Ben E. King and Charlie Thomas sitting backstage at the Apollo swigging a bottle of wine when Screamin' Jay Hawkins comes down the stairs. Jay then gets ready for his performance by climbing into the coffin.

"I heard the lock go click, but I didn't pay it no mind," Thomas recalls. "We walked away from the coffin because they started playing Screamin' Jay Hawkins' music." Charlie tells Ben E. that he wanted to see the entrance with Screamin' Jay coming out of the coffin, so the two walk back, just offstage. They saw the coffin being placed on stage and then saw it shaking violently about, like "a leaf in the wind." Charlie and Ben E. realize that Screamin' Jay was locked in the coffin. Charlie says, "Oh hell, that was a lock I heard click." Ben E. turns to Charlie and suspiciously asks, "Did you lock Screamin' Jay Hawkins in the coffin?" Charlie says no, "but I heard the lock click."

Frank Schiffman, who managed the Apollo, ran onto the stage yelling, "Close the curtains, close the curtains!" Screamin' Jay climbs out with his eyes red, looking to kill someone—in particular Charlie Thomas and Ben E. King. Frank Schiffman finds Charlie and Ben E. first and said, "You better take a walk behind 125th Street until Screamin' Jay cools down."

Charlie conjures up the incident: "When we came back to the Apollo, Screamin' Jay sees us and says in his deep baritone, 'Come here. Come here.' I said to Ben E., we should get out of here; but Ben E. said we should stand and take our medicine, which we did. Screamin' Jay Hawkins said to us, 'I know you locked me in that coffin when you were backstage drinking. I know it was an accident and I'm going to forgive you.'"

"I told Jay I heard the lock but I wasn't sure it was the lock," Charlie said.

Recalling the event decades later, Charlie adds, "Every time I saw Screamin' Jay after that, I said I was sorry. I know he wanted to put a spell on me when he got locked in that coffin."

The incident happened, cooler heads prevailed and no one got beaten up.

Jay once did a radio interview with Johnny Otis and relayed a very weird and contrite version of this story. He told Johnny:

> They thought they were just having fun but they didn't realize there is only three minutes of air in a locked coffin with all that upholstery. Don't play with coffins, it's for keeps. I'm the only crazy man who will get in a coffin knowing that I can get out. The Drifters made it impossible to get out so therefore they became my enemy. I instantly put spells on them. I prayed to God, saying what have I done to offend thee? If you allow me to live, I promise never to get into this coffin again and while I'm jumping to the left and to the right and kicking and screaming and crying and praying and somehow the good Lord heard me, helped me knock the coffin off the display it was on. Whereupon when it hit the floor, it busted wide open. I forgot where I was or what I was supposed to do. I made a side-step to the right and made a bow to the audience and said, please forgive me for I must go. I would not be here tonight if I could not shake it off its foundation.

That was years ahead.

After the Ahmet Ertegun incident at Atlantic Records, while in Philadelphia, Jay quietly slipped away from the Rocking Highlanders. In later years, Jay would recall his Rocking Highlander days by saying he and Tiny did not get along.

For a while, he ended up with Johnny Sparrow and His Bows and Arrows in Philadelphia. Johnny Sparrow was born in 1920, and beginning in the 1940s played with jazz greats Louis Armstrong, Jay McShann and Lionel Hampton before starting his own band in 1949. Johnny was known as the "Mad Sax," and in the early 1950s was a big deal in the Philadelphia area.

Jay was scrapping around, attaching himself to any band that would take him. Next in line was the Lynn Hope Quintet, fronted by another jazz wanderer who ended up on the pre-rock 'n' roll trail. Born in 1926, Lynn Hope was a tenor saxophonist, having a minor hit in 1951 with "Tenderly," a fine, soft-bluesy instrumental. Jay probably met him in 1954 when the Lynn Hope Quintet was playing a series of clubs in Philadelphia. Lynn Hope was an unusual fellow for his time. Before Jay hooked up with him, Lynn converted to the Muslim faith and changed his name to Al Hajj Abdullah Rasheed Ahmad. He still recorded under the Lynn Hope moniker, but took to wearing a turban-like headpiece.

It was also in Philadelphia that Jay met Fats Domino, who was looking for a piano player to do opening sets for his show. Fats wasn't yet the megastar of the mid-1950s, where he would have such huge hit records as "Blueberry Hill" and "Blue Monday," but he already had numerous records that not only scored on the R&B charts but had crossed over to the pop charts as well. Fats was a squarely built man with a head that looked too large for most people. His thick hair was tightly trimmed at the sides and piled on top where it was carefully coiffed in a flat line like a football field. He had a welcoming smile and could have been anybody's favorite uncle.

Jay, who was already dressing wildly and perfecting his "screaming-blues" singing style, would have seemed an unlikely pianist to open for Fats. However, as calm and straight-as-an-arrow-looking Fats was on stage, he had a penchant for employing the outrageous. At one point in the late 1950s he had the flamboyant Esquerita open for him. Born Eskew Reeder Jr. in 1935, over the course of a professional career he worked under numerous monikers before settling on Esquerita. Little Richard tells of meeting him in 1951 in Macon. Esquerita's skill at the piano led Little Richard to focus on the instrument. In regard to demi-monde, Little Richard's dazzling pompadour is said to have been a nod to Esquerita's skill at elegantly piling so much hair atop his head—with an elaborate drift over the forehead.

In the early years of rock 'n' roll there existed a whole subset of gay, overtly lurid and sometimes cross-dressing musicians who played clubs that catered to this type of crowd. Down in New Orleans, most R&B singers would play the Dew Drop Inn when in town; but the club was also famous for its drag shows.

The club, which was opened in 1939 by Frank Painia, was a place African American musicians could play in the highly segregated city. Although New Orleans' Jim Crow laws specifically prohibited "mixed-race mingling," white music enthusiasts would be allowed inside the Dew Drop Inn anyway, with only occasional raids by the police. White people would flock here because in the 1950s and 1960s, this was where Southern soul was brewing. Irma Thomas got her start here and it's where Allen Toussaint met Dave Bartholomew, two guys who virtually created the New Orleans sound of early 1950s rock 'n' roll. It was also the home venue of Patsy Vidalia, the famed female impersonator who began working at the Dew Drop in 1947. Little Richard certainly took note of Patsy's act on his many visits to the club. The Dew Drop Inn was a legendary venue whose defiance helped propel rhythm and blues and rock 'n' roll against all odds.

According to Jay Halsey, who tracked the career of Esquerita, Screamin' Jay also played the Dew Drop Inn and similar clubs. Either in the late 1950s or early 1960s, Jay met Esquerita. They became friends, then, later in life, bitter enemies.

In the mid- to late 1950s, Jay toured on package shows with

Little Richard, but he had met him in the early 1950s. They had something in common and it wasn't just music. In 1956, Lee Angel (Audrey Sherbourne) began her burlesque career on the East Coast with a show called the World of Mirth. She later went on to become the only striptease dancer to headline rock 'n' roll shows on the Chitlin' Circuit, earning wide acclaim as an international star of the trade before retiring in 1977. Back in her robust days of 1956, Lee Angel was dating Little Richard when she attended a party at a guest house on West Broad Street in Philadelphia. Although she told a documentarian that there was a lot of sex activity going on at the party, Little Richard wouldn't let anyone touch her sexually. Then she met Jay. "I turned to Little Richard for friskiness," she said, "and to Jay for satisfaction." She claimed to have had a relationship with Jay for 44 years and with Little Richard for 50 years.

Before all that, Fats Domino decides to let Jay open for him. Jay had a set story that he often related about his short stint with the Fat Man. This is the version of the tale he told Alex Kalofolias, who did much of the interviews for the documentary *I Put a Spell on Me:* "He was playing second piano with Fats, when the latter realizes the girls were looking more at Jay than at Fats. One day Fats comes into rehearsal and says to Jay, 'I want you to go up there in the balcony and when I play let me know how many times my [diamond] ring flashes.' So, Jay goes to the balcony. Fats played a song. When Jay came down, he said Fats' ring flashed 40 times. That episode was a reflection of their relationship; Fats was jealous of him."

That's the point of Jay's tale: that Fats was envious of all the attention he was getting. In every Jay tale, there was always a hyperbolized version of himself who was far greater than the real Jay at the time. Other pundits point out that Jay was too outlandish for Fats; and that he was let go after showing up at a gig in a loud leopard-skin suit. However, as noted, Fats had a tendency to have outlandish performers open for him so he wasn't afraid of the bizarre. More than likely, it was his ego that got him fired. Needless to say the Fat Man gigs didn't last too long.

Hirshey writes about the breakup this way: "The bookings got classier, and Fats' diamonds have grown larger with his rise on the charts. Now he is given to sending Jay up to the balconies for reports on how his flashing rings irradiate the cheap seats. Disgusted, Jay places a call to Wynonie Harris, who gets him his first solo gig at Smalls Paradise in Harlem."

In a letter to a British record publisher, Jay wrote, "Being an avid record collector especially of the original artists of rhythm and blues and having Wynonie Harris in the year of 1952 take me under his wing as his personal protégé and get me my first night club job in New York City ...."

Jay moved on because he wanted to be a star. The Fats Domino gigs were a stepping stone, just like his tenure with Tiny Grimes.

Jay had returned to New York to try to make it on his own.

Someone else trying to make it on his own in 1953 was Hy Siegel, who had been the founder and president of Apollo Records, which at one time had signed gospel singer Mahalia Jackson to a contract. Hy had retired from the business and left New York for a while. Upon his return, he founded in September of that year a new label for rhythm and blues music called Timely Records. The first two groups Hy signed were The Ambassadors and The Gay Tunes. In a nod to Hy's success with Mahalia Jackson, Timely also signed what was called a "spiritual" group, the Colemanaires.

In February 1954, Hy decided to record a new R&B singer, Jalacy Hawkins. The result was two records, "Baptize Me in Wine" with "Not Anymore" on the B-side, and "Please Try to Understand" with "I Found My Way to Wine" on the B-side. They were Jay's first singles, all in the classic R&B format, heavy on the saxophone and with the histrionic Jay way over the top of his backup band.

Bill Millar, who befriended Jay in England and wrote extensively about him, is a fan of these recordings. He commented:

> Two of Hawkins' records for Timely ["Baptize Me In Wine" and "I Found My Way to Wine"] echoed the rumbustious drinking blues which [Wynonie] Harris had already popularized. Another, "Not Anymore," with slide guitar wizardry from Mickey Baker, was perfectly illustrative of blues at its most exquisite.

Hawkins, who apparently knew what was happening in the R&B world at that time, could have been trying to catch the buzz from Stick McGhee's "Drinkin' Wine, Spo-Dee-O-Dee," which rose to Number 2 on the *Billboard* R&B charts in 1949, but was so popular it stayed on the charts for close to six months.

The original lyrics to the song before it was cleaned up for radio went like this:

Drinkin' that mess is our delight,
And when we get drunk, start fightin' all night.
Knockin' out windows and tearin' down doors,
Drinkin' half-gallons and callin' for more.
Drinkin' wine motherfucker, drinkin' wine!
Goddam!

The blues performer Hawkins probably tried to emulate on these early recordings was Amos Milburn, who made a career singing about hard drinking. Milburn's best-known songs include "Bad Bad Whiskey" (Number 1 on R&B charts in 1950), "Thinking and Drinking" in 1952 and "One Scotch, One Bourbon, One Beer" (Number 2 on R&B charts in 1953).

Lyrics for "One Scotch, One Bourbon, One Beer":

One scotch, one bourbon, one beer
One scotch, one bourbon, one beer
Please mister bartender, listen here
I ain't here for trouble, so have no fear
One scotch, one bourbon, one beer
I don't want soda nor bubble gum
You got what I want, just serve me some
Since my baby's been gone, everything is lost
I'm on this kick and I can't get off

The Timely label proved to be tinier than Tiny Grimes. The unsuccessful record firm was bought out by Hy's former company Apollo Records.

In 1954 or 1955—the years differ depending on the source—Screamin' Jay Hawkins was back in Philadelphia to record with Grand Records. The label, founded by Herb Slotkin, only lasted from 1953 to 1956, specializing in the doo-wop group sound, featuring ballads loaded with great harmonies, minimal instrumentation and tenor leads. Among the doo-wop groups who recorded on Grand were The Belltones, Castelles, Silhouettes (who in 1958 had a Number 1 record, "Get A Job," on the Ember label) and Lee Andrews and The Hearts (two pop hits, "Long, Lonely Nights" in 1957, and "Tear Drops" in 1958 for Chess Records). Into this dreamy mix of soapy ballads and soaring tenors came Screamin' Jay Hawkins. Only one record was released under his new moniker, "Take Me Back" with "I Is" on the B-side. Grand didn't release it until 1956 or 1957 (again, different sources give different years).

Supposedly, Jay recorded a number of songs for Grand, but as far as any researcher has noted, none of the others made it to a 45 (seven-inch disc played at 45 revolutions per minute [rpm]).

The Grand recordings, according to one writer, took place in June 1955. What happened was Stan Pat, a Philadelphia-area radio personality (broadcasting from Trenton, New Jersey) became head of A&R for the label. Pat was also acting as Jay's manager.

In a 1983 interview Jay did in England, he said, "We had a record called 'I Put a Spell on You,' which was recorded previously for Grand Records, and it was a ballad, something like Johnny Ace or Roy Hamilton would sing. And I'm only sorry I didn't bring a copy with me, it is right here in England, it's at the hotel. I brought a whole cassette—it's got about eight songs I did on Grand Records: '$10,000 Lincoln Continental,' 'Take Me Back,' 'I Is,' 'I Put a Spell on You.' They wanted to destroy the master, or they were supposed to, that's why you see on this one, if I'm correct, it would say 'Hawkins and Slotkin' underneath the title. Slotkin had Grand Records; he wanted a piece of the pie." In the 1950s, some record company executives (such as Slotkin) or disc jockeys adopted the sleazy practice of taking co-composer publishing credits. It was considered a form of payola—extra payment through composer royalties. Even Alan Freed took co-composer liberalities.

Also in 1955, Jay caught what looked like a career break. Mercury Record Corporation was a decade-old recording company that had established a fairly successful stable of pop stars, including Frankie Laine, Buddy Rich and Patti Page. Even from its beginnings in the mid-1940s, the company also recorded R&B singers such as Eddie "Cleanhead" Vinson. Mercury jumped into the more modern rhythm and blues world in the early 1950s when it hired Bobby Shad as director of blues and jazz records. Shad supervised sessions across the genres from Illinois Jacquet, to The Platters, to Dinah Washington, who became the queen of R&B after her first recording "West Side Baby" for Mercury back in 1948. For a time in the early 1950s, Johnny Otis worked for Bobby at the label. In 1953, Johnny cowrote and played drums on Big Mama Thornton's legendary recording of "Hound Dog" and in

1954 he produced Johnny Ace's "Pledging My Love." With Shad at the helm, Mercury became a go-to destination for many up-and-coming R&B acts of the time.

In 1955 and 1956, now recording as Jay Hawkins, he cut another set of records for the Mercury label and for its new subsidiary Wing label, which had ventured into doo-wop territory later recording The Penguins, who had a big hit in 1955 with "Earth Angel." Mercury was willing to take chances on all the different styles coming out of the rhythm and blues world. If anything, the label could be accused of churning musicians, but these were heady days with teenagers buying records in increasing numbers and the music scene changing daily. Record producers had to move quick or be left behind. Hawkins came into Mercury/Wing with a head of steam and growing reputation. He put in the time and the effort and did some of his best recordings: "This is All" with "(She Put the) Wamee (On Me)" as the B-side; "Well, I Tried" with "All of My Life" on the B-side; and "Even Though" with "Talk About Me" on the B-side.

If Bill Millar liked Jay's earlier recordings, he was positively ecstatic about the Mercury numbers:

> These are dark, sere, seemingly inebriant performances with few equals in blues or rock ... "She Put The Wamee On Me" is demonic voodoo blues at its best; it demands to be played during a 3 a.m. thunderstorm with the lights out ... "This Is All," "Well I Tried" and the Latin-style "Talk About Me" are essentially straightforward R&B wrought out of the ordinary by Hawkins' vocal inflections—that amazing whiskey-stained baritone with blocked-sinus clearings, constricted screams and low, dissolute moans.

The Mercury/Wing performances are notable not only for Jay's unusual recording style, but also for the musicianship of his backing band including tenor men Sam "The Man" Taylor and Big Al Sears, drummer Panama Francis and guitarist Mickey Baker. The arrangements were by Hawkins and Leroy Kirkland. Kirkland was a top-tier record producer and was responsible for putting together such a notable backup group.

While none of Jay's early records made a dent in the music charts, by the mid-1950s he was a known musician in the East Coast R&B scene with high-level contacts, a coterie of other players and singers who could be of help in a pinch, and a comfort level in the recording studio that bordered on destructive.

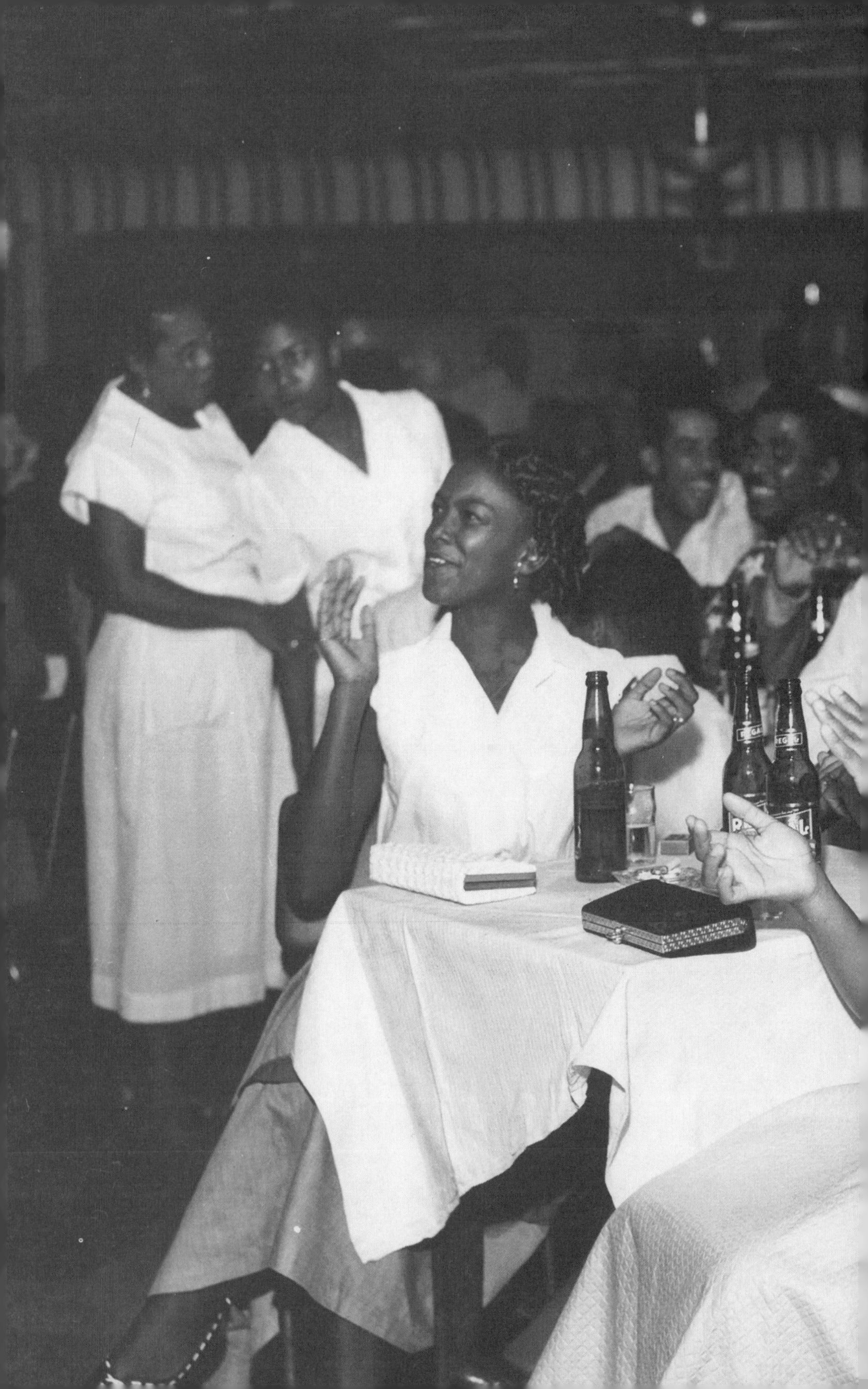

CHAPTER

4

the ReCOrD

label OKeh took its name from a derivative of the word *okay*, or *OK*. In other words, it's a slang version of a slang word. When the Otto K.E. Heinemann Phonograph Corporation decided to branch out into phonograph records in 1918, it adopted that name: OKeh Records. It was also a play on Otto's full initials.

OKeh Records produced all sorts of odd recordings in addition to popular songs, but it is best known for its early blues and jazz recordings, including New Orleans Jazz Band, Mamie Smith, Bix Beiderbecke, King Oliver and Bennie Moten. By the mid-1920s, it became a true American success story, at least in the purely economic sense, acquired by bigger and bigger firms until it was completely neutered. Its particular strengths—blues and jazz recordings by black musicians—came to an end in 1938 when CBS bought American Record Corporation, which owned OKeh's parent company, Columbia Records.

However, as the post-World War II years galloped into the 1950s, white teenagers bought the records they heard on rhythm and blues stations without the discriminatory considerations of their parents or society at large. In addition, a growing urban population of African Americans and their children, with better paying jobs and more money to spend, were interested in the new music they were hearing, which is why new record labels appeared almost every week tapping into the burgeoning market that the big companies had ignored.

While the OKeh label was phased out in 1942, Columbia Records still recorded R&B artists on the Columbia 30000 Series. In May 1951, Columbia decided it was going to get competitive again in the R&B market and revived the OKeh Record label starting with some of its African American performers from the Columbia label.

Columbia's best move was to hire an aggressive up-and-comer named Danny Kessler to take over the revived label. Kessler began life in the music industry at the very bottom, as a record picker—a job title that explained what he did. He eventually worked his way to salesman. Then, when Manie Sachs, who headed Columbia's A&R department, came down to Philadelphia because Columbia was unhappy with the local distributor, he appointed Kessler as promotion manager.

Sachs took the ride to Philadelphia because the city boasted a strong group of disc jockeys who could break a record. Philadelphia was an important market, and its disc jockeys were one of the reasons so much musical talent and record infrastructure was based in the city.

Kessler did well in Philadelphia. Sachs promoted him to Connecticut and New York. About the same time Columbia was considering reviving OKeh, Sachs resigned and went to work for RCA Victor. A new regime was installed and they realized Kessler had a feel for rhythm and blues records, so they made him head of

A&R for OKeh. One might say Kessler's biggest coup was signing an unknown Johnnie Ray who, between Frank Sinatra in the mid-1940s and Elvis Presley in the mid-1950s, was the biggest draw for teenage females. His record "Cry" was Number 1 on mainstream and rhythm and blues charts in 1951. More importantly, Kessler began signing new African American artists to the label, the first being The Treniers, who in 1951 had a Top 10 hit on the R&B charts with "Go! Go! Go!" Bridging the gap between swing and jump, The Treniers were not just musicians but entertainers, with a live act that was comedic and often acrobatic.

Not all the records were hits, but OKeh was bringing in a lot of talent, some new and some old, who would one day become big stars. Saxophonist Johnny Hodges recorded for OKeh as did The Ravens, who in 1952 had the group's biggest hit, "Rock Me All Night Long." By 1954 some of its original artists began to break out.

At the start of 1956, Jay signed with Wing Records where he recorded two records, "Even Though" with "Talk to Me" on the B-side and "Well, I Tried" with "All of My Life" on the B-side. Nothing happened and by the summer he was looking for a new record deal. Over at OKeh, he had a lot of contacts. From his days playing in Philadelphia he knew performers like Chris Powell, Mickey Baker and even Chuck Willis, whom he met on the club circuit.

Danny Kessler was no longer head of A&R; his position was taken over by Arnold Maxim, another white guy who looked more like the accountant who sat next to you on the Long Island Rail Road on your commute to New York every day. However, one can't judge a book by its cover. Maxim not only had a real feel for R&B and rock 'n' roll, but liked the music as well. He later became head of MGM Records.

Maxim also had his moment in rock 'n' roll history. In 1957, when Sammy Davis Jr. inaugurated a syndicated radio talk show, he had a round table discussion with two guests, Columbia Records producer Mitch Miller and MGM Records president Arnold Maxim. Davis and Miller smugly denounced rock as "the comic books of music," but Maxim disagreed, saying, "I don't see any end to rock and roll in the near future."

So with all Jay's contacts in the music business, his sounds found their way into the ears of the aggressive and forward-thinking A&R man Arnold Maxim. Jay signed with OKeh Records in the summer of 1956. His first recording session is scheduled for September 12.

While Jay was toiling away in a record studio for Wing Records, a Southern singer named Elvis Presley released "Heartbreak Hotel," his first record for his new label RCA Records. It would become his first Number 1 single, adorning the top of the charts for the first time in early March.

In 1955, Bill Haley and His Comets unleashed "Rock Around the Clock," the first rock 'n' roll record to dominate the American music charts. It was the Number 2 biggest song of the year, according to Billboard. The other four records in the Top 5 of the year were all mainstream, Broadway/swing-derivative songs, mostly instrumentals, from Pérez Prado, Mitch Miller, Roger Williams and Les Baxter. Not one name that would excite a red-blooded teenager, whether white or black.

One might say the advent of rock 'n' roll started with "Rock Around the Clock," but 1956 is generally considered the first year of the era of the new sound that would come to dominate the world. However, if one looks at the pop charts of that year, 1956 was a time that the old guard of music was still holding strong against the new onslaught of rock 'n' roll and the crossover to the pop charts of rhythm and blues. So for every record by Elvis, The Platters, Carl Perkins, Gene Vincent or Frankie Lymon and the Teenagers, there were twice as many records by mainstream musicians such as Nelson Riddle, Les Baxter, Morris Stoloff, Perry Como, Doris Day and Dean Martin.

The key to the change was the individual radio stations, particularly those that shifted to the teenage market, and played mostly rock 'n' roll and rhythm and blues. The top records for 1956 at one of these key stations in New York were: #1, "In the Still of the Night," The Five Satins; #2, "Don't Be Cruel," Elvis Presley; #3, "My Prayer," The Platters; #4, "Why Do Fools Fall in Love," Frankie Lymon and The Teenagers; and #5, "The Closer You Are," The Channels. Of its Top 40 records, only three mainstream songs appeared.

In the early 1950s, the rhythm and blues world was dominated by the group or doo-wop sound, but there was also space for the jump musicians and singers such as Big Joe Turner. As evidenced by his early recordings, Jay was trying to find his way through both strands of the R&B world, shifting from a ballad to something raw and powerful such as "(She Put the) Wamee (On Me)." His schizophrenic approach matched his personality. He was strong for the outré, the shock and the demented; a crazed performer, but also a very intelligent, introspective, literate man. He was tall and handsome with an inviting smile. He would appear in early photos like an African American movie idol or as he was wont to do, screw up his lips in a cross between a snarl and a scare and open his eyes wide in a mock tribal caricature.

The genesis for "I Put a Spell on You" is a broken-heart tale and when Jay put it to music he opted to make it a kind of ballad. Jay has often explained the origin of the song. Although he is an unreliable narrator when it comes to key events in his life, this story remains consistent.

In a simple version, he recalls, "I wrote the song because I was going out with some girl who decided she was gonna put me down. I decided that I didn't want her to put me down. So, I wrote a song to her, and the song was 'I Put a Spell on You.' It was just a sweet ballad the way I cut it for Grand."

The most in-depth version begins in the summer of 1954 and Jay is playing at a club called Herman's Bar in Atlantic City.

The New Jersey coastal town steadily declined as a resort area through the twentieth century. Then with an influx of African Americans from the 1930s through the 1960s, Atlantic City remained a popular spot for nightclub entertainment. There were well-known places for the white music aficionados such as the 500 Club and the Jockey Club, but the real excitement was on the north side of town, which was populated by African Americans, and home to four major nightclubs: Club Harlem, Paradise Club, Grace's Little Belmont, and Wonder Gardens.

Club Harlem opened in 1935 and relied on African American acts, but the crowds were evenly mixed with blacks and whites. As Ben Alten, who owned the club for almost 40 years, remembers, "The whole town of Atlantic City slowed up after 2, 3 o'clock in the morning. The 500 Club closed, this closed, that closed, but Kentucky Avenue at 9 o'clock in the morning you couldn't put a car through there. Everybody, white and black, was on Kentucky Avenue. And that is the truth."

In February 1936, papers for Herman's Bar as a New Jersey Trade Name was filed. In 1954, it definitely was no longer one of the big four music venues in Atlantic City. In short, the perfect place for an up-and-coming singer who had yet to make a name for himself—the perfect place for Jay to introduce himself to future audiences.

After walking out on his marriage to make his name in the world, Jay definitely didn't adopt celibacy. In Atlantic City, he had an unnamed girlfriend from Philadelphia, who had a key to his apartment. She came inside with him to Herman's bar when he got the gig. That didn't mean Jay was suddenly a one-man, one-woman guy. Opportunity was opportunity for a young musician in his mid-20s. The young lady catches on, and one night while Jay is singing, she walks up to the stage and tosses the key in Jay's direction. She blows him a kiss and disappears for good.

In most versions of this story, Jay discusses the problem with the barmaid after the show, who says, "I have warned you, I have warned you, leave these other women alone. You had a good woman. She has left you." Jay answers, "No woman would leave me, are you crazy?" Then, after the club closes, he goes back to his apartment and sees that she has cleared out, taking all her clothes, pictures and, God forbid, even their records.

The next day, he tells the barmaid he is hightailing it for Philadelphia to talk his now ex-girlfriend into coming back. The barmaid asks, "You think you can get her back?" Jay responds, "No problem, even if *I have to put a spell on her.*" After a moment, he adds, "That's it—put a spell on her. I'll write this song, she'll hear it and she'll realize I'm madly in love and she'll come back."

Jay said he also wrote "Darling, Please Forgive Me," which he recorded in the OKeh sessions, for the lady. It's a strange spoken word song, where Jay intones solemnly over a languid Chuck Willis beat. The song begins with a cheesy organ, perhaps to invoke memories of church, then Jay's voice drops in: "My heart is crying, my soul is dying, all because I've been lying. Yes, I admit I've been lying to the one I love." Meanwhile, in the background, sounding far, far away in another world, someone is moaning and singing and sighing. Later, Jay sings, "forgive me, I know I've been cheating on the one I love." It's hard to tell if Jay himself recorded the background haunts and then spliced it onto the record. The whole end product was so strange, it was hard to tell what Jay was thinking—certainly not something the record-buying public would warm up to. Record sales aside, one has to appreciate Jay recognizing the consequences of his womanizing behavior and his willingness to bare his soul, even if it was partly theatrical, in the process. Jay was forced to confront his own demons in the studio.

The unnamed woman in the plot didn't take to the song, even though Jay later said this was the record that should have won her back. In the end, she did come back, but the record that warmed her heart was not "I Put a Spell on You," but the B-side cut, a more upbeat form of craziness called "Little Demon." Not exactly a love song; more of a fun song, with Jay making what would become his usual sounds and mumbles. In between, he sings:

> He had steam in his soul for the one he loved so;
> he had death on his mind 'cause my demon let him go
> He gonna run through the world 'til we understand his pain
> Somebody help him get his demon home again.

He could be very witty and in "Little Demon" he lightens the song:

> He made the sky turn green, he made the grass turn red
> He even put pretty hair on Grandma's bald head
> He made the moon back up, he even pushed back time
> He took the frutti out of tutti, he had the devil drink wine

The last line of the song could have been a nod to Little Richard, who in January of that year reached the pop charts for the first time with a Top 20 hit, "Tutti Frutti." Not knowing when Jay first wrote "Little Demon," the question is, who was listening to whom?

In any case, Jay said the unknown lady fell in love with "Little Demon" and came back to him. They were together for four more months before Jay ended the relationship, saying he only came back to her so he would be the one to leave.

The person who brought the tale of "I Put a Spell on You" to life was not the man himself, but the writer Gerri Hirshey, who inadvertently stumbled into the role as Jay's amanuensis while writing her book about soul music. Normally, no one can top Jay in being the public crier of his own story, but Gerri's literary take in *Nowhere To Run: The Story of Soul Music* is beautifully written:

Backed by a house band, Jay is onstage singing when the woman walks into the hot, smoky room and pushes her way through the crowd to the front of the stage. She is staring fixedly at the singer, rummaging in her purse. At the glint of metal a few patrons back off. The lady lobs a shiny object toward the stage, and it lands between Jay's feet. He recognizes his apartment keys.

He looks up to see the woman blowing him a kiss before she disappears back into the crowd. There are still two songs left in the set, and Jay wails through them before he replaces the mike in the stand.

"And how about a nice hand for the band that been shakin' up this land …?"

While the band takes its bows, Jay makes his way to the bar and Mom, Herman's barmaid, a woman so wise Jay calls her Solomon.

"You done lost the best thing you ever had." Mom shakes her head over a tray of beer glasses. "That girl is either out of Atlantic City right now or in the process of gettin' out. Those were your keys, right? Well, she's done locked up your pad. You can get in, but you won't find no girl. The girl left you, Jay."

Jay walks next door to his apartment and finds it locked. When he gets in there is no woman. Her clothes are gone. The mirror has been stripped of photographs.

"Good-bye my love" was all she wrote, in scarlet lipstick, on the glass.

And there is loosed upon the waterfront a terrible scream. Jay will remember it as the most painful moment of his life. "Only one," he tells Mom later, "that found its way out of my big mouth directly through my heart and guts."

The soulful moment.

Jay sits down on the bed and commences to write. Already he knows the key and tempo. The song would be dedicated to her. He would just conjure her face and scream out the words.

Imagine the performance Jay gave in telling this story to Gerri. It could have been Oscar-worthy. Although there are still traps, it is doubtful this was the most painful moment in his life. There was never only one woman. His ego was likely more scarred than his heart.

Nevertheless, the song comes out of his soul in a ballad-like form, which is how he sings it on Grand Records and how he intends to sing it for OKeh. One must ask why Jay felt the need to re-record the song for the OKeh sessions, when he had already recorded it for Grand, which was still in business at the time. One suggestion is that Arnold Maxim heard the recording and saw something in the song that even Jay hadn't seen, that the song was darker and even eerier than how Jay performed it in the initial recording. This was validated when Jay and his band went into the studio, and Maxim didn't like what he heard at all.

In Jay's words this is what happened. "Maxim said, 'With a song title like that it's got to be unusual. I heard the original on Grand, and it was a straight ballad, this song must be weird, it's got to be scary. So how do we go about it?' And nobody said nothing. Nobody said nothing."

In the studio that day were some very good musicians, many of whom had played or recorded with Jay in the past, particularly with Jay's Mercury/Wing recordings. Leroy Kirkland had been the primary arranger for those recordings and he had a group of musicians he worked with often, guys like drummer Panama Francis, tenor sax men Sam "The Man" Taylor and Big Al Sears, and guitarist Mickey Baker.

The record credits this group, listing the artist as Screamin' Jay Hawkins "Orch. under the dir. of Leroy Kirkland." The unknown engineer on the record could have been the legendary Luis Pastor "Val" Valentin, who later worked for Maxim when he headed MGM Records, and eventually worked with such diverse talents as Ella Fitzgerald, Stan Getz, Mothers of Invention and Velvet Underground.

Maxim, wondering how to get the band loosened up, decides to send out for a large order of chicken and barbecue ribs along with plenty of hooch. Not only did the band get loose, they were drunk as pub dwellers on St. Paddy's Day. Jay claimed he sang parts of "I Put a Spell on You" while lying on his back on the floor; Mickey Baker was completely drunk and Sam "The Man" Taylor had trouble getting his lips around the mouthpiece of his tenor sax.

Most of Jay's band came of age in the 1940s playing for jazz bands. The musicians in that era were always dressed to the nines—so they weren't about to crawl all over the floor like Jay. Drummer Panama Francis played and toured with Cab Calloway so he had seen many an unusual turn of events in his day, from drugged days to boozy nights. One drunken recording session was not an unusual sight for him. Al Sears wore glasses and with a tidy mustache looked almost academic until he started rocking back and forth while working the saxophone. He was an upright player and an upright musician. Sam "The Man" Taylor also played with Cab Calloway in addition to guys like Louis Jordan and Big Joe Turner, so one more liquored-up recording session was just another day for him. Despite Jay's assertions, Sam "The Man" could sip with the best of them and still play the best sax solo in New York. If there was one young buck at the recording session it was Mickey "Guitar" Baker and he was almost 30 years of age when he bopped into the recording session with Jay. Mickey scraped by on both coasts before becoming a red-hot session musician in the early 1950s. His advantage was that he wasn't necessarily a jazz musician by trade or experience, and could easily slip from doo-wop to rhythm and blues to pre-rock 'n' roll. He was a man in demand and completely at home in any recording studio under any circumstance. Drunk as a skunk he could still play better than most guitarists. This crew could perform a rock 'n' roll rendition of Beethoven's 9th Symphony stone-drunk, and people would sing their praises.

Over the years, Jay has told different versions of how this recording came about, and although some of the facts changed, the basic tale is the same.

Version one:

Arnold Maxim decided it was too quiet and he said, "Look, what do you guys do when you do it in a nightclub and you're really having a good time?" And we said hell, we're so drunk we don't know what we're doing. And he said, "That's it." And he turned around and he spoke to somebody and a half hour later, they came in with boxes and boxes of booze, and boxes and boxes of chicken. He said, "this is a party, it's not a recording session—a party, everybody drink, everybody eat. Then when I think you're right, then we'll make it a recording session."

Version two:

We were gonna cut a new version of "I Put a Spell on You." Arnold Maxim, who was head of Columbia at the time, felt that we had to do something different in regards to the song. So he brought in a case of Italian Swiss Colony Muscatel, and we all got our heads bent ... 10 days later, the record comes out. I listened to it and I heard all those drunken screams and groans and yells. I thought, oh, my God.

Version three:

The producer plied the band singer with enough muscatel to kill an ox before rolling the tape. "We all went there sober. We had no idea the man wanted us to get drunk! We made all those records drunk. I don't even remember the man telling us when to stop eating and drinking and when to pick up our instruments. I sat down and listened to all that gruntin' and groanin' and screamin' and said 'Uh-uh, That wasn't me. No way.'"

Jay was being very ingenuous in the comments because if there was one thing he had perfected in his previous recordings it was the unusual sounds, the grunts and groans, the mumbles and moans, the unique trill that turned simple words in something sinister. By the time Jay rolled into the recording of "I Put a Spell on You," those sounds were already a staple of his songs and performances.

In addition to "I Put a Spell on You," the group recorded "Little Demon," which was then followed by "You Made Me Love You," and "Darling Please Forgive Me"—basically two 45s with B-sides. Then the group came back the next day to record more songs for an album that became *At Home With Screamin' Jay Hawkins.*

Jay was 27 years old and had been honing his craft since his days in the military. On the way up, he played with some great musicians from Tiny Grimes to Fats Domino and Bill Doggett. He was in the end determinedly idiosyncratic, and from the moment he decided to forge his own path, it was going to be his very, very own path. His sound from the start was both lurid and entertaining, an act no one else was doing at the time or had done with any great success before. It wouldn't be until the end of the 1960s that any musician or band caught up to the kind of performance Jay had pioneered. Jay was decades ahead of his time.

"I Put a Spell on You" was the apogee of Jay's hard-earned brilliance. It was either haunting or romantic, depending on how the listener felt as the song unwound. And it was either solid rhythm and blues or borderline novelty.

After the Screamin' Jay Hawkins recording sessions, Maxim realized he had something special in "I Put a Spell on You," a groundbreaking record that could really excite the teenage radio audience. The trouble was, it straddled the genres of rock 'n' roll and novelty, leaving audiences and, most importantly, disc jockeys to guess which genre best categorized the avant-garde classic. Plus, the moans and groans were creepy and unearthly to the general public at the time who preferred more "safe" tastes when it came to music. As good as the record was, it was questionable how it would be received by radio stations around the country. America's parents were already upset about the salaciousness of Elvis Presley; the rise of the new, hedonistic music called rock 'n' roll; and that their children were listening to African American performers. Something like "I Put a Spell on You" could be their worst nightmare.

There were two ways to market Screamin' Jay Hawkins. OKeh could try to normalize the performer: make him out to be a cuddly singer that you could invite into your home; or it could accentuate the true strangeness of "I Put a Spell on You." OKeh tried both, and neither worked very well.

First to arrive was the single, "I Put a Spell on You," which was welcomed by listeners, radio buyers, and then the deejays. However, a quick backlash soon followed, and some radio station owners were reluctant to play the song out of fear of public disapproval. The grunts and groans of "I Put a Spell on You" sounded "demented," "cannibalistic" or "erotic," depending on the particular gripes of the parents and other disapproving adults listening at any given time.

OKeh realized it had a perception problem and decided to pitch it as a novelty record. In *Billboard* magazine, next to the Top 100 playlist of November 14, 1956, which featured "Love Me Tender" by Elvis Presley at Number 1 (RCA Records), novelty record "Green Door" by Jim Lowe at Number 2 (Dot Records), "Just Walking in the Rain" by Johnnie Ray at Number 3 (Columbia Records) and even "Honky Tonk" by Bill Doggett (King Records) at Number 9, OKeh ran a top-of-the-page to bottom-of-page ad that "hawked" Screamin' Jay Hawkins. Jay was photographed wrapped in a cape, his arms crossed, gloved hands stiff, in grappling mode, his bottom lip dipped at one corner as if he was waxing unstable for shock value. He looked a bit silly, but at the same time provocative and rebellious. The copy on the ad, in many different typefaces, from top to bottom ran this way: A WILD WEIRDIE (boxed and in background color); Screamin' Jay Hawkins (in color type moving into larger letters from left to right as if in a comic "someone was screaming the name"); (then in increasingly bigger type) rock, rolls, grunts, groans, shouts, screams; (in very dominant, large black letters with curious white lines through the letters of the words), I PUT A SPELL ON YOU; at lower right some notes about the record and the words "A Billboard R&B Best Buy 'POPPIN' AS A POP HIT!'"; at bottom of page, the words "OKeh" records (no capital R) then in red type, in screamin' hifi. However, the oddity of the ad was a box on the lower left that read, "D.J.'s Be brave ... Put a spell on your fans ... Tie up your switchboard ... Get on this hit ... it happened in New York, Chicago, Philadelphia and Hartford—if you get fired, we'll get you a job." This was a clarion call to music aficionados to support Jay's weirdness against the conformity of the 1950s.

The writer Ed Ward, when writing a history of rock 'n' roll for Rolling Stone, reported that no deejay got fired except for a guy named Bob Friesen, who worked at radio station CHWK in Chilliwack, British Columbia. In February 1957, CHWK station management was outraged by the song and fired poor Bob. The unemployed deejay had read that Billboard, saw the ad, and so appealed to OKeh Columbia to get him a job. The company dithered and dithered until some warmhearted fellow at a Columbia record pressing plant got Bob's story into Billboard. A station finally contacted Bob, which turned out to be good publicity for the station.

There was a lot of chatter about the record, which helped boost sales even without blanket play at radio stations. "I Put a Spell on You" has often been called a million-seller, but that would have to be cumulative. Using *Billboard* charts, the list of Top 100 R&B singles of 1956 shows Jay at Number 97.

Challenging radio stations to play the record amid public backlash didn't work out well, despite the fact that "raucous" rock 'n' roll was exploding all over the country. 1956 was the year of "Rip It Up" by Little Richard, "Stranded in the Jungle" by The Cadets, "Be-Bop-A-Lula" by Gene Vincent, "Why Do Fools Fall In Love," by Frankie Lymon and The Teenagers, and "Blue Suede Shoes" by Carl Perkins.

"I Put a Spell on You" was left off the playlist of many a radio station aimed at the teen market, but somehow the word got out—in record stores, on jukeboxes, in local gatherings and inside the apartments of urbane music fans looking for that sound that would take them miles above the manufactured cookie-cutter hits of the 1950s. As one writer inscribed, "the relative lack of chart statistics from the time belies the fact that 'I Put a Spell on You' soon became immensely popular." It was testament to the power of teen communication, the networking of sophisticated music fans and informal marketing.

Nick Tosches, never one to hold back on the psychotropic, pulp fiction prose, wrote: "The record became an underground sensation. Screamin' Jay Hawkins' vocal hallucinations were perceived as being invocatory of all manner of horrible things, from anal rape to cannibalism."

As parents made their displeasure known to the record company, Tosches claims that the record was remastered so that its closing "groan-coda" was censored to a fast fade-out. Even that didn't stop radio stations from tossing it in the dump file. Finally, Tosches concludes, "the pubescent sleaze-seekers of America continued to buy the record in great numbers."

Hawkins later recalled, "The record sold, the record did good. They claimed it had cannibalistic sounds, that's why they changed the ending of the first 'I Put a Spell on You.'"

Hawkins complained to Tosches, "Man, it was weird. I was forced to live the life of a monster. I'd go do my act at Rockland Palace and there'd be all these goddam mothers walking the street with picket signs: We don't want our daughters to look at Screamin' Jay Hawkins."

Despite it all, "I Put a Spell on You" became a hit without a major chart position—a nearly unparalleled feat in the music business.

The problem that Jay and his record company faced was how to translate the sales from his singles into making Jay a star. After all, in the mid-1950s, such acts as Little Richard and Jerry Lee Lewis were considered outlandish or revolutionary, and yet they crossed over into the world of teen popularity and continued record sales.

Just like today, rock 'n' roll stars in the 1950s reached out to the public through two primary venues, new records and concerts.

However, the world was a different place back then. Singles were the primary market for the recording industry. Albums wouldn't supplant the 45 in popularity until late in the 1960s. In the mid-1950s, except for jazz musicians, or specific singers such as Frank Sinatra, the best-selling albums were mostly film and theater soundtracks. In 1957 and 1958, the best-selling album for both years was the original cast recording of *My Fair Lady*. In 1959, Henry Mancini's *Music From Peter Gunn* was the best-selling album, then from 1960 through 1965, the best-selling albums were *The Sound of Music, Camelot, West Side Story* (for two years), *Hello Dolly* and *Mary Poppins*.

Still, it was important to produce an album for a singer, as it was a good secondary market. With no follow-up singles, Jay didn't get his first album recording until 1958, when *At Home*

With Screamin' Jay Hawkins was released by Epic Records, a label founded in 1953 for jazz and classical music by Columbia Records, which made it a sister company to OKeh.

OKeh released a couple of more of Screamin' Jay Hawkins' records in 1957, including "You Made Me Love You" with "Darling, Please Forgive Me" on the B-side and "Frenzy" with "Person to Person" on the B-side. The best of the new singles was "Alligator Wine" with "There's Something Wrong With You" on the B-side, which came out around late 1957 or early 1958. The record was written by the famed songwriting team of Jerry Leiber and Mike Stoller, who had also written such songs as "Kansas City," "Jailhouse Rock," "Yakety Yak," and "Hound Dog." The song began this way:

Take the blood out of an alligator, heh
Take the left eye of a fish, heh-heh
Take the skin off of a frog, heh-heh
Heh, and mix it all up in a dish

Either the radio stations were still frightened of Screamin' Jay, or some of these records just flat-out weren't very good, like "You Made Me Love You," because audiences just weren't buying like the record execs anticipated. Even with the help of red-hot tunesmiths Leiber and Stoller, the record failed to rise on the charts.

With no follow-up to "I Put a Spell on You" to make the charts, it was decided that Jay had to be normalized to market him to the public. The result was a very bizarre album that was the antithesis of Screamin' Jay Hawkins. Even the title of the album *At Home With* was designed to make Jay more inviting, as if to say, "come into my house, look I'm just an ordinary fellow." The album cover design is equally as strange as the recordings. Jay is pictured in situ among with a variety of household objects scattered about the room and resplendent in an informal white smoking jacket, bolo tie, sunglasses and a determinedly weird hat. This is set upon a Halloween-orange background contrasted with the pink, yellow and white titles. His head is tilted to the left of the album cover and he has a perplexed look as if to say, "What the hell am I doing here?"

The real shame is in the grooves of the record, where tunes by Hawkins are balanced against a whole group of American songbook classics: "Ol' Man River," "Give Me My Boots & Saddle," "Deep Purple," "You Made Me Love You," "I Love Paris" and "Swing Low, Sweet Chariot."

The real marketing of Jay was in his live performances, but the man appearing in the photograph on the album cover belied his stage presence in every way. His concert days coincided with the release of his record, a standard practice then and one that continues today. The electrifying man on stage would have to convince audiences to buy the sanitized music on that album—a daunting task for any musician.

The Apollo Theater in New York and other Chitlin' Circuit venues, which catered to African American music and audiences, would usually run a stocking-stuffed lineup of performers, who would sing a couple of songs, and then make way for the next act. The Apollo sometimes would do two or three shows a day—all with numerous recording acts. When Alan Freed attempted the first rock 'n' roll concert in Cleveland it was a multi-act program as well. In regard to touring, country-music cavalcades were no different. The big shows that catered to teenagers generally lined up anywhere from a half-dozen to a dozen acts, who would tour regionally, with some acts getting subbed out with different per-formers as the locales changed. For example, a 1957 package tour called "The Biggest Show of Stars for 1957" featured Fats Domi-no, Clyde McPhatter, LaVern Baker, Frankie Lymon, Chuck Berry, The Crickets, Paul Anka, The Everly Brothers, The Spaniels, The Bobbettes, Johnnie and Joe and The Drifters. This tour ran for 80 days, with some of the black groups getting substituted for white singers on the West Coast, or the white singers leaving the show in the South because of segregation laws. At that time, white and black performers could not appear on the same stage.

In 1954, Alan Freed moved his radio show to WINS in New York and within months it became the Number 1 program in the city. In April 1955, Freed organized the first of his rock 'n' roll concerts at what would become his main venue, the Brooklyn Paramount Theater. It was called "Alan Freed and his Rock 'n' Roll Easter Jubilee" and featured his standard, racially integrated lineup of established and up-and-coming singers. The program noted: "In spite of ... mis-guided and ill-advised criticism, 'ROCK 'N Roll' has rapidly gained the affection and esteem of millions of music lovers throughout America. In fact, to such a degree that we are now privileged to present you in person, and on the stage of one of the most beautiful theaters in America, many of the highly accomplished artists whose compositions and recordings have placed them in the 'Hall of Fame' of musical Americana."

The show's lineup included LaVern Baker, The Three Chuckles, Danny Overbea, The Moonglows a.k.a. The Moonlighters, Eddie Fontaine and The Penguins. The backup band would look very familiar to Screamin' Jay: Red Prysock, Sam "The Man" Taylor, Al Sears and Mickey "Guitar" Baker.

Freed's success was good for the music business; for integration; and for African American performers, all of which put him at odds with the musical establishment at the time, and various groups upholding what they perceived was the morality of America in trying to save teenagers from themselves.

As one writer noted, "Freed's programming not only increased WINS' ratings but forced the other largely white pop music stations into a scramble for a black pop presence. He also alarmed the pop music establishment by the success of his concerts and dances, which flushed hundreds of young black performers off the street corners and into recording studios."

After a brawl at an Alan Freed concert in Boston, in May 1958, numerous cities including Boston banned rock 'n' roll shows. The *United Press* reported: "Mayor John B. Hynes banned teen-age rock and roll sessions in public halls following a Boston Arena 'big beat' jam session that erupted into slugging and stabbings. Hynes said, 'These so-called musical programs are a disgrace and must be stopped.'"

The day after the Boston brawl, an editorial in the small Massachusetts paper the *Woburn Times* suggested Alan Freed should be barred from ever conducting a youth entertainment session in Boston or anywhere else, citing an episode at the Paramount Theater "where teenagers danced on the seats, necked in the aisles and screamed and shouted as wide-eyed Freed gazed in ecstatic joy."

Freed put together three more Brooklyn Paramount Shows in 1955, then did three more in 1956 culminating with a December "Alan Freed Christmas Jubilee." The headliner and singing act to close the show was Screamin' Jay Hawkins.

While there is some debate as to how many records "I Put a Spell on You" actually sold after it was released earlier in 1956, the platter and all its controversies caught the attention of Freed. Freed had been promoting rock 'n' roll since the early 1950s and was no stranger to contention when it came to the music. He might even have remembered the young Jalacy J. Hawkins he met back in Cleveland. Jay believed he did.

"Alan Freed was the first man, the first white man that I ever met, that acted like he cared about black people," Jay once told an interviewer. "I mean not just myself alone; I'm talking about Fats Domino; I'm talking about Ruth Brown; I'm talking about Sarah Vaughan; I'm talking about The Clovers and The Coasters and Lloyd Price. Because he not only played our records ... he went into the Fox and the Brooklyn Paramount out there and he carried us everywhere he went."

Freed was uncanny in his ability to tap into the teenage zeit-geist in the mid-1950s, and his selection of Screamin' Jay Hawkins to close his Christmas Jubilee show spoke to that. Freed had a plan and it was just a matter of getting Jay to go along.

As young war babies and postwar babies grew up in the 1950s, they were as mad for all things monsters as they were for rock 'n' roll. Horror B-movies proliferated in the 1950s, many of which were aimed at the teen market. In 1956 alone, two classic horror/monster films were introduced, *Godzilla* and *The Invasion of the Body Snatchers*, although *The Mole People* and *The She Creature* were more in tune with B-movies of the time, many of which were shown at drive-in theaters. In 1957, John Zacherle introduced his first iteration of *Shock Theater* on a local station in Philadelphia and by the next year would have a Top 10 novelty record, "Dinner with Drac." Shlocky horror was abound in pop culture in the '50s; the question was how to capitalize on it.

Freed sensed the inherent campy horror of Jay's song and came up with the idea of a stage act involving Jay climbing out of a coffin before singing. Freed was so confident of his plan that earlier in the day he had a coffin delivered to the Paramount, and had the stage manager figure out how to mic it and wheel it onto the stage.

"The coffin," Jay would always point out, "was Alan Freed's idea." The trouble was that Jay, who was no stranger to doing "supernatural" things on stage, found the coffin idea a little too gruesome. Jay might sing about bad juju, but he wasn't going to challenge the gods by climbing into a sarcophagus.

How Freed talked Jay into using the coffin in his act involved serious bribery, which was a story Jay told often. The only significant change over the years was how much Freed forked over to Jay. By the time Mike Armando joined his backup band in the 1970s, the amount of the bribe had risen to $5,000. In the 1980s, when interviewed by *New York Times* reporter Gerri Hirshey, he brought the number back down to $2,000, although that was probably an exaggeration as well. Louise Harris Murray, who recorded with The Hearts in 1955, remembers getting paid as one of four girl singers $75 for a full week's work at the Apollo Theater. In 1956, the average American salary was $4,450. Getting $2,000 would have been a lot of money in those days. Numerous accounts of that story suggest the sum was actually $300.

Freed corners Jay in his dressing room and starts talking about the hit record and the wild man stage act before getting to the point. He says to Jay, "But you need one more thing."

Jay perks up and asks, "What's that?"

At that point Freed casually responds, "A coffin."

Thinking it's a joke Jay laughs it off, but Freed explains what he's thinking.

Years later, Jay would tell his response to Freed in this off-color way: "Now you don't show this nigger no coffin. 'Cause he knows he gets in that only once. And when he does, he's dead." Undoubtedly, this wasn't what actually was said, because in the 1950s African Americans didn't sling around the N-word and certainly wouldn't have done so in front of someone who hired him for a big show. In either case, Jay's initial response was clear: he wasn't getting into that coffin.

Then Freed begins peeling off bills. Money was always tight for Jay, and in the mid-1950s, up-and-comers like Jay weren't getting a lot of money from record sales or prior gigs. Jay's breaking point would have been reached fairly early.

When Jay told Hirshey he got $2,000, he also bragged to her that Freed told him: "I would have gone another thousand. I've got cameras down there ready to photograph you tonight in that coffin. I want this to be the weirdest show I've ever done, and on top of that, Jay, I can tell you it will be the last one 'cause they're gonna stop us from doing the shows here. They're claiming we're creating too many riots."

That was a great deal of bullshit. For one thing, Freed was just starting out in his relationship with the Brooklyn Paramount. He would do a dozen more shows until his last in 1960. Although there had been some issues in the early shows, Freed's real legal problems with concerts didn't begin until the Boston melee two years later when he was charged with incitement to riot.

Jay was nervous the first time in the coffin and said he got liquored up before he went on stage. He also says he kept one finger resting between the bottom of the coffin and the lid to make sure it didn't close tight on him. Ready or not, Jay was about to experience one of the biggest moments of his music career, one that would forever change his stage presence and influence generations of performers after him.

Freed guessed right. The coffin idea was a "monster" hit with the audience! Even Jay was overwhelmed by the reception he got.

In May 1957, *The Alan Freed Show* premiered on ABC-TV, and among the guests in the first transmission was Screamin' Jay Hawkins. Predating *American Bandstand*, the half-hour show featured a mix of white and black performers, and enjoyed an immediate popularity with the expectation that it would be renewed for the 1957–58 television season. Then the unexpected happened. In one early episode, Frankie Lymon, a black performer, was seen dancing with a white girl. In the thick of segregationist America, this otherwise innocuous dance threw ABC's Southern affiliates into a tizzy. The show was immediately canceled.

Freed tried to do one more thing for Screamin' Jay: get him into the movies.

In 1955, a grim little movie about rebellious teenagers hit the big screen and became an overnight sensation. Called *Blackboard Jungle,* it starred Sidney Poitier and Vic Morrow as unruly students in a class taught by Glenn Ford. The soundtrack was propelled by the first rock 'n' roll hit of the 1950s, "Rock Around the Clock" by Bill Haley and His Comets.

Suddenly, there was a teenage movie market, and the smaller, independent studios crashed around for a decade trying to find a way to reach those school-age kids with an extra dollar in their pocket to spend on a flick. One way to reach them was the Pied Piper of teenagers, Alan Freed, who starred in five rock 'n' roll movies between 1956 and 1959. The plot lines were irrelevant. The key to all these movies was to introduce as many current rock 'n' roll acts to teenage moviegoers as possible within the confines of a 90-minute script.

The first film in the Alan Freed genre was an obvious rip-off of *Blackboard Jungle,* a movie called *Rock Around the Clock* featuring Bill Haley and His Comets, The Platters, Freddie Bell and The Bellboys, and Lisa Gaye. That same year Alan Freed also appeared in *Rock, Rock, Rock,* featuring Teddy Randazzo, Tuesday Weld, Chuck Berry, Frankie Lymon & the Teenagers, Johnny Burnette, LaVern Baker, Flamingos and Moonglows. Every movie in which Freed was involved struck a balance between black and white performers. This was at a time when Hollywood movies, and television beaming from the studios in New York, hardly showed African American actors or performers, so it was a very courageous position by Freed and the small studios that developed his movies.

Although Freed would do three more movies in this genre, the format went off the tracks in his third film, *Mister Rock and Roll.* Released by Paramount Pictures in 1957, it was ostensibly about how Alan Freed discovered "Rock and Roll" (an establishment wording, not the true term used by the fans and musicians, "rock 'n' roll"). Somehow into the mix and the plotline wandered the boxer Rocky Graziano, and jazz musician Lionel Hampton. Then came the usual roll-out of singers: Ferlin Husky, Frankie Lymon, Little Richard, Brook Benton, Chuck Berry, Clyde McPhatter, LaVern Baker and Screamin' Jay Hawkins—or not.

All the acts made it onto the screen except Screamin' Jay Hawkins. To his credit, Jay never blamed anyone else for the idea to appear in the film as a half-naked African tribesman. If it was better for Jay not to do something, then he would certainly do it. If the problem with "I Put a Spell on You" was that the sounds Jay made were too "cannibalistic," and the solution to that would have been to appear in the film well-dressed like all the other singers in the movie, then Jay was going to do the opposite—shove that cannibal business in the audience's face. It was a serious miscalculation, because Paramount decided not to allow that segment in the final movie. Freed deserves some culpability here as well. Part of the underlying reason his films were made was to show America what wonderful, clean-cut, everyday people their teenage children were listening to on the radio. If the message was that rock 'n' rollers weren't bogeymen, why allow a singer to be filmed as some kind of bogeyman?

"I walked on naked apart from a loincloth; white shoe polish marks on my face; my hair combed straight up; a spear in one hand and a shield in the other, like one of those wild Mau Maus," he recalled.

He was not in a loincloth, but what looked like a big sheet that was tied around his waist at the top, and hung down to his knees. Shell necklaces adorned his neck, sandals were on his feet, and in his hand was a tambourine.

The song he was singing for the film was called "Frenzy," and as written, it was tamer than one would imagine.

Dig this crazy mood I'm in
Listen to my heart as it starts to spin
When you kiss me, do it again I'm in a frenzy
Watch my eyes when you light them up
Listen to me whine, like a harpsichord
When you touch me I warm right up I'm in a frenzy

The song, written by songwriter Don Hess, boasted a fine rock guitar lead, with deeply baritone vocals from Jay. Then after singing the word "frenzy" he would venture off into that unknown musical ether of Hawkins mumble-jumble.

The Paramount executives didn't spark to Jay's desire to stand out from the crowd of popular musicians at 200 decibels, nor did they spark to his portrayal of black stereotypes. Jay noted, "The movie people claimed it would be an insult to the black people of the United States." The scene was soon excised from the final film.

It wouldn't be the last time Jay would be accused of insulting black people. The NAACP also took issue with Jay, especially when he began using a fake bone through his nose.

During a radio interview in England, Jay ranted: "The NAACP came after me and said, 'Do you know what you are doing to your own race?' I said, 'You take your own race and you know where you can stick 'em. I'm trying to make a living. Will you get outta here and leave me alone?' Sammy Davis wrote me a letter saying give $500 and join the NAACP. I said show me one thing they've done for black people and I will join. I never heard from either one again."

Regarding that bone in his nose, Mike Armando recalls, "Someone wrote a story about it. He didn't care. He used to say, 'I was born naked, black and ugly and when I die, I'm going out naked, black and ugly.' He never cared what people thought about him."

Paramount cared, and Jay was tossed out of the movie. Another opportunity missed in the post-"I Put a Spell on You" days.

CHAPTER

5

when

Alan Freed peeled off cash to entice Screamin' Jay Hawkins to do the coffin act, it wasn't a financial hardship to the rock 'n' roll impresario. He was making very good money on his concerts and could afford slapping Jay's palm with some green. Freed's first show at the Brooklyn Paramount in April 1955, the Rock 'n' Roll Easter Jubilee Stage Program, grossed $107,000, which overwhelmed the house record set in 1932 by the now-forgotten crooner Russ Columbo. His second show in September of the same year grossed $154,000, netting Freed $125,000 to split with promoter Morris Levy and his radio station WINS.

For a promoter, there was good money to be made running concerts. For performers, there was enough income if they weren't cheated (which was often) to keep them on the road.

"By the fall of 1957, the package tours were crisscrossing the land again, hitting even the smaller towns," wrote Ed Ward in *The History of Rock & Roll*.

Jay could be a charming, funny personality when he wanted to be, and that's the side of him Freed saw. He liked Jay, and really tried to help him get his career launched, including adding him to a Big Beat tour he put together in 1957. As a headline in *Cash Box* magazine read, "Alan Freed Pacted for Six Week Tour" that included Buddy Holly, Chuck Berry, Frankie Lymon, Danny and The Juniors, The Chantels, Sam "The Man" Taylor, Milt Shaw and two prickly, spontaneously unreliable piano players, Jerry Lee Lewis and Screamin' Jay Hawkins. Lewis has often been quoted about touring with Jay, whom he liked very much. As Lewis told friends in England, he never thought of Jay as competition. Lewis thought of him as "something of a vaudeville act rather than a musical act."

By 1958, the hierarchy changed on the Big Beat Tour. At the end of 1957, Jerry Lee Lewis, a pretty good showman as well, had his biggest hit with "Great Balls of Fire," which reached Number 2 on the pop charts in the prior December. He followed those up with two more hit records in 1958, "Breathless" and "High School Confidential." As a result, Jerry Lee Lewis was the new headliner for the tour with Buddy Holly, Chuck Berry, Frankie Lymon and the secondary headliners. The Diamonds and Billy and Lillie headlined what could probably be called the third tier of stars. They were followed in the advertisements by other down-listed acts like The Chantels, Danny and The Juniors and Screamin' Jay Hawkins, all of whom were fading due to lack of new hit records.

There were already hints of Screamin' Jay Hawkins' impending position at the bottom rung of a show roster. An ad for The Jubilee of Stars show in the Akron, Ohio newspapers in August 1957 boasted headliners Roy Hamilton, The Clovers, The Spaniels and what looks to be the new addition to the lineup, Johnny and Joe. The down-listers were Screamin' Jay Hawkins and two singers who never made the big time, Donnie Elbert and Ella Johnson.

Just when things couldn't get worse, they did. Screamin' Jay

Hawkins had been a popular singer at the Apollo Theater in New York, but a flyer for a November 29, 1957 show illustrates just how far down Jay had fallen. This was a concert presented by Tommy "Dr. Jive" Smalls, another popular deejay in the New York metro area. The headliners were Ray Charles and former backup bandmate Mickey Baker, now part of the duo Mickey and Sylvia. The next level of singers were the doo-wop groups The Velours, Kodaks and The Jesters, followed by a lower listing of Bobby Day. Finally, the lowest listing of the concert featured Screamin' Jay Hawkins and Tiny Topsy (a 250-pound singer whose real name was Otha Lee Moore)—as if the bottom rung was for circus acts.

Position on the tour roster was a big deal, and Jay, who put a lot of soul into his act to make it stand out from the noise, began to chafe at perceived slights when others who he thought were lesser acts appeared ahead of him. He began to create, antagonize, if not quiet enemies.

Jay told Nick Tosches a story about being on a package tour in 1957 with Fats Domino, The Cadillacs, Billy Williams and Billy and Lillie when a young kid by the name of Paul Anka was added to the show. Anka was a timely addition as he had a Number 1 hit that summer with a song called "Diana." "I'm already tired, I just come off the road," Jay says. "Fats Domino was slated to close the show, but Fats canceled out for some reason which we don't have to go into here. My manager asked me to go in Fats Domino's spot, so I insisted on the closing spot of the show, and I was politely told that Paul Anka was going to close the show. I said, 'To hell with Paul Anka.' So Paul Anka walks over to me and he says, 'I'll come to your funeral.' What a goddam punk."

Discomfort was part and parcel of the tour schedule. However, the real problem for performers on package shows, whether on the road or at a permanent venue such as the Apollo Theater in New York, was hierarchy. At the Apollo, newcomers and those with lesser hits were assigned dressing rooms on the third floor while headliners got the bigger dressing rooms on the second floor. All that mattered on the tour were hits. You either had one, or you suffered immensely for not having one. Sometimes, if you had a big hit while touring, you got moved up on the show. As time went on, if your act failed to hit the charts again or never did, you would be dropped at a moment's notice. Then you were left to your own devices and those of your management company—if you still had one.

Tommy "Dr. Jive" Smalls, like Alan Freed, would also put together tours, mostly focusing on black performers. In November 1956, he brought his New York show to the Howard Theatre Washington, D.C. The flyer for the show reads: "Dr. Jive, the disc jockey who has all New York rockin' and rollin' now sends to Washington his ALL STAR RHYTHM AND BLUES JAMBOREE, direct from a record smashing run at Harlem's famous Apollo Theater." This was the year of the "I Put a Spell on You" release, but that didn't matter to Smalls who organized the show in order of hit songs. From the top, the featured singers with their featured songs were The Dells, "Oh What a Night"; The Debutantes, "Song Sweeties"; The El Dorados, "A Fallen Tear"; Screaming (Screamin') Jay Hawkins, "Take Me Back."

When Screamin' Jay Hawkins was still an up-and-comer, he would play anywhere he could get a gig. For example, in May 1955, he appeared at The Fat Man in Delaware County, Pennsylvania. An advertisement in the local paper read: The Fat Man; Jam Session Saturday 3:00–6:00; Starting Monday, May 30; Screamin' Jay Hawkins; our specialty Chicken—Spaghetti; Mattero's "T" Bar."

After Jay hit with "I Put a Spell on You" as a solo act, he played slightly better joints. A set of *Philadelphia Inquirer* ads atop one another in October 1957 showed Count Basie at Pep's on 516 South Broad Street while Screamin' Jay Hawkins was headlining a bill with Tiny Grimes playing Tunick's Show Bar on Broad above Erie.

OKeh released a smattering of the Screamin' Jay Hawkins singles between 1956 and 1958, starting with "You Made Me Love You" with "Darling, Please Forgive Me" on the B-side and "Frenzy" with "Person to Person" on the B-side. In 1958, it finally released "Alligator Wine" with "There's Something Wrong With You" on the B-side. None of the new releases were successful. Going conservative with classics was as fruitless as experimenting with a more swamp-like release such as "Alligator Wine."

With nothing working, Jay headed down to Philadelphia where he hooked up with Red Top Records, which was trying to make a name for itself pushing doo-wop with groups The Students, The Turbans and The Quin-Tones.

At Red Top, Screamin' Jay Hawkins doubled down on "Screamin' Jayness" with a record that no radio station in America would play even if a deejay could be found to try it. Taking aim at popular perfume Chanel Number 5, the record was called "Armpit #6" with "The Past" on the B-side. The refrain:

You dig for yourself my chick from the sticks
with a whole kinda perfume called Armpit #6

"Armpit #6" was a long way from The Quin-Tones' "Down the Aisle of Love":

We exchange our vows to love one another
No matter how things may be
We promise to always stay with each other until eternity

Meanwhile, Jay was touring incessantly, continually refining his act. Not every show had a coffin, but Jay was continually adding zaniness. In 1957, a local news magazine in the New York area sent a reporter to interview Jay, who was playing a one-week stand with Dr. Jive's Rhythm and Blues Revue at the Apollo Theater. He reported that Screamin' Jay was wearing a zebra tuxedo, complete with zebra cape, zebra gloves and zebra shoes. Looking around the dressing room, the reporter saw in the closet an array of loud suits in white, green, pink, yellow and fire-engine red.

Jay opened a drawer in the dresser and pulled out a full-length set of polka-dotted long underwear. "When I wear that tux, I finish with a strip and jump down into the audience in these. I get a bigger kick out of it than the audience. I try to do anything that's impossible when I'm on the stage." Never one for modesty, Jay said of his stage performance, "Man the chicks were gassed when I grabbed the spotlight."

The Apollo Show which took place in early summer 1957 included Screamin' Jay Hawkins, Bo Diddley, The Cardinals, Larry Birdsong and El Boy, among others. One of the New York newspapers spotlighted the upcoming show, writing: "Screamin' Jay Hawkins who has his own way of putting over a song has become a favorite with the Apollo fans. His recording of 'I Put a Spell on You' caught the fancy of the record buying public. A dynamic stage performer, Hawkins has his own style of delivering a song." The accompanying photo showed Jay in his matinee idol pose, looking dandy with a Rhett Butler oversized tie.

Bo Diddley was once interviewed for a documentary about Screamin' Jay and told this tale: "Somebody told me, you're playing Detroit and the Flame Show Bar, and I said, yes. They said Screamin' Jay Hawkins is coming after you to close; so my band and I, we played the gig and we were hanging around Detroit for a couple of days and Screamin' Jay came in, and the promoter came running up to the hotel and asked us if we wanted to work another couple of nights, and we said sure, we weren't doing anything. We found out Screamin' Jay Hawkins had ran all of the people out. He did 'I Put a Spell on You' and…the people freaked out and ran out of the club. He tore the place up! It was kind of hard to go on stage behind an act that kids want to see again and again and again with the bones and flashing. Even me, I would stand and watch."

Michael Ochs, brother of folksinger Phil Ochs, and well-known rock-music photographer, recalls that in 1957, when he was 14, he went to see one of Alan Freed's shows at the New York Paramount Theater. "It was before the coffin phase and what he did was, they would announce Screamin' Jay Hawkins and the stage would be bare but across the stage would come these clattering teeth. Then the curtains would open, and this guy would have his back to you, and then he would jump into a turn-around. As a kid you would just jump back."

Although accoutrements to the act such as a cane topped with a cigarette-smoking skull would come later, in the mid-1950s, Jay mostly employed garish suits and weird ties to accent his strangeness. As Jay told a reporter in 1957, "My records are selling pretty fine, but I think you have to see me to appreciate me."

The Apollo show was important for one eventual addition to the act, Graham Knight. Knight, who helped Jay when he toured England with an updated smoke machine. Jay's original fuse box was created by one of the Schiffman brothers, whose father Frank owned the Apollo Theater. The original smoke machine was a simple device, basically a box with a fuse wire. Once the box was plugged in, it would emit a spark, which would light up flash powder. The resulting smoke could be colored by adding different elements; for example, if you wanted purple you could add potassium to the powder. The fuse box would cause endless problems in the years ahead.

For young male performers, the package show tours were, to use 1950s terminology, a real gas. What was not to like? The package shows consisted of playing music, associating with talented recording artists, camaraderie, boozing, more boozing and plenty of women to meet.

A Screamin' Jay story about boozing:

Now, the Chitlin' Circuit, we used to use that name in the United States when talking about opening at the Apollo Theater in Harlem. We do seven days and from there we would go to Washington at the Howard Theater and from Washington to Baltimore to the Royal Theatre. From Baltimore to Cleveland to the Circle Theatre and Cleveland to Chicago to the Regal Theater, that's the Chitlin' Circuit. So in between shows we drank. We drank, and we were drunk when we went out before the audience, but we always managed to stand up straight. Nobody could tell we were drunk....Guys like Jesse Belvin, Johnny Ace, Guitar Slim, we had drinking sessions with a gallon of Italian Swiss Colony Muscatel wine, and we'd sit in the hallways of the Teresa Hotel, which is very famous in Harlem, or the Cecil Hotel, which is another famous one on 118th Street and Lennox Avenue. And we would sit there, and after we got about halfway down the gallon I would say, "we've got a show tomorrow." And while I'm talking, I'm pulling off my clothes and the next thing I know I'm sitting in the hallway naked and Slim's naked, then somebody wakes us up early in the morning and says, "You can't lay in the hallway naked. And besides it's time to go back to the theater and do the show."

This was an extremely talented, wonderfully handsome, and very unfortunate group of young men.

Guitar Slim, whose real name was Eddie Jones, is best known for his million-selling record, "The Things I Used to Do," which resided at Number 1 for 14 weeks on the R&B charts in 1954. This was an important song in the eventual development of soul music in the 1960s, especially because it was produced by a young Ray Charles. Unfortunately for Guitar Slim, he was a one-hit wonder and became an alcoholic, dying of pneumonia at the age of 32.

Jessie Belvin, a talented singer and songwriter, is credited with writing and cowriting a number of R&B hits including "Earth Angel." He is best known for his single "Goodnight My Love," a Top 10 R&B hit, which Alan Freed used to close his radio program. He died in a car accident at the age of 27.

Johnny Ace, whose real name was John Marshall Alexander Jr., was the most popular R&B singer in the country in the early 1950s. His first record, "My Song," topped the R&B charts in 1952 for nine weeks, and his last record, "Pledging My Love," was Number 1 on the R&B charts for 10 weeks in 1955. It was a posthumous hit, as he died by allegedly killing himself playing Russian roulette at a Christmas Day concert the year before. He was just 25 years old.

In Ace, Belvin and Jones, the music world lost three legends at far too young an age.

Perhaps it was a miracle Hawkins was able to avoid such calamities—although he did come close to an early demise.

Hawkins claims to have stopped drinking in 1957. As he told a reporter later on, "You're talking to a man who for over 28 years stayed pickled and then stopped. I mean I drank everything I could get my hands on; in the Army, Air Force and in civilian life I drank a 190 proof grain alcohol, mixed with Black & White Scotch and a Jack Daniels for a chaser. I went to bed like this and woke up like this."

The reporter was dubious, not about Hawkins' feats of alcoholism, but that he stopped drinking. If Jay did stop drinking, it didn't last. When Mike Armando played in Jay's backup band in the 1970s, he recalled, "Jay was a heavy drinker, smoked a lot of marijuana, and took a lot of prescription pills."

In 1962, Jay finally went back into the studio with another small independent label to record the songs "I Hear Voices" and "Just Don't Care." The company was called Enrica Records, which was formed in New York four years before by Theodore "Teddy"

McRae and Eddie Wilcox. The company was located at 1697 Broadway near the epicenter of pop music at the Brill Building 1619 Broadway and 1650 Broadway. Jay migrated down Broadway to the Brill Building and began working with one of the best songwriting duos in the history of pop music, Gerry Goffin and Carole King. Also briefly recording for Enrica was a familiar name yet slightly altered, Fender Guitar Slim, who likely could have brought Jay to the label, because in 1962, Jay needed all the help he could get to jump-start a dormant career.

The best summation of what happened to Jay, and why he needed all the help he could get, comes from Bill Millar, Jay's lifelong friend from England, who was always willing to write a positive review, or touch up the liner notes on one of Jay's albums.

"Independent labels like Red Top ("Armpit #6") and Enrica ("Just Don't Care") were separated by a prison sentence imposed for a misdemeanor more serious than flashing," Millar wrote. On October 3, 1958 Hawkins pleaded guilty to the "carnal knowledge of a 15-year-old girl and the possession of cannabis."

Jet magazine of September 25, 1958, ran the story with this headline: "Singer Jay Hawkins Admits to Rape Charge." The small story read: "Rock 'n' roll singer Screamin' Jay Hawkins, 28, pleaded guilty to charges of statutory rape of a 15-year-old Akron girl and possession of narcotics in Cleveland, Ohio. Hawkins and the girl were allegedly found in the singer's room at the Majestic Hotel. If convicted, he could get as much as three to 35 years in prison."

Millar, who gained Jay's prison records, wrote that the minimum sentence was recorded as two years and the maximum sentence as 20 years. Jay was luckier than most as he was granted parole on October 15, 1959 and released in November 1960. His prison records also contained some interesting notes about Jay having a few run-ins with the law, for delinquency in 1943, "suspicion" (of what we don't know) in 1954, charges of bastardy

PHILIPS
PROMOTIONAL COPY
NOT FOR SALE
40606
1-43954
MRC
Music, Inc.
(BMI) 2:17
STONE CRAZY
(J. Hawkins)
SCREAMIN' JAY HAWKINS
Arranged by Jay Hawkins
String arrangements by
Shorty Rogers
WKINS
a spell
you
ttle
mon
I HEAR VOICES
(Jay Hawkins)
SCREAMIN' JAY HAWKINS
and the CHICKEN HAWKS
45-127-A
Vocal with
Rhythm
45 RPM

ENRICA

1697 BROAD

ENRICA
HIGH FIDELITY
45 RPM

1010-A

"I HEAR VOICES"
(Jay Hawkins)
"SCREAMIN" JAY HAWKINS
And The Chicken Hawks
With Teddy McRae Och.
PRODUCED BY ENRICA RECORDS INC.

AT HO

SCREAMI
JAY HAWKINS

Including:
I PUT A SPELL ON YOU
ORANGE COLORED SKY
HONG KONG
OL' MAN RIVER
YELLOW COAT
TEMPTATION
...and more!

45 R.P.M.
OB 7460

U.K. SUBJECT TO
PRICE CONDITIONS
E PRICE LISTS

THE WHAMMY
(Hawkins)
SCREAMIN' JAY HAWKINS
with Orchestra conducted
by Sammy Lowe
Producers Hugo & Luigi

MADE IN GT. BRITAIN

featuring
Screamin'
Jay Hawkins

SIDE A
1. **Tiny's Jump
2. Hey Now
3. Why Did You
   Waste My Time?
4. St Louis Blues
5. Drinking Beer
6. My Baby's Left Me
7. *Frankie And Johnny
   Boogie – 1

SIDE B
1. **Hey Mr J B
2. **Battle Of The Mass
3. **I'm In Love With You
   Baby
4. My Baby's Cool
5. Hawaiian Boogie
6. **No Hug No Kiss
7. *Frankie And Johnny
   Boogie – 2

No.121 September/Octobe

Unlimited
Blues

MANUFACTURERS OF THE WORK RESERVED COPYING. PUBLIC PERFORMANCE AND BROADCASTING OF THIS RECORD PROHIBITED

PLANET

33⅓ r.p.m.

PLL 1001
℗ 1966

Side One

'THE NIGHT AND DAY OF,
SCREAMIN' JAY HAWKINS,'
1. Night And Day (Porter) Chappells.
2. In My Dream (Hawkins) Robbins.
3. I Wanna Know (Cop. Control)
4. Your Kind Of Love (Hawkins) Robbins.
5. Change Your Ways (Hawkins) Robbins
6. Serving Time (Hawkins) Robbins

SCREAMIN' JAY HAWKINS
A Contemporary Record
Production

MANUFACTURED AND DISTRIBUTED BY PHILIPS RECORDS LTD.

45 RPM

CRE

"Okeh" Trade Mark Reg. U.S. Pat. Off. Marca Registr

ALLIGATOR WIN
- Leiber - Stoler -
SCREAMIN' JAY HAWKINS
Orch. under the dir. of
Leroy Kirkland

(a lawsuit filed to determine payment for a child born out of wedlock) and non-support in 1954 and 1958.

One of the more unusual coincidences about Jay's time in prison was that he became friends with a tough white kid who also had musical aspirations. Outlaw country singer David Allan Coe spent time in Ohio's Mansfield State Reformatory, and when he wrote his autobiography called *Just for the Record,* he referred back to his incarceration with this note: "Screamin' Jay Hawkins played saxophone in the band and I spent many hours with him writing songs and learning some basic piano structures."

Immediately upon release, Jay was able to get back on the package tour circuit. A Pittsburgh show at the Syria Mosque on December 5, 1960, was put together by local deejay Porky "The Daddio of Radio" Chedwick and it was simply called "The Hit Makers." In order of listing were Hank Ballard and The Midnighters, The Drifters, Dee Clark, Jerry Butler, Isley Brothers, Bo Diddley, The Spaniels, Blue Notes and Screamin' Jay Hawkins. If anyone is curious how much money the acts made on the road, it could be useful to see what the promoter expected from the gate. For this set of shows at 7:30 and 10:30, the cheapest seats were $2 and the most expensive were $3. The Syria Mosque seated 3,700 people so even if the average ticket came to be $2.50, the maximum gate was less than $10,000, which had to be divided up among many players including nine acts.

In May of the next year, The *Delaware County Daily Times* ran a promotion for a place called El Rancho Club featuring Carmen G and his Band, with a plug for Jay that read, "Also Sunday Only, Screamin' Jay Hawkins Quintet."

With his career in flux, Jay was trying his hand at different music formats, such as heading up a small group emulating the jazz bands of the early 1950s when he started out in the music business. Club work didn't pay a lot of money so it was difficult to keep a quintet in business. Then, an unfortunate accident sent his career in an entirely different direction. The timeline is a bit cloudy as Jay's stories shift. The year was now 1962, and Jay was performing in Miami when one of his fuse boxes exploded in the face of a young singer named Pat Newborn (real name Patricia Williams). This quickly led to an affair. Jay was almost twice her age: he was 33 and she was just 18 years old.

In 1962, Jay was still scatting around the country looking for gigs—and then he met Pat Newborn, sometimes known as Shoutin' Pat Newborn. With Pat recovered from her burns, he forged an act with his new lover. As he often did, Jay returned to the Philly area where he still had some contacts.

Jay's long association with the Philadelphia music scene helped him get a recording session with locally based Chancellor Records, owned by Bob Marcucci, who also managed two teen idols, Frankie Avalon and Fabian. They were the two recording stars of Chancellor Records. The teen idol kind of soft, gurgley pop sound was Chancellor's specialty, with Avalon, Fabian, Jodie Sands, even an early Johnny Rivers. It was also the antithesis of Screamin' Jay Hawkins. Nevertheless, in June of 1962 Jay and Pat recorded a new song by Jay called "Ashes" with "Nitty Gritty" as the B-side for Chancellor.

This was as teenybopper as Jay could get with a basic late-1950s rock 'n' roll beat. Jay sang lead, and Pat followed behind as the one-person chorus. The record was more Frankie Avalon than Screamin' Jay.

Jay: Ashes, ashes, ashes of a broken heart
Pat (chorus): Ashes, gray, gray ashes, ashes, gray, gray ashes
Jay: Since we're apart

Jay and Pat got together because of a burn injury and now they were singing about ashes. The B-side was an equally bopperish song called "Nitty Gritty," not to be confused with the Shirley Ellis hit record "The Nitty Gritty," which was a Top 10 record the following year. Jay was a talented singer, who could move from rock 'n' roll to blues and standards, but Chancellor's young teen sound was way beyond (or below) him.

The record did get released although not picked up. A music trade publication in September 1962 posted a small notice about the record: "SCREAMIN' JAY HAWKINS WITH PAT NEWBORN; Four Stars; Nitty Gritty—CHANCELLOR 1117; Screamin' Jay returns to the disk scene after a long absence with a strongly R&B-oriented rocker side, based on a new dance, the Nitty Gritty. Good beat here and the chatter is worth some play (Rambed, BMI) (2:27); Three Stars Ashes—(Rambed, BMI) (2:26) Moderate Sales Potential."

Looking back, a reviewer in 1975 wrote, "The original 'Spell' will always remain a World Classic of Soul Music (nothing can ever detract from that side's place in the history of our music), and his CHANCELLOR outing, 'Ashes,' was undoubtedly the best of his rest …"

Pat got something out of it. On both sides of the single, the artist attribution read SCREAMIN' JAY HAWKINS on the first line and the words WITH PAT NEWBORN on the second line.

With the Jay and Pat act not really going anywhere, the two hit splitsville for a while and it appears Pat fell apart emotionally before they got back together on the cusp of the new year.

A curious gossip item in the *Pittsburgh Courier* of December 8, 1962 read: "Screamin' Jay Hawkins quickly became engaged to his vocalist-partner Pat Newborn as soon as she rejoined his act. Pat's mother learning that her daughter, disgusted with show business, had flown from New York to Washington, packed Pat's belongings and took her home to Long Island. Screamin' Jay, taking no more chances of losing Pat, again sealed their 'partnership' with a huge diamond engagement ring."

Jay and Pat, now engaged, were back at it early the next year. On January 18, 1963, the *Courier-Post*, which serves South New Jersey near Philadelphia, ran an advertisement for La Maina's Musical Bar in Cherry Hill, New Jersey, exclaiming that a week before the big show with the Carroll Brothers, the club was featuring The Nite-Cappers, "The Rage of Wildwood" plus an added attraction, Screamin' Jay Hawkins and Pat Newborn.

The following week, the *Philadelphia Daily News* ran a La Maina's advertisement promoting the "added attraction" of Screamin' Jay Hawkins and Pat Newborn, behind the headliners the Carroll Brothers featuring Peter Carroll, a five-person combo of white musicians that had been recording since 1958. The ad publicized the fact that Pete Carroll had "starred in the motion picture *Don't Knock the Twist*," which, ironically, was a knockoff title of an Alan Freed vehicle called *Don't Knock the Rock*. By 1962, teenage movies hadn't changed much, and although there was no Alan Freed, the movie featured a truckload of black and white performers including Chubby Checker, Gene Chandler, Vic Dana, Linda Scott, The Dovells, Len Barry and the Carroll Brothers.

It's awfully cold in Pennsylvania in January, but wonderfully warm in Waikiki. Jay and Pat decided to relocate. The version that Jay tells of this move is that he heroically nursed Pat through her injuries then went with her to Honolulu.

To reporter Richard Guillatt in the 1980s, a bitter Jay explained the move to Hawaii this way: "I got sick of the whole thing because I was stereotyped. When I came along they didn't know if I was a novelty, a comedian...they billed me as a rock 'n' roll clown, the Man of Many Faces, the Voodoo Prince, the witchdoctor. I've been called everything in the world and I still am to this day. Because of my act, and because of the weird things I was doing, in 1958, I decided the people of America just wasn't ready for me. I wasn't making money, I wasn't in the clique."

Maral Nigolian, who met Jay later in his life and after his death tried to find all the children resulting from his sexual encounters, was interviewed in a documentary talking about Jay and Pat. The story that Jay had told her, which she related in the interview, ran like this: "He had a girlfriend named Pat Newborn and was trying to get away from her. He caught a flight to Hawaii and she got the traffic controllers to stop the plane and join him on the plane to Hawaii. The escape to Hawaii to get away from her didn't work because she followed. In 1962, Jay moved to Hawaii."

Jay has a third story to explain the reason they went to Hawaii. When he arrived in England for his first tour, he told Bill Millar that he was heading to Japan by ship when Pat fell sick on board. Since Honolulu was the nearest port, they stepped off in Hawaii and liked it so much they stayed for two years.

However, a fourth story is the most likely. Jack Cione, who ran a string of nightclubs in Hawaii, was looking to bring rhythm and blues singers from the mainland to work his clubs. "He was touring as a singer and I bought his act," says Cione.

To a documentarian, Jack added, "I was the first one to bring Screamin' Jay Hawkins to Paradise. At that time, his career was taking a slowdown on the mainland. He was working joints in Atlantic City at that period of time. He fit in perfect for my joints in Hawaii, the budgets were the same."

Hawaii sounded better than Atlantic City or Philadelphia, so Jay decided to take up Jack Cione's offer. Everyone was in for a shock. When he arrived he brought along Pat, whom he introduced as his wife. "Everyone who first met him thought he was married," laughs Jack. "Then he started fucking this little blonde chick. He was quite a character in his love life."

Pat, a very beautiful, light-skinned African American woman, had a sexual appetite about as kinky as that of her partner. She would sometimes seduce women and then bring them back to her apartment to share with Jay. It was here where Lee Angel (Audrey Sherbourne) got her revenge. "I met Pat Newborn in New York before they went to Hawaii," says Lee Angel. In a British documentary Lee calls Pat a "female Satan." "I didn't like her, but I had fun with her. She had a reputation of picking up girls for Jay and I let her pick me up on purpose. She didn't know I knew Jay. When we came to the apartment, I said, 'Nice meeting you, Mr. Hawkins.' He didn't say much of anything."

Was Pat interested in a threesome? Angel says no, "not with me. She watched Jay and I have sex."

Milan Melvin, an actor and friend of Jay's, says in the documentary *I Put a Spell on Me* that when he met Jay in Hawaii, Jay explained the attraction of Pat Newborn: she was a wonderful lover because she brought home other women and he got to ball them both. "Three-ways were common with Pat," says Melvin, although Jay took umbrage if Pat brought a woman home to make love to without Jay.

If Jay and Pat were still "engaged" at this point, there was definitely a looseness about the relationship. Jay was now working for a guy who ran a series of strip clubs with a lot of beautiful, young Asian and Hawaiian women. As Jack noted, "He was like a fox in the chicken coop." The abundance of so many available women was a big surprise to Jay and certainly made him think twice about having brought Pat to Hawaii. Again, a pertinent observation from Jack: if Jay had known about the environment he was going to be working in, "he would never have brought his sandwich to the banquet."

Jay and Pat recorded one other record at the Forbidden City Nite Klub. Released on The Sounds of Hawaii label, the A-side was a remake of "Whammy" with "Seems Like You Just Don't Care," an appropriately titled song considering what happened next.

One of Jack's waitresses, who instantly caught the attention of Jay, was Virginia (Ginny) Sabellona, whom he eventually decided to marry in 1964. There were two problems with that announcement. The first was that Jay was already engaged to Pat Newborn, and even if that had ended, he was still in a relationship with her. Pat was not the most emotionally stable woman, and the pronouncement by Hawkins of the upcoming marriage caught her by thunderous surprise. Outraged, she stabbed Hawkins with a nine-inch kitchen knife.

According to Lee Angel (Audrey Sherbourne), the event unfolded this way. "Jay was living with Pat. On this particular day he was packing his shit to leave when Pat walked in. He told Pat, 'It's over; I just got married.' That's when Pat tried to kill him." There are numerous, gruesome stories of this stabbing, with some reports of Pat opening up a wound from the back of Jay's neck to the base of his spine. In the most heroic, if not outlandish, rehash of this event, Jay told Bill Millar that Pat plunged the nine-inch butcher's knife into his back, puncturing both his lung and diaphragm. He was hospitalized for several weeks, but not before chasing Pat several blocks, before fainting through loss of blood.

One eyewitness to Jay's hospital stay was Jack Cione, who said all that *Psycho* movie horror stuff was absolutely fictitious. "I visited him in the hospital after the incident. It wasn't a bad wound, just a little hole. Nothing serious."

A local paper headlined the story this way: "Waikiki Nitery Singer Stabbed; Girl Questioned." The brief article read: "A Waikiki night club singer was stabbed in the back this morning in the apartment of a 20-year-old girlfriend who told police that they were arguing and she stabbed him. Jalacy J., Screaming Jay, Hawkins, 36, is in 'fair' condition at Queens Hospital today. Police are holding the woman for further questioning."

Jack's story about the small wound is probably accurate, as it doesn't appear Pat served time for stabbing Jay, and the incident was treated as no more than a domestic disturbance. "After she was arrested, she eventually left town. She wasn't put in jail," says Jack. "She found a boyfriend who took care of her. I think she ended up in New Zealand."

Fortunately, Jay survived, but his troubles with women would follow him wherever he went.

The second problem with his marriage to the woman he called Ginny was that he was still married to his first wife Anna Mae. According to Ohio divorce records, Anna and Jay weren't divorced until February 2, 1970. The divorce was granted to Anna on grounds of "extreme cruelty," which technically means either physical violence or acts of mental cruelty which endanger safety or health.

Jack Cione ran a dozen entertainment venues in Hawaii, and not all of them were strip clubs. One of his properties, the Dunes, was a supper club and brought in big-name talent including a host of African American performers like Pearl Bailey, Sammy Davis Jr. and Redd Foxx.

As Jack liked to say about Jay, "he liked it so much here, he stayed for three years." Besides the tropical weather, one of the reasons Jay stayed so long in Hawaii was because he and Jack got along like two old army pals. In fact, Jack opened a nightclub called the Show Bar, specifically for Jay to host. It was a good spot for a guy like Jay, because the Show Bar was located on Hotel Street. Hotel Street was popular with American servicemen looking for booze, women and a place to hang for those long, languid nights when one didn't have to return to the confines of a ship or barracks.

"I always wanted to open a nightclub for the black community in Honolulu," says Jack. "There was no hangout for black people; and with the Navy, Air Force and Marines in town, Hawaii had a lot of black people and they had no club of their own."

The Show Bar became the number one club in town and it wasn't even burlesque. Jay was there every night as the host, which was the big attraction. Anyone who came into town to play would hang out there and it was the go-to place if you were African American.

Besides playing host, Jay sang and played the piano. He eschewed his outlandish garb, and dressed in sport clothes, even adorning the ubiquitous "aloha" shirts popular in Hawaii. He would do his more garish, full-blown Screamin' Jay Hawkins act on special nights such as Halloween and New Year's Eve, even bringing in the coffin. In Honolulu, Jay added girls to the show.

Jay was paid a good salary for back then: about $250 a week, along with a percentage of the liquor sold at night. Financially speaking, Jay was in a groove. Jack says otherwise. "I only saw him when he had a business problem or had money problems, which he always had. Then he would come to see me." If he was making such good money, what was the problem? "Women," says Jack. "He liked white women and they liked him. He was a big shot and he treated the girls. They came to him because he had big money, big tongue and a big cock."

Jack, as noted, also enjoyed rhythm and blues music, which was why he brought Screamin' Jay Hawkins to Hawaii, and why he would pay top dollar, about $10,000 a week, for black R&B headliners such as Sammy Davis Jr., Lena Horne or Sarah Vaughan. Sometimes, Jack would hear about a mainstream R&B singer whose career was on the skids and bring him or her to Hawaii to play one of his lesser clubs. That's how Earl Grant ended up playing piano at the Forbidden City, one of Jack's strip clubs, for about $1,000 a week.

Earl Grant was two years younger than Jay, born in 1931 in Idabel, Oklahoma. Like Jay, Grant ended up in the service, where he augmented his income by playing piano in local clubs near the army base in Fort Bliss, Texas, where he was stationed. He signed with Decca Records in 1957 and over the next 12 years had a handful of hits, the biggest of which was the Top 10 record *The End,* in 1958. Earl Grant would eventually have another top-selling platter, a Christmas album, in 1969, but between 1958 and then, it was lean years for Earl Grant, which worked out perfectly for Jack Cione.

"Nobody knew him in Hawaii, but I heard him on the mainland so I brought him over here with his brother, who was a drummer." They also liked Hawaii, and the steady gig with Jack, so they stayed for a while, playing the lounge at Forbidden City, the most famous strip club in Honolulu at the time.

One day Jack comes into Forbidden City and he hears Earl tickling the piano keys for three of the club's strippers, who are singing in unison. Jack listens, taken aback by the girls who almost sound professional. The young ladies were Deedee McNeil, Audrey Lovett and Helene Harris. Jack told them, "You girls are good. You don't have to strip anymore, let's make you an act—the Soul Sisters."

In 2001, Jack reminisced for the *Honolulu Advertiser* about the time in the mid-1960s when Frank Sinatra visited Honolulu, and he and his entourage were hanging out at the Forbidden City. "The lounge at the Forbidden City featured Screamin' Jay Hawkins and the Soul Sisters on one of Sinatra's visits," he told the reporter. "He hated soul and rock music but did love one of the Soul Sisters, who had a Sarah Vaughan-type of singing style. That soon became his favorite hangout."

Around 1963, Jack teamed Jay with the Soul Sisters for a locally produced album called *A Night at Forbidden City,* a rarity of rarities—the label noted the producer as Sounds of Hawaii.

With an itch to get back into the mainland gigs, Jay left Hawaii to tour again. Soon after, Jack sold the Show Bar.

Jack enjoyed Jay's company and patiently took the time to listen to his many stories. Asked what he thought of these fascinating tales of derring-do, Jack surmised, "Jay was full of bullshit." Bullshit or not, Jack benefited from having rock 'n' roll's wayward son performing at his clubs.

CHAPTER

the Twisted

Wheel nightclub in Manchester, England, has become legendary as the birthplace of the "Northern Soul" movement of the 1960s and beyond. Northern Soul was basic, hard rhythm and blues music that eschewed the more commercial soul music such as the Motown sound that was popular at the time.

The club opened in 1963 and Roger Eagle began working at the club as its first R&B disc jockey. Later in the year, the club also began pioneering the all-nighters.

Every Saturday, the club spotlighted pop groups like Herman's Hermits, then at 11 p.m. the club closed and the pop music crowd departed, explains Roger Fairhurst, a regular at the Twisted Wheel in the mid-1960s. The club opened again at midnight, and from that point on, it was all R&B until sunrise. "This became a movement all over the country," Roger adds.

Roger Eagle, who was the main man at the all-nighters, had an insatiable hunger for R&B music and certain esoteric musicians, one of which was Screamin' Jay Hawkins. That is how Brian Smith became a regular at the Twisted Wheel, and photographer for its short-lived blues magazine, *RnB Scene*.

The all-nighters proved to be a big success. Roger Eagle, their resident deejay, began proselytizing about Screamin' Jay Hawkins. Says Brian, "Roger introduced a sort of running *Jay Must Not Be Forgotten* theme—almost a crusade." Brian, Roger and other like-minded regulars at the Twisted Wheel jumped on board the Screamin' Jay bandwagon, contacting anyone who might know anything about Screamin' Jay, including U.S. record companies, and theaters like the Apollo.

Brian wrote to CBS/Epic Records because its Memory Lane series re-issued "I Put a Spell on You," but the corporate reply said there had been no contact with Screamin' Jay for years, and that if Brian had ever talked to him, please inform Jay small royalties were sitting at CBS/Epic, waiting to be collected.

A breakthrough came in May 1964 when Brian and friends went to see Little Richard play at another Manchester club called the Oasis. Grabbing an opportunity to talk with one of Little Richard's entourage, Brian asked a man in the entourage if he knew Screamin' Jay Hawkins. The man turned out to be Don "Sugarcane" Harris of the singing and songwriting duo Don and Dewey (Dewey Terry), who wrote "I'm Leaving It Up to You," a Number 1 hit for Dale and Grace the year before. In addition to being an old friend of Screamin' Jay, Don had also just visited with him three weeks before in Honolulu, Hawaii, where Jay was working at the Forbidden City. Brian quickly scribbles a letter to the Forbidden City, and unexpectedly gets a reply. The letterhead reads, "From the Desk of Jack Cione." In the response, Jack said he would pass Brian's letter on to Jay. Soon afterward, Brian received a letter directly from Jay. At the time, Jay was recuperating from his stab wound delivered by a jealous Pat Newborn. Somehow he found the time to reply to the Twisted Wheel regulars who so admired his music, while licking his wounds. Says Brian, "He seemed genuinely knocked out to get these letters from kids around Manchester."

Roger Eagle started his pitch to bring Screamin' Jay to England with an opinion piece he wrote in the August 1964 *RnB Scene* magazine:

> *For those of you who may be shipwrecked in the Pacific in the near future, I offer the following advice, head for Hawaii. There is a club in downtown Honolulu, where you will find one of the great ravers of all-time, the legendary Screamin' Jay Hawkins. Those of you who still treasure his release of the frantic "I Put a Spell on You" will be glad to know he is still in touch with the world of records and has got two songs from the Sounds of Hawaii label, "The Whammy" and "It Seems Like You Just Don't Care." The former is a voodoo number with references to mojo bones, moonlight and shotguns, while the second is a more conventional rock 'n' roller. Jay's voice is more powerful than ever and according to Don & Dewey, who saw him recently, the stage act remains one of the most exciting in the world … Jay was one of the great characters to emerge from the golden rock 'n' roll era. Today, married and looking forward to settling down and raising a family, he still has countless admirers … Although bringing him here today seems somewhat in the nature of a dream, stranger things have happened. He should make the trip …*

A few months later, Roger Eagle again took his pen in hand and wrote, "Screamin' Jay Hawkins, one of the world's great ravers, is due to tour the country in February next year. His manager John Cann and his charming wife Gloria visited the country in October to arrange the trip."

John Cann, a TWA executive from New York, was on holiday in Honolulu with his wife Gloria when they met Screamin' Jay. They were longtime jazz and blues fans who became huge fans of Screamin' Jay Hawkins. They made a point to see him at Forbidden City, where he was more a piano man and emcee than a star.

The story Gloria told Bill Millar, while they were both waiting for Jay's plane to arrive for a tour of England, went something like this: She and John were vacationing in Hawaii in August of 1964 and could not believe their eyes when they saw a neon sign advertising Screamin' Jay at this small club. John was a longtime fan of Screamin' Jay. He and a small clique of friends sat around for hours playing the records of jazz legends like John Coltrane, Dizzy Gillespie and Miles Davis. The only rock 'n' roll vocalist they ever played was Screamin' Jay Hawkins!

Jay, Bill and Gloria got to talking. The Canns thought it was a waste that someone as talented as Screamin' Jay was reduced to playing a strip club in Hawaii. They offered to manage him. Jay accepted, so they moved him and Ginny to New York. John Cann must have had some contacts in the music world, because he was able to set up a recording session for Jay at Roulette Records soon after.

Roulette Records was founded in 1957 by a small group of investors including George Goldner, and Morris Levy, the latter of whom became a powerful but controversial member of the American music publishing community. He was eventually convicted of extortion in 1990, part of an FBI investigation into the infiltration of the record industry by organized crime. This isn't to say that Roulette wasn't a very successful record company on its own. In the 1950s, Buddy Knox, Jimmie Rogers, The Playmates and Ronnie Hawkins all had hits on Roulette. In the early 1960s, Joey Dee and The Starliters scored for Roulette with "Peppermint Twist," a Number 1 record in 1961. It was a major break for

Screamin' Jay to secure a recording session there. The resulting 45 had "The Whammy" on the A-side and "Strange" on the B-side. "The Whammy" was a remake of the 1955 recording "(She Put the) Wamee (On Me)."

The B-side was an original composition, yet it too was supernatural, with riffs ripped from other songs and lyrics that asked such pertinent questions as "how many ringers in a pickle; how many hams in a head, how many waves in the ocean; how many crumbs in bread"; or "where do eyeballs come from?"

But the Canns were trying hard. Jay had shown Gloria all his correspondence with the Manchester, England fans and a copy of the Twisted Wheel magazine *RnB Scene,* and they hit upon the idea of bringing Jay to Europe. She and John flew to England to scout the scene.

"One day, Roger Eagle rang me at work and said a lady called Gloria Cann had called at the Wheel and wanted to discuss bringing Jay to the UK," says Brian Smith. "We both had dinner with her that night but were a little nonplussed as to where to send her. We only knew promoters who'd brought jazzmen and rock 'n' roll packages, but only Don Arden at close quarters. There had been problems with [Chuck] Berry and [Carl] Perkins tours, but in the absence of any better idea we just said, 'Try Arden.'"

Don Arden was born Harry Levy. Although no relation to Morris Levy in the United States, the two men had similar reputations of disreputable business habits and connections to organized crime. Arden was sometimes referred to as the "Meyer Lansky of Pop." Incredibly, he was also the father of legendary reality TV personality turned talk show host Sharon Osbourne, and father-in-law to Ozzy Osbourne.

"The thinking was, if a bunch of kids in Manchester know you well enough, maybe there is a tour in it," says Brian. "The Canns came over, saw the people at the club where Roger [Eagle] worked and then met a London promoter."

Jay left the details to the Canns, but being rookies at the promotion game, the Canns got taken for a ride by the shrewd operator Don Arden. Says Brian, "Arden took him to the cleaners. According to Jay, Cann was persuaded to put up several thousands of dollars and work on Arden's terms for the first tour, with the famous 'Arden option' for another tour, which would then be on Cann's terms."

One of the complaints about Jay's tour of England was the lack of promotion, which should have come from Don Arden's offices. John and Gloria fought hard to get bits and pieces of information to appear in the local press. Some blurbs of newspaper ads read:

> John and Gloria Cann send greetings to all fans of Screamin' Jay Hawkins, and look forward to Jay's tour of England in February 1965. Why not be at London Airport to welcome Jay. Details of exact time of arrival to be published when known.

> [A paid advertisement] Screamin' Jay Hawkins Tours England; THE WORLD'S WILDEST MAN IS TOURING THIS COUNTRY IN FEBRUARY—WHATEVER YOU DO—DON'T MISS HIM.

> Screamin' Jay Hawkins, one of the world's greatest ravers, is due to tour this country in February next year. His manager, John Cann, with his charming wife Gloria, visited this country on October 27th to arrange the trip … We wish him the very best of success, and would like to assure him of a great welcome when he sets foot in this country. We also extend a warm welcome to Junior, a great friend of Jay's. Junior is a skull attached to a pole, which Jay carries with him wherever he goes.

JAY HAWKINS HERE: Screaming (Screamin') Jay Hawkins, the American negro rock 'n' roll singer whose reputation here rests on his wild wax release of several years ago, I Put a Spell on You, is coming to Britain in February for a month of TV, radio and club dates, impresario Don Arden told RM this week.

Screamin' Jay Hawkins' first tour of Great Britain began ominously. He missed the flight to London. The story was that he had left his passport at home, so he arrived in London a day late. The Canns and a bunch of Twisted Wheel regulars and friends were at the airport waiting. Gloria Cann bought everyone drinks and handed out promo copies of "The Whammy" that was recorded on Roulette Records.

"The Whammy" disappeared without a trace in the United States, but the Canns were able to get the record some notice in England. A review in the *RnB Scene* purred: "This is powerful stuff from the master raver. As reported in an earlier edition of *RnB Scene*, this is a voodoo number, with references to moonlight, mojo bones, shotguns and spells … it should be issued here before long. The flip is a faster dance number, but filled with Jay's own special lyrics. In the States they don't know which to class as the A-side, but here I think the voodoo side has the edge."

Many of the Twisted Wheel regulars and fans stayed at the airport, including Bill Millar.

"We decided to stay the night at London airport and were certainly not disappointed," Bill Millar wrote in his diary at the time. "Jay arrived at 9:30 on Tuesday morning and was truly an astounding sight. I felt like I could have waited all week for this." Jay stepped down to the Customs Hall dressed in black from head to foot. He was wearing a fur cape with a gold emblem on the back, a black and white turban, black high-heeled boots, black trousers and was carrying Henry in his hand. Jay also sported what Bill called "way-out jewelry" such as a three-inch-thick engraved bracelet, huge emerald rings on fingers of both hands, and a large medallion around his neck.

Somehow Bill was lucky enough to join the entourage. Don Arden sent a chauffeur to pick up Jay, Ginny, the Canns, Bill, and his buddy Cliff White in a Jaguar to take them to the Washington Hotel.

"At once it became evident that his knowledge of the R 'n' B scene was utterly fantastic," Bill wrote. "Throughout the ride from the airport to the hotel he was incredibly friendly and most helpful even though I constantly plagued him with questions, which a lesser artist would have thought aggravating, especially after a tiring plane journey."

When he came to England on that first tour, Jay played small clubs and those who came to see and hear him were the selective few, the very dedicated rock 'n' roll fans, who might have heard about him from what other blues artists might have said. Don Arden arranged a backup group.

On that first tour, Jay was backed by a simple blues band that adapted to his music, says Graham Knight, who first met him on that tour and became lifelong friends. "Jay could read music and was a very good musician. He preferred to work with people who had a jazz background because among other things he transported all the charts for every record he ever made, so he would have the first trumpet part, the first violin part, the first drum part and the first guitar parts."

On one of Jay's tours to England he did a television show called *Gadzooks!* and one of the band members backing him was Jimmy Page, says Graham. "Because this band was professional, Jay just passed out the original music and told them to play the dots. Most of Jay's songs had the same beat—it was well within Mr. Page's capability."

The other good thing about Jay's act, says Roger Fairhurst, another English superfan, was that it was transferable in that it could work in an R&B club, a rock 'n' roll stage, or at a nightclub. "He would do a standard, such as the Jule Styne and Sammy Cahn classic 'It's Magic,' but would insert his own words," says Fairhurst, "so 'It's Magic' in Jay's version would go like this: 'She went upstairs to get undressed, and suddenly she had no chest, so what was once her sex appeal was all foam rubber, stainless steel. It's tragic.'"

Jay was very funny, say Fairhurst. The day he arrived in London, Fairhurst along with Brian Smith and several others went to visit him at the Washington Hotel. "There was a wedding taking place across the road from the hotel. It was a Jamaican couple getting married. The couple came out of the church—they were about 50 yards away. Jay leaned out the hotel window and started shouting, 'Don't do it, baby. Don't do it.' The guy looked up, really stunned. Jay did stupid things like that all the time."

Roger Eagle wrote in the *RnB Scene*, "The first time we took Jay to a restaurant in Manchester, Brian Smith showed him how to produce sound out of a half-filled glass of water. Immediately, Jay started to compose a new number! The Indian waiters were panic-stricken, for they only found out at the end of the meal what was happening. As we were leaving, we heard the noise coming from the kitchen—so naturally Jay burst in and asked them if they would mind not copying his sound without his permission."

Writer Jack Watkins retells the story of Jay being driven through Manchester, when he produced a revolver, rolled down the car window and began firing blanks at innocent pedestrians. "What the hell are you doing?" screamed Roger Eagle, who was in the vehicle with him. "Just keeping 'em on their toes, man," replied Hawkins.

Jay refrained from performing the coffin act on his first tours of England, but that didn't mean he wasn't outlandish. "Occasionally, he would drop his trousers, and on the back of his long underwear he had a kick me sign," says Graham. "He did other things that were crazy such as with the elastic [rubber] bands. He would have some of us in the balcony with the bands and three-in-one oil. He would tell the audience, 'This is a very old theater and early today I saw worms dripping from the roof.' This was the days of the woman's beehive cut and we would shoot these elastic bands and some would end up in the girls' hair. They would put their hands up and scream. Jay was the greatest at emptying places. I remember him doing that in Halifax. The promoter there thought it was a stupid thing to do."

The first Screamin' Jay Hawkins tour of the UK got off to a rough start, smoothed out over the next few weeks, and then ended abruptly. Part of the problem was the lack of promotion, but it was also because Jay was mostly unknown in the country except to a small coterie of die-hard fans. In addition, the venues were small, and because of that, it was hard for anyone—Jay, the Canns, or Don Arden—to make good money from the tour. On a positive note, Jay made lifelong friends who supported him for the next 30 years, and word of mouth about his fantastic shows began to percolate among club-goers. Eventually the crowds would follow.

A small notice ran in a local listing of events: "American rock star Screamin' Jay Hawkins opens first British tour at Town Hall, Wallington, Surrey (7 pm)."

Jay burst on stage doing his own number "Yellow Coat," dressed in a bird's eye suit with black-and-white diamond patterned pockets, a black jeweled turban, black and white moccasins and a shiny black cape, observed Bill Millar. "His movements are out of this world with legs quaking fit to shame a '57 Presley. He is the undoubted epitome of explosive, dated rock 'n' roll … his piano playing was limited to a few chords but his screamin' vocalizing continued for over an hour."

However, the show was completely lost on the audience from the start. The "local-Wallington thugs-*cum*-delinquency-department" booed, while the remaining adolescent females just sat about disinterested. Bill later wrote about the show, "Hawkins was never in better form: he ran on and off-stage, did splits, played piano, waved his cloak like a rabid bullfighter and screamed a slew of rock 'n' roll classics for well over an hour. Sadly, the louder the half-dozen fans cheered, the more the locals booed … eventually fighting broke out and we escaped via the dressing room and car park."

A small tombstone ad read: "Europe's Greatest R&B Centre—The Fabulous Flamingo Club, 33/37 Wardour Street, W.1 Presents American R&B Star Screamin' Jay Hawkins, Wednesday, February 3rd." Jay toned down his act for this show, which was covered by a couple of the music industry magazines.

An even smaller tombstone ad: "BROMEL CLUB; Bromley Court Hotel, Bromley Hill, Kent, Sunday, February 7th; Screamin' Jay Hawkins." This visit was the third stop on the tour and Screamin' Jay still hadn't created an audience in the UK. Bill wrote, "… he comes on stage at 9:15 p.m. and bursts into his usual opening number 'Yellow Coat.' Twelve numbers, all of them rockers, followed in a half an hour with Jay tearin' up and down at one point knocking over an amplifier and beatin' Henry with his well-worn tambourine … Audience reaction was poor without being impolite—'What'd I Say' was given the largest applause probably as it is the sole tune that the masses recognize."

The most humiliating instance of the whole trip occurred in a club outside Manchester when drunken patrons tried to steal Henry. They failed.

For this tour Jay came back to the Flamingo three times. On his second show, he eschewed the cap and wild-man outfit, going for the top hat and tails look, or as Bill Millar noted, "looking like the Duke of Earl with facial hair." By his third visit, the audience had expanded, attracting true R&B fans from far and wide.

The tour was a very busy one for Jay, as he also appeared on the television show *Thank Your Lucky Stars,* where he sang "The Whammy." The performance was strained. Jay mimed to a prerecorded version of the song, which is not easy for the screaming wild man used to bellowing from the depths of his soul for songs like "The Whammy."

Jay, along with Bill Millar and others, stopped in to see an old friend of Jay's, Larry Williams, who had charted in America with a couple of weird rockers of his own, "Short Fat Fannie" and "Bony Maronie." Larry was recording a live album for Sue Records and on seeing Jay, made up some new lyrics on the spot: "Saw Screamin' Jay Hawkins with Long Tall Sally in the coffin; she don't love him but she do it very often."

For most of Jay's tour in the UK, Jay was backed by a local Manchester musician Ronnie Carr, who had a band called the Beat Boys. According to the publication *Manchester Beat,* the group changed its name to "The Blues Set" to accompany Screamin' Jay Hawkins on his first British tour, having been matched up with the R&B singer by Don Arden. While in the UK, Jay gets the chance to go back into a studio to record an album. He returns to the Twisted Wheel and rehearses hard with the Ronnie Carr Blues Set, but when it was time to go into the studio, Arden bounces the group and brings in session musicians.

The Ronnie Carr Blues Set was a part-time band from Leigh, a town in the Greater Manchester area. Ronnie Carr's one claim to fame was that he gave Clive Powell a start in the 1950s before Clive changed his name to Georgie Fame, becoming a very successful British R&B singer.

Ronnie Carr's band had rehearsed the entire album, and just a couple of days before going into the studio, Arden dismissed them. Regarding their midnight removal, Brian Smith says, "It nearly wrecked their careers and I saw Ronnie a few days later driving a laundry van."

Arden's presence in the Screamin' Jay camp had one huge benefit. Using his pull in the industry, he secured the use of EMI's Abbey Road studio on May 3, 1965 to record most of the songs used on the album that would become known as *The Night & Day of Screamin' Jay Hawkins*.

The use of the Abbey Road studio was unique, in that it rarely hosted artists outside the EMI roster. Alec Paleo, who wrote the liner notes to the rerelease of *The Night & Day* album along with other songs, maintains that the recording session happened because the release of "The Whammy" on UK Columbia permitted the use of the studio.

The cover of the album was tame by Screamin' Jay standards. Jay stands right of frame donning a dark suit with a white shirt and tie. His hair is slicked back and his shoes shine brightly. His posture is crooked, as he seems to be looking down at his wife, Ginny, who is sitting on the floor with her long hair winding all the way to the ground. Next to her is a statue that looks playfully Buddhist. She looks up at Jay, who is smiling back at her. Of the 12 cuts, almost all are ballads with the lead song being "Night and Day."

The stream-of-consciousness liner notes to the albums read: "Many can sing in tune—few (even less) can scream. Jay Hawkins was, and is, unique. He enjoyed his monopoly which straddled the fence of Rhythm and Blues. He was young and screamin' was a means to an end—this album isn't the end—nor the beginning of—it is one side of Mr. Hawkins—his night and day. You can't tell a book by looking—read it—you can't tell a man by a name—unzip and acknowledge—Night and Day—Cole Porter—beautifully resurrected—beautifully baritone—with care. Alright, O.K. You win, another classic … He writes—in fact he has written most of the tracks on this album …."

The album was released on the Planet label, but not until the next year.

All things seemed copacetic for the tour, but Graham told otherwise. Jay had a lot of squabbles, mainly with the promoter Don Arden. Brian Smith believes that when Arden summarily dismissed Ronnie Carr's band, Jay and Arden fell out.

There were other issues between Arden and Hawkins. Arden was promoting a John Lee Hooker tour at the same time he was promoting Screamin' Jay. Jay's ego could not reconcile playing second fiddle to anyone else, especially when it involved someone he knew. Unfortunately for Arden, Jay could do a wicked impression of John Lee Hooker, who had a slight stammer. Jay rang up Arden's office one day and pretended to be Hooker. When he got Arden on the phone, Jay, "playing Hooker," said he was in jail, and that Arden would have to get him out immediately if he wanted him to play the next show. Arden took the call for real and sent someone to the north of England to get John Lee Hooker out of jail. "There was no end of trouble because of it," says Graham. One can only imagine the interaction between Hawkins and Arden after Jay's "jail house shuffle."

Graham had volunteered to do some of the driving for Jay on the tour. "Jay was very professional in his operations," says Graham. "Most musicians stay up late after a show, go to bed late and then hustle the next day to make the next gig. Jay did not have that problem. We would drive to the next gig as soon as we finished the prior show. He had this postcard and he would put it in to the venue he was going to. The postcard basically said 'I'm in town and I will see you XX time.' Jay was always at the next place."

Being very garrulous, Graham would impart his opinion about the tour and what could be done differently to make it better. Some of his unwarranted jabber got back to Arden, who got into it with Jay. The verbal conflict amped up quickly. Jay yelled, "Don't tell me who I can talk to!" and appeared to be threatening. Arden responded by pulling a gun on Jay. Brian Smith says the issues were deeper, involving poor accommodations and the backing band not being paid. "Jay was a hard-nosed character and reportedly carried his own service revolver around with him. He wasn't a soft touch," says Brian. Nevertheless, Arden had a reputation of being involved in organized crime. Jay, having spent many years dealing with recording companies in New York who were tied to the mafia, was well prepared to deal with any such threats. Jay wasn't going to mess around. Supposedly, when Arden pointed the barrel of his gun at Jay, the performer said, "Right, that's me out of here!"

That evening, Bill Millar and friends had decided to visit with Jay and maybe catch Donnie Elbert at the Flamingo. Instead they got a frantic and irate Screamin' Jay who commandeered Bill to "deflect" phone calls from Arden's office while steadily oiling his revolver.

Millar's deflecting effort served as the only break for Jay that evening, who was frantically trying to get out of Dodge as fast as humanly possible. Unable to stuff his entire wardrobe back into his luggage, he started to trash his own belongings, tearing up his beloved suits. Ginny told Bill not to worry; Jay did this periodically. When Jay left for the airport, Bill and Cliff White were loaded down with Henry, capes, shoes, records and a suitcase full of flash powder and fuse boxes.

Ignoring the hasty departure, an ecstatic Roger Eagle summed up Jay's first visit to the British Isles in *RnB Scene*:

> Screamin' Jay Hawkins, the man this magazine helped to introduce to this excitement starved scene, came, saw, and definitely conquered in his recent British trip. Here's why. Firstly, his stage act. Jay is a tremendous personality. Merely having a cup of coffee with him in his hotel room can reduce a fan to

hysterics. A meal in a restaurant can be nearly fatal...Besides being one of the wildest entertainers of all-time, he is also an extremely charming and courteous man. Neil Carter, his mother was terrified at having Jay around, but she was absolutely knocked out when she met him. He is very well read and will talk on any subject ... His beautiful wife Ginny accompanied him everywhere on the tour and made a great impression on her own account.

"He went back home," says Graham. "And the letters we got back from him didn't give an address. That convinced us he needed a low profile for a while."

These letters were always rich in affection and anecdote, says Bill. He would write tidbits of news, such as he and Ginny were guests at Lady Iris Mountbatten's wedding; or Esquerita had gotten into a tussle outside the Colony Record Shop. Bill was told to take good care of Henry. Then after a brief sojourn in Hawaii and another Apollo appearance, Jay forwarded along some exceptionally good news. He wrote to Bill: "I must let you know that on 30 March 1966, I shall be putting in a very weird appearance at London Airport for a thirty-day tour. I hope that Henry, the fuse boxes and the capes are ready to be used again."

This next jaunt of Jay's was put together by Global Promotions, run by Roy Tempest, a UK music promoter and agent. The backing band for this tour was Herbie Goins and The Nightimers.

A British music publication noted: "Blues guitarist Freddy King, rock and roller Screaming (Screamin') Jay Hawkins, and blues giants Lightning Hopkins and Chuck Berry are all set for Britain tours organized by promoter Roy Tempest."

Jay arrived on April Fools' Day and played the Ram Jam Club that night. Bill writes, "Luminous-socked rockers turned out in force, displacing Afro-Caribbeans for the evening, and Hawkins came on as if it were still rock 'n' roll's finest hour. He eclipsed everything around at the time, agitating his way through 'The Whammy' and concluding with 'Shout,' a feat of improvisation."

This tour proceeded without complication, but also with the same kind of uneven reception that Jay experienced on his first go-round in the UK. The clubs were still small.

A tiny tombstone ad read: "The New Scene Club; Ham Yard, Gt., Windmill Str., W.1.; Proudly Presents, Screaming (Screamin') Jay Hawkins with Herbie Goins on Thursday, April 14th, 1966; Nightly 8 p.m. to 11:30 p.m., Friday and Sat. ALLNIGHTERS; The Greatest American Sounds."

Less than a dozen people turned up at the New Scene for Jay's show, but one of the few was Lee Dorsey, the New Orleans R&B singer whose record "Ya-Ya" was a Top 10 hit in 1959.

Despite all his good efforts, Hawkins didn't appear to bolster his fan base in the UK in any measurable way, despite two tours and recording an album at Abbey Road studio. So, it's surprising to realize how much impact he had on the British music scene in the 1960s. The most obvious example was the ephemeral career of David Edward Sutch, who dubbed himself "Screaming Lord Sutch," a direct rip-off of Jay's legendary moniker. Grabbing an appellation wasn't enough for the young punk of a performance artist. Lord Sutch stole the soul of Jay's stage performance as well! Copied straight from Screamin' Jay's playbook, Sutch's performances included horror-themed performances, dressing as Jack the Ripper and even emerging from a coffin. Lord Sutch even got trapped inside his own coffin, a staged mishap that mimicked a Screamin' Jay incident from a decade before.

While an entertaining performer, Lord Sutch wasn't really much of a musician. An album of his called *Lord Sutch and Heavy Friends* was voted the worst album of all time in a 1998 BBC poll, despite the fact that he had such great musicians as Jimmy Page, John Bonham and Jeff Beck backing him up.

Lord Sutch was one of those gadflies that only the English could invent. Although his wild, uninhibited, but very untalented music career defused, he still craved the media spotlight. He eventually went into politics, running for office on one nonsensical splinter group after another such as the "Go To Blazes" party, before forming the Official Monster Raving Loony Party in 1983. He died in 1999, having committed suicide by hanging himself.

Lord Sutch also met his rock 'n' roll idol, Screamin' Jay Hawkins, on Jay's second tour of England. Before that happened, a small gossip item appeared in a British music rag. It read: "American blues singer Screamin' Jay Hawkins starts a month-long British tour this week, and although it's his first British visit there's one person he wants to meet—Screaming Lord Sutch …'I'm certainly not gunning for the guy, or anything like that…In fact, I've already spoken to him on the phone for a couple of minutes, and he seems like a real nice feller.'" Clearly, Jay knew he had a white doppelgänger in the UK.

On a free weekend during the second tour, Jay came up to Manchester to see his friends at the Twisted Wheel. "We happened to notice Lord Sutch was on tour in Manchester that night," says Brian Smith. "Sutch freely acknowledged that he'd got a large chunk of his act from him [Screamin' Jay Hawkins], so we arranged to take Jay to see him."

Jay wasn't interested in the show, but he was interested in Lord Sutch, and was happy to play along when Brian took a few pictures of the two brandishing knives. Sutch, who certainly knew how to work the British press, came up with a loony promotion right on the spot. He said to Jay, "Look, I'm going into a London clinic for a minor operation, why don't we show pictures of you threatening me with a knife and we'll say you took umbrage at me for stealing your act. Then a few days later I can reappear saying, 'What are you doing accusing my friend Jay?' and we'll get a few more days' coverage."

"Jay smiled and just shook his head," Brian recalled. Jay finally met someone who was crazier than he was.

Lord Sutch wasn't the only British performer with less talent and a somewhat nuttier personality than Jay, who also freely stole Jay's performance theatrics.

A Screamin' Jay Hawkins performance, on stage or off, usually ended in flames, whether it was flash-pots, smoke bombs, or his little trick of flashing fire from his fingertips. Jay loved pyrotechnics. The man who took that concept one step beyond was a British performer named Arthur Brown, and his group was called The Crazy World of Arthur Brown. This band only had one hit record, "Fire," but it was a good one, charting at Number 1 in the UK, and at Number 2 in the United States in 1968, selling over one million records. "Fire" was an appropriate song for Arthur Brown. Brown began his weird stage performances by brandishing a burning metal helmet, which soon radically progressed to Brown flat-out setting his head on fire! His song was "Fire," his show was fire, but that was the limit of Brown's creativity. Though his creativity and talent may have been lacking, Brown boasted some good people behind him, including Pete Townshend of The Who, who executive-produced the group's first album. On an interesting note, The Crazy World of Arthur Brown paid homage to Jay by recording "I Put a Spell on You" on its self-titled album.

Another British group to record "I Put a Spell on You" was Manfred Mann, which released an EP (extended play) seven-inch record called *No Living Without Loving* in 1965. One of the four songs recorded was "I Put a Spell on You."

The British group that made the biggest impact with the song was the Alan Price Set, led by singer Alan Price. As an organ player extraordinaire, he was an original member of the group The Animals, which had many hit records in the 1960s, most notably the Number 1 single "House of the Rising Sun" in 1964. The next year he left the group, founded the eponymous Alan Price Set, and in

1966 had his first big hit with "I Put a Spell on You," which was a Top 10 record in the UK, and the group's only record to chart in the United States. The band remained a constant hit maker in the UK into the 1970s. Coincidence or not, the same year the Alan Price Set boasted a hit with "I Put a Spell on You," The Animals released an album called *Animalisms* with its own version of the song.

The writer Dave Marsh once noted, Nina Simone "still stands as the greatest interpretive singer of the 1960s, having pounced on songs by Bob Dylan, Leonard Cohen, George Harrison and Randy Newman." Marsh leaves out Screamin' Jay Hawkins, which is odd, because Nina Simone's reinterpretation of "I Put a Spell on You" turned the song inside-out and upside-down. A shouting, voodoo-tinged blues number became a sultry, jazzy whisper of a song; menace evolved into seduction in Simone's version. Some Nina Simone fans think that it is her masterpiece. Maybe she did too, which is probably why she titled her biography *I Put a Spell on You*. As a single during the swinging sixties, it only made the R&B charts in United States, topping out at Number 23, but it was also her first record to chart in the UK, at number 28. The single came from the album *I Put a Spell on You*, which fared poorly in the United States, but was a Top 10 seller in the UK. The album boasted a number of songs by such European singer-songwriters as Jacques Brel and Charles Aznavour, although the lead song and the big hit was the Screamin' Jay Hawkins' classic. Screamin' Jay's legendary song found many homes throughout its lifetime, but there would be only one true title holder to its magical place in music history, and that was Hawkins.

CHAPTER

7

jAZz-pOp

chanteuse Nina Simone first burst onto the music scene in 1958 with the albums *Little Girl Blue,* and *Nina Simone and Her Friends*, on independent label Bethlehem Records. The albums were bolstered by her best-selling single "I Loves You, Porgy" (from the folk opera *Porgy & Bess),* which was a Top 20 hit on the pop charts and a Number 2 bestseller on the R&B charts. It wasn't until two years later that she finally had mainstream success with her live album *Nina Simone at Newport,* which reached Number 23 on the American album charts.

Simone remained a popular album artist, but with the major radio stations almost solidly pop-obsessed, there was little room for esoteric, soulful jazz singers like Nina Simone—at least not in America. In Europe, where jazz was surprisingly more mainstream than in the United States, there was space on the charts for Simone's musical talents. In 1965, Simone virtually re-invented Screamin' Jay Hawkins' classic *I Put a Spell on You*, turning it into a sultry, jazzy song about as far away from the original as Elvis Presley's "Hound Dog" was to the primordial version of Big Mama Thornton's bluesy classic. The album was also titled *I Put a Spell on You*.

The single reached Number 23 on the R&B charts in the United States, failing to chart at all on the pop charts. In the United Kingdom, the song only reached Number 49 on the pop charts, but her penumbra soon changed, and the record-buying public in the UK made room for her in their collections. Over the next three years, she had three Top 5 records in the UK and in 1958, a reissue of "I Put a Spell on You" charted once again. The song is probably Nina Simone's most popular, singular recording, which is likely why she titled her autobiography *I Put a Spell on You*.

Oddly, in her autobiography, Nina makes scant reference to the record, other than to complain that at the time, other recording artists were getting hit records from songs she had already recorded, such as the British singers like Manfred Mann and the Alan Price Set recording "I Put a Spell on You." Nina wrote, "This list [of records] started to get me down after a while, especially when some of my audience thought I played those songs because they were familiar crowd-pleasers, as if I only cover other artists' hits like some second-rate cabaret singer."

Despite Nina's complaint, no one sang "I Put a Spell on You" like she had.

In the United States, the record and album barely made a dent. While Europeans continued to rediscover Screamin' Jay Hawkins through the songs of other performers, he was forgotten in the United States. His time would come again—and relatively quickly.

Mike Armando, who played guitar for Screamin' Jay Hawkins in the 1970s, points out that Jay's career took a major turn when Creedence Clearwater Revival unleashed its first album, the eponymous *Creedence Clearwater Revival* in 1968, with a swamp-rock version of "I Put a Spell on You." In Creedence Clearwater Revival's version, the song launches with a thunder of drum beats before John Fogerty jumps into howling vocals. It is on this recording where "I Put a Spell on You" really crosses the threshold from R&B into rock.

Initially, the Creedence album was just a moderate hit, not even breaking the Top 50 in album sales in 1968. Eventually, however, it would go platinum. The most successful cut from the album was the remake of "Susie Q," a hit record for singer Dale Hawkins in 1957, and now a moderate, first-time hit for Creedence Clearwater Revival, rising all the way to Number 11 on the pop charts.

The album was interesting as it introduced a number of CCR records, mostly showcasing John Fogerty's songwriting skills, while retooling a few oddball classics like the Wilson Pickett soul recording "Ninety-Nine and a Half (Won't Do)," the rockabilly "Susie Q" and, of course, Jay's R&B standard, "I Put a Spell on You." The latter two songs were released as singles. The CCR version of Jay's song peaked at only Number 58 on the pop charts.

CCR's next four albums were juggernauts, and hit singles spilled out like the floodwaters in the bayou. The group was immensely popular and at the top of their game, but they never forgot the great ones whose songs they reimagined for a new generation of music fans. "I Put a Spell on You" was a staple of their live performances. The career of Screamin' Jay Hawkins was dragged back to the limelight in the oceanic wake of CCR's success.

Like Jay, Nina Simone moved around from one record label to the next throughout her career. With increasing fame and success she hopscotched from a small independent to Colpix to the even bigger Philips Records in 1964. She recorded five albums with Philips including *I Put a Spell on You.* With Screamin' Jay back in the mainstream thanks to Creedence Clearwater Revival and

Nina Simone, he found Philips receptive to the idea of taking him on as a new recording artist.

Philips Records produced records in a wide variety of genres, from classical, to jazz, to pop. In the series of records surrounding Jay's studio sessions for Philips, the company released dozens of pop albums from the likes of Blue Cheer ("Summertime Blues"), San Francisco psychedelic rockers The Charlatans, the orchestral Paul Mauriat ("Love Is Blue"), Steve Miller, The Four Seasons and Tex-Mex rock band Sir Douglas Quintet ("She's About a Mover").

The first of two albums from Screamin' Jay to drop for Philips was the 1969 release of *What That Is*, which featured a cover photograph of Jay inside a coffin with one hand pushing up the top lid of the burial box. On the backside of the album was a close-up of Jay in the coffin. He's fully dressed with a tan jacket and what looks to be a gold chain around his neck. He sports a goatee and still combs his full head of curly hair in a modified 1950s style, with a pompadour front, as if he just left the stage of an Alan Freed show. In a musical tour de force, all the songs were written by Jay. He had a gonzo knack for phrasing:

From "Do You Really Love Me":
Do you really love me baby? Like a rat loves cheese.

From "Feast of the Mau Mau":
Cut the fat off the back of a baboon; boil it down to a pound in a spoon; scoop the eyes from a fly flying backwards; take jaws and the paws off a 'coon.

From "I'm Your Man":
Stop flapping your jaws, because you know you can't get away.

From "What That Is":
Shut your mouth! [grunting]; What'd you say? [grunting]
Now! There's a sack hanging in your head with your brains
in it eating scalp chop suey, corroded biscuits, and bat's
knees soup, in a gas mask!

Bill Millar, in his liner notes for the compilation album *Scream-in' Jay Hawkins,* writes, "Hawkins' female characters are generally alien, mephitic creatures with double chins, flabber mouths and bald heads; 'Thing Called Woman,' with its compound eyes and solitary upper limb, doesn't disappoint."

Despite all that good stuff, there was one clear topper on this album, Jay's second best-known song, "Constipation Blues." Unlike "I Put a Spell on You," this song is not really adaptable for a jazzy chanteuse to sing, nor was it a classic R&B composition. In fact, "Constipation Blues" is really not much of a song; its notoriety is due to its audacious grossness, and Jay's performance art in carrying out the sound effects of what one might associate with constipation and its inevitable "relief."

The song begins with Jay speaking about the background of the song before he sings:

Let it go! Let it go! Let it go! Let it go!
I don't believe I can take much more
Let it go.

Got a pain down inside
Won't be denied
Yeah, every time I try
I can't be satisfied
Let it go!
Let it go

..... Splash!
Feel, ah, I-I feel alright
Yes-ah, I'm beginning to feel alright now
Splash!
Yeah, yeah, I tell ya, everything's gonna be alright
Splash!
Flush .....

Behind a slow blues beat, and lot of horns, Jay grunts and groans in a manner people might find humorous in a sophomoric way or just straight off-putting. Although, one has to admit, he gives the song his all in a soulful way. There is never a "halfway" with Jay when it comes to the absurd. He feels "alright" at the end, and we are all relieved because Jay's noises are anything except foul. One wouldn't think this is the kind of song that makes it to a single record given its guttural grunts, references to bowel movement, and its raw, if lurid vocals. Yet it ended up on the B-side of his first single in four years, "Do You Really Love Me."

Of course Jay has a story for the creation of "Constipation Blues." Bill Millar quotes him as saying, "I never had been constipated in my life and it didn't dawn on me until I was five hours on the stool in the hospital that nothin' was gonna happen. I had doctors give me enemas and still nothin' happened. I had tears in my eyes, and I noticed this beautiful roll of toilet paper and I took out a pencil, and at the bottom of the toilet paper, I started writin' the song backwards, from the bottom up. The more I rolled out the toilet paper, the more I got into the song. I wrote exactly as I felt; each movement, each sound, each pain ..."

Like most Jay stories, this one morphed into one or more versions, some closer to the intro of the song itself. The Millar recounting is the most prosaic version. As the years went on, Jay would sometimes use the song as a cudgel against staid audiences. For the younger crowd, it was just a funny song that

Jay could dramatize with facial expressions. This was always a good song for a live crowd; on a single or album it wasn't as easily "digested."

Millar, in the same liner notes for the *Screamin' Jay Hawkins* album, paraphrases a reviewer, writing, "one critic was moved to ask whether the man who once opened his act by rising from a coffin now closed it by flushing himself down a lavatory."

Pardon the pun, but Jay managed to quickly squeeze another album out of Philips, the equally unglamorously titled *Because Is In Your Mind (Armpitrubber)* in 1970. Although, the cover art is exceptional, a kind of electrified-Aztec-graffiti version of Jay—like something from the underground comics of the 1960s. While the subheading "Armpitrubber" makes the record sound like another Screamin' Jay grunt-and-groan noise-fest, this is a grand album highlighting Jay's talent as an R&B singer. He does a wonderful rendition of the classic "Good Night My Love," complete with violins and female voice-over. "Our Love Is Not for Three" is worthy of Otis Redding, and "Bite It" is Screamin' Jay in his prime. He yells "let's bite it one time" and other phrases (smell it, lick it, etc.) over a thin Mar-Keys' "Last Night" instrumental track. If there is one fault with this album, it is that it is derivative of what had been going on with soul music for the past decade.

In 1970, Jay recorded two songs to be released as a single on a small independent label, Queen Bee. The A-side was "Monkberry Moon Delight," written by Paul and Linda McCartney, but on the record, credit is given to "Paul & Linda Mac." The B-side was "Sweet Ginny," a real rocker, and, one assumes, a dedication to his second wife Ginny, whom he claimed to have married while in Hawaii, even though he was technically still married to his first wife Anna Mae at the time.

During his years with Ginny, the two were like conjoined twins. They rarely went anywhere without each other. This was for two reasons. First, Ginny liked to keep an eye on Jay, knowing from her days in Hawaii that he had a tendency to stray. "When Jay was with Ginny there was nothing going on with anyone else," says Graham Knight. Secondly, Jay wanted to have someone with him at all times, especially at night, since he had trouble sleeping. Being a wife to Jay was like having a 24-hour job with no vacation. Jay's wife had to be his sex kitten, nurse, secretary, travel companion, ego-booster and stagehand. With all of these demands, Jay still managed to find women who loved him, no matter how demanding the "ask."

Mike Armando, who only knew Jay when he was married to Ginny, recalled, "Jay would say, 'Clean my toenails.' 'Rub my feet.' And she would hop to it." Jay confided in Mike, telling him, "the reason she would do anything I say is because she is not Americanized." Or, she was afraid. People who knew Jay said that he was physically abusive to Ginny.

Jay's stage act was always an elaborate affair, whether he employed the coffin or not. He was a showman and he gave a good show. He placed clip-on bones under his nose, with ends that curled up toward his eyes, in a half-menacing, self-mocking version of an African tribesman. Pyrotechnics were an essential, hence the fuse boxes. At times, he had a mechanical hand that would crawl across the stage. His most common prop was a cane with a skull that smoked cigarettes—affectionately known as Henry. Sometimes, he would sport a huge medallion that hung from a heavy chain around his neck. While the chain swapped in and out of his performances, his rings never left his fingers. He always flashed at least six silver rings, a gimmick he picked up from Fats Domino.

When he first came to England in 1965, he brought his "fuse box," with him—the one made by Jack Schiffman, the son of Frank Schiffman, who managed the Apollo Theater in New York.

It was a very simple device consisting of a box with a fuse wire. Someone would plug the box into an electric socket and the fuse would spark flash powder. Graham Knight took one look at the dangerous fuse box and made him four new ones, safeguarded with asbestos. The mechanism was the same, with the exception of the fuse wire sparking Johnson's Flashpowder, which was easy to use and adaptable to coloration. If you added salt, the smoke would turn green; with potassium, the smoke turned purple; and with other chemicals came every shade in the spectrum of the color wheel. With Graham's addition, the smoke could be pointed as well. Graham also put the motor into the walking hand that was used in Jay's shows.

"It was Ginny's job to control the fuse box, but she didn't take part in the show. Mostly it was used for the big finale when Jay sang 'I Put a Spell on You,'" says Graham. "Nevertheless, the fuse box was always mayhem. Sometimes you would get a terrible smell, or the clouds of smoke hung over the stage refusing to dissipate."

In 1968, Graham visited Jay in New York. At the time, he was staying at the Alvin Hotel at Broadway and 52nd Street. The hotel was a real dive, popular with ladies of the night, says Graham, although a lot of musicians on the fringe stayed there including Esquerita and the band that backed Jackie Wilson. The whole area was rough. He and Ginny were living in one room. There was no kitchen, and he had what Graham called "a small cooker." Jay was getting some work around the New York metro area, mostly playing piano in crappy nightclubs. At some point afterward, Jay was being pressed for payment by the hotel and in danger of being thrown out. Graham sent him money, a kind act which was repeated.

Graham noticed in Jay's apartment three suitcases, which constituted his whole life. The suitcases had a written address pasted on the side that read, "where the wind blows." Jay told

Graham, "when you had as many gigs as I've had, you got to keep moving."

He did.

The recordings for the first Philips album in 1969 took place in Los Angeles. The arranger was Shorty Rogers and the producer Milan Melvin. The sessions for the second album, *Because Is in Your Mind (Armpitrubber)*, took place in Houston under the production guidance of Huey Meaux, who bragged a long track record in the business, producing such records as "She's About a Mover" (*Billboard* Number 13 in 1965) by the Sir Douglas Quintet and "Wasted Days and Wasted Nights" (*Billboard* Number 8 in 1975) by Freddy Fender.

With the money he received from the Philips sessions, Jay and Ginny went back to Hawaii. "He was living in a nice house with several rooms and a swimming pool," says Graham. "It was about six or seven miles from downtown Waikiki."

At the time, Jay was involved with the local mafia in running an after-hours club on Hotel Street in downtown Honolulu, says Graham. Hollywood celebrities such as Don Johnson and Sal Mineo would come to the club on the down-low to hang out with Jay.

On Sundays, the club would have a jam session for local musicians, and all sorts of people one wouldn't expect would come to play along. The jam sessions were led by jazz musician Trummy Young, who played with Earl Hines, Jimmie Lunceford, Benny Goodman, Charlie Parker and Dizzy Gillespie. In 1964, Trummy quit the road and settled in Hawaii, becoming of all things, a Jehovah's Witness. One Sunday, when Graham was in Honolulu, he accompanied Jay to see one of the jam sessions, where Jay sang an amazing version of "St. James Infirmary." It went so well that Trummy asked Jay, "Can you come back next week?" To Trummy's surprise, Jay said no. The reason? Jay didn't want to be associated with the Sunday crowd because they were mainly "old musicians." Jay still thought of himself as young, fit, and at the nexus of music stardom. Trummy was 10 years older than Jay.

"When he came back to Hawaii he wasn't working for me," says Jack Cione. Wherever he was working, Jay wasn't doing much singing. Graham recalls him telling jokes between strippers. He might have also been the house bouncer. One person who did work for Jack was Lee Angel. After working in London, she returned to the United States, eventually making her way to Honolulu and the Forbidden City nightclub, where she worked as a stripper. "Lee Angel was one of my star attractions," says Jack. "And one of my favorite girls. She was good entertainment, always on time, a crowd-pleaser and very professional."

Angel arrived in Honolulu in 1972. "I knew how to work a room and this particular night I had the guys right where I wanted them," she said. "I turned toward the door," which was stage right, and in walks her old lover Jay with Ginny. "I said to myself 'no, no, no, no, no.' And it took me a few minutes to get myself together and back into dancing. Afterward, I confronted him and instead of raising a scene in the club I convinced him to go outside and talk. We really fought. I agreed to meet him the next day, but I had no intention of doing it. Soon afterward he returned to New York."

After every sunny Hawaiian holiday, Jay returned to the depths of gloomy New York. Hawaii could heal his wounds, but it couldn't boost his ego, make him a star or keep him famous. So, it was always back to the big city hoping to launch his career one more time.

The 1970s weren't a great time for New York City, and they weren't a great time for Jay. The deep R&B soul that fueled Jay's lyrics was mostly a memory, appreciated only by the early rockers and the aficionados from Europe. New genres steadily creeped in. Folk acts with singer-songwriters from sunny Los Angeles like Jackson Browne, James Taylor and The Eagles became increasingly popular. Motown, Memphis soul, and the "Philadelphia Sound" soon faded out, until they were all replaced in wholesale fashion by disco. In the aftermath of their collapse, Jay found comfort in emerging rock acts who borrowed their very existence from his early performances. Alice Cooper, Kiss, and the New York Dolls, among other acts, all wore makeup, dressed in theatrical attire, and performed their songs with a larger-than-life stage presence in front of packed football stadiums. Jay witnessed his influence on rock 'n' roll unfold in a way that he never thought possible, yet he was still relegated to the shadows of rock 'n' roll and R&B. He was a man stuck in time, hoping to re-emerge triumphantly, years past his prime.

It didn't help that Jay wallowed in alcohol and drugs, which only fueled his anger at the Music Gods for deserting him and leaving him to make a living in small clubs and oldies shows. He was the great Screamin' Jay Hawkins—where was the respect?

In the 1970s, says Mike Armando, "Jay was a heavy drinker, smoked a lot of marijuana and took a lot of prescription drugs. It was Ginny who would help him sort out his pills." The good thing about Jay was that his tolerance for booze, weed and pills was extremely high, so no matter how much he imbibed or ingested, he would always be able to perform. On the downside, there was one thing Jay's tolerance to booze and pills could not escape: the loss of memory that came with years of abuse. Robert Cutarella, who played drums for Jay, spoke to this: "Jay always had Ginny with him. She would give him pills all the time. I always joked that the pills erased his memory because he couldn't remember the names of the guys in the band from one minute to the next. It was the standard joke with the band."

When he returned to New York, Jay had no real band. He picked up musicians here and there when he had a gig. Although cheap to operate that way, it was a hectic and rarely satisfying way to perform. Gradually, he wised up, and found a regular group of musicians to back him up. The musicians may have got more than they bargained for because Jay had issues at almost every gig—with the venue, the promoter, or with the other acts. As one can imagine, the disputes all had to do with two things: money and ego.

Robert Cutarella had been playing drums since he was nine years old, and it showed in his adult years. He was a top studio drummer and his skills were in high demand. He played on nights or weekends when big acts needed a drummer to fill in. He did a lot of oldies shows including backing Dion and The Belmonts, The Chiffons and The Shirelles, with a brief stint in the jazz world backing Joe Williams. He even auditioned for Bruce Springsteen when his first album came out. Eventually, Robert hooked up with Jay. The year was 1973, and he joined what he recalled was a mixed bag of players. "We would go out for a gig, come back, go out, come back," says Robert. "He was so confrontational with some of the agents they kept not wanting to give him gigs. I could only do it for a few months."

In the early 1970s, Jay was only paying his musicians $50 a night because he wasn't getting much. Robert suggests Jay was being paid no more than $500 a night. "He was desperate for money," Robert continues. "His time had passed. He felt he didn't get what he was supposed to get when he first started out. In the early 1970s, everything was bigger including record sales. Concerts were bigger but Jay had come up in a time when anyone was just happy to get a gig. Sure, they didn't get what they should have, and in the 1970s they were living off his performances and income from ASCAP or BMI. Maybe it was substantial at one time but I never saw him live very high."

Mike Armando began playing as Jay's lead guitarist after being contacted by Robert. He stayed with Jay's backup band through the 1970s. His take on the business is much different than Robert's. According to Mike, in the mid- to late 1970s Jay's manager had full-time work at the post office and would ask for $5,000 for Jay and his band. Band members got $300 a gig.

Mike explains the difference: "Robert was playing drums for Jay when Jay needed a drummer for a few gigs. They were trying to form a band; the effort did not last very long as it all fell apart. So Jay was mostly using freelance musicians whenever he needed someone to back him for a gig. This is the reason they got paid $50 each. After that, Robert worked for MCA Records and that is when he asked me if I wanted to join the Screamin' Jay Hawkins band. Robert was not in the band with me. Jay's band began after Robert, and formed when I got in."

He adds, "Jay never screwed the band members out of money. He was honest with the money and always looked out for the band."

At the time, Jay and Ginny were living right off Broadway, around the corner from the old Ed Sullivan Theater, which was on Broadway between West 53rd and West 54th streets.

The problem with Jay was that he was always trying to shock everybody, says Robert. "That was his whole thing. Some recording acts have more solid songs behind them, but Jay liked to shock."

"If people didn't know him, he was a rough character, but if you knew him or played for him, he was like a lamb," Mike claims. "He would do anything for you. When I was out there, he would scream, 'take another solo!' He would announce your name on the mic. He would give a spotlight to the musicians."

For someone who had such a great stage act, Jay, at this point, was inconsistent, yet very demanding at the same time. "Sometimes Jay would forget the words and just look at us," says Robert. "The band would just play straight-ahead blues and shuffles, not really rock 'n' roll. It was a slow, down-tempo blues with a heavy backbeat. As a drummer I didn't have much to do." But, woe was you if you tried to stand out. "If you over-played, he would get pissed off," says Robert. "We in the band stayed in the pocket. If you didn't just sit there, Jay wasn't going to be a happy camper.

"And the band played on" was the unofficial motto of Jay's team of backup musicians, no matter what the circumstances— even when Jay set himself on fire at the Virginia Theater in Alexandria, Virginia. The year was 1976 and it was a concert that began in strife and literally blew up from there.

Alan Lee at Roadhouse Productions was promoting oldies concerts in the Washington, D.C., area and one of his first shows included Screamin' Jay Hawkins. The ad in the local paper read: "Virginia Theater; Sat. Feb 7; 2 shows only 8 p.m. and Midnite. With ... THE WILDMAN OF THE 1950S, SCREAMIN' JAY HAWKINS, *I Put a Spell on You*." The undercard were local singers such as "D.C.'s own Velons." Tickets were $7 in advance and $8 at the door.

Since Screamin' Jay was going to use a coffin in his act, Roadhouse Productions was obliged to supply a coffin.

"So, where do you get a coffin? I was friends with someone who did local plays and at one venue there was a coffin in the prop department; we made arrangements to have it delivered to the theater," explains Alan Lee.

A rehearsal was scheduled for that Saturday afternoon for the evening shows, of which there would be two shows. Jay arrived at the theater late in the afternoon.

"Jay walks in and I introduce myself and my partner," says Alan. "He goes over and looks at the coffin and says, 'It's no good. I don't come out of a coffin, I come out of a casket.' I thought what's the difference, and we get into a 20-minute argument. He says, 'That would be silly if I come out of a coffin [and] not a casket. A coffin would work if Dracula came out, and you were doing a show about vampires.' The argument went on and on, and finally we prevailed, because at 5 p.m. on Saturday, where the hell are you going to get a casket? I remember thinking to myself, here I am arguing with an adult about it being OK to come out of a casket, but not a coffin. We were lucky to find this coffin prop. He said he'll go with it, but he was not happy."

"The problem with Jay was he would burn a lot of bridges," says Mike. "There were always arguments. Producers and club owners didn't want to be bothered with him because things would always end up on the wrong note. Jay would argue about anything and everything."

There was one thing about the Virginia Theater that did make Jay happy. It had an old pipe organ that was placed stage left. It was built on rails so that it could move electrically out to the audience. Jay was the opening act, and he began his performance by climbing out of the coffin with his cane, which was topped with Henry, the smoking skull, and then moved over to the organ and played it as the organ moved out to the audience. "It was incredible," says Alan.

"When we played the Virginia Theater, Jay used his fuse boxes with flash powder to create the colored smoke effect," says Mike. "He could trigger the fuse boxes with a button on the stage that he could manipulate with his foot. That night, he was hitting the button and hitting the button, but nothing was happening. So, he bent down and hit the damn button with his fist. *Boom*, the fuse box went off, singing his hair and face. He fell to the floor."

"My partner and I were sitting in the back of the theater watching the show, and then Jay went down to the floor and started crawling around," remembers Alan. "We were thinking he was singing 'Alligator Wine,' and he was mimicking an alligator. Then we noticed he didn't get up. The band continued singing the song."

"The stagehands came out," Mike continues. "And when they were carrying him off the stage he was yelling to me to keep playing. We were playing basic blues. The crowd rose up, standing and clapping, thinking it was part of the show."

The theater called an ambulance. Jay suffered minor burns on his forehead and his eyebrows got singed. Twenty minutes later he came back out to perform again!

Jay performed the second show and Lee says, "he was tremendous. His midnight show entrance was much safer. At the time, Jay was living in a boarding house in Manhattan, was hard to reach, and before we got to the show, told me about a hit man who was coming to D.C. to do some 'work.' I immediately said, 'I don't want to know about this.'"

The *Washington Post* covered the story in the Monday paper under the title "Burnt Offering," which was a play on the name *Burnt Offerings*, a popular novel by Robert Marasco in 1973, which was made into a movie three years later with '70s horror icon Karen Black.

The article read:

> The rhythm 'n' blues revival show at Alexandria's Virginia Theater Saturday might had a little bit of everything: oldies, new songs, bizarre theatrics—and a very nearly serious accident.
>
> The mishap occurred at the end of the Screamin' Jay Hawkins set when an incendiary that was part of his act exploded in his face. Hawkins, who suffered minor burns on his fingers and a small cut on his tongue, was stunned by the flash and crawled offstage. The audience, thinking it was all planned, applauded the departure.
>
> Their confusion was understandable, Hawkins has been performing weird theatrics since long before there was an Alice Cooper. He began his set Saturday by emerging from a black casket and staggering to the microphone where he sang songs such as I Put a Spell on You, Alligator Wine and the highly graphic Constipation Blues using an incredible series of snorts, grunts, groans and screams.
>
> Hawkins' outrageous posturing doesn't quite obscure his ability as a blues singer, as he proved on Stormy Monday, a song on which he also played the theater's giant Wurlitzer console organ ...

"Every tour date was a crazy adventure," says Mike.

A lot of this had to do with ego. Jay believed he was a star of the first order, when he was just an esoteric rock 'n' roll classicist to music fans at large. If you were really into the bluesy origins of rock 'n' roll, or simply knew of and appreciated the song "I Put a Spell on You," then as a potential concert attendee, someone like Screamin' Jay Hawkins would be of interest to you. Like the Brits in the early 1960s who were dedicated Screamin' Jay fans, he represented the real heart of rhythm and blues, and one might see him as he or she would want to see Muddy Waters. This was in comparison to their contemporary Bo Diddley, who boasted a slew of major R&B and pop hits, such as the two-sided hit record "Bo Diddley" and "I'm a Man" that earned a Number 1 spot on the R&B charts in 1955. If Bo Diddley and Screamin' Jay Hawkins both performed at a show in the 1970s or beyond, Bo Diddley would get top billing, since he was more well-known because of his hit record, and the wide radio play that it received. Unlike Jay, Diddley had a large built-in audience. Jay's audience was much smaller. One had to have a deep affection for rhythm and blues to appreciate his talents. Battles between Jay's view of his self-importance, and how he was perceived by ticket-buying audiences, would be a source of deep internal conflict throughout the rest of his life.

As an example, sometime in the mid-1970s, Jay's booking agent calls him at home and asks if he wants to do a college gig on Long Island. Always looking for gigs, Jay says yes immediately.

The show was just two performers, he and Bobby Lewis, an R&B singer from the Midwest who had a couple of Top 10 hits in 1961. One of those hits, "Tossin' and Turnin'," was a Number 1 record for seven weeks, making him one of only seven solo male recording artists to have a Number 1 hit for such a long period of time until the 1990s. Others to accomplish this rare feat in music history included Elvis Presley, Marvin Gaye and Michael Jackson.

"The lineup, which was set up and advertised by the promoter, was Screamin' Jay Hawkins to open and then the star, who was Bobby Lewis, would close," says Mike. "When we get to the college, Jay, as usual, wants to change the order of the performance, which was already set. I was in the dressing room when I hear this big commotion, yelling, screaming, cursing and fighting. I went to see what was going on. Hawkins was cursing at Bobby Lewis and Bobby was not taking any of Jay's shit and cursing back. Cooler heads prevailed before it all went to fisticuffs. Hawkins wanted Bobby Lewis to go on first because Jay wanted to be the main act. The outcome didn't change; the bill stayed the same despite all the tumult."

There were always arguments, Mike says. "There was always craziness everywhere we went. One time we were to appear at a club in New Jersey. Again, it was a two-act show, Screamin' Jay Hawkins and the folk/rock group The Critters. Jay was to go on first and The Critters to close. Jay wasn't happy."

One could argue that Jay was a much more important musician than The Critters, but The Critters boasted a number of hits, including "Younger Girl," "Don't Let the Rain Fall Down on Me" and their biggest-selling record, "Mr. Dieingly Sad," was a Top 20 record in 1966. Not only were The Critters more recent hitmakers, but they were somewhat of a local New Jersey phenomenon.

"When we get to the club to check out the equipment and the stage, no one was there yet," Mike says. "Then The Critters walk in, and Jay approaches the lead singer, Don Ciccone, about changing. They said no because the show wasn't booked that way. Immediately, Hawkins gets angry, and starts calling them all kinds of names before Jay settles on calling them The Crickets, which just made us laugh. It went on and on and on with Jay yelling he was the main star and that the show was booked wrong. 'You are the fucking Crickets. I'm a bigger star than you!' he yelled to Don Ciccone. The people who had booked the show were going out of their minds because they had booked the show a certain way and didn't want it changed. It was getting pretty hot, and looked like the yelling was moving on to the pushing and shoving stage. At some point after Jay carried on with the manager and the people who ran the venue; The Critters give in, and decide to go on first. They do their performance and leave quickly. After we set up and go on stage we realized the PA, the electronic sound amplification system, was dead. It was chaos at first because everyone was running around trying to figure out what went wrong. Someone eventually discovered there was no power to the PA; the tubes were missing. Our guess was someone from The Critters removed the tubes from the amps. We couldn't perform and therefore never got paid. Jay wanted to kill someone. Lucky for The Critters, they were gone. We didn't talk to the manager, we just walked out of the place."

Sometimes, Jay would just piss off an audience for the hell of it.

Another tour date in the '70s was at an upscale supper club in Connecticut. The audience was well-dressed; men in suits and ladies in dresses, much older and whiter than Jay's normal audience. Being a supper club, the band would be performing when folks were eating. Jay liked playing "Constipation Blues," sometimes at the start of a show. The patrons looked wealthy, and the dinner appeared to be "fancy." Mike leaned in to Jay and said, "Maybe we shouldn't start that song at the beginning of our gig." Jay didn't care. The first song was to be "Constipation Blues." People were in shock. They started getting up and leaving. If there were 50 people in the audience, 20 of them walked away. Jay didn't care if he offended whites, he didn't care if he offended blacks. He looked at himself as a performer, take it or leave it.

The NAACP took issue with Screamin' Jay Hawkins' act, saying it created an irresponsible association of the black race and cannibalism. Jay didn't care. Mike reiterates, "He used to say, 'I was born naked, black, and ugly, and when I die, I'm going out naked, black and ugly.'"

One time, at about 4 a.m., Mike was driving Jay back from a gig when they hit the outskirts of Washington, D.C. where Jay's sister lived. He starts banging on her door. Mike says, "It's four in the morning, your sister may be sleeping." Jay keeps banging until his sister finally answers the door. "My band just got through playing and are tired. Give them something to eat and drink." She did.

They get back on the road and immediately get lost. Jay sees someone on the street and tells Mike to stop the car so he could ask for directions. Jay was still dressed in his performance getup, with a bone through the nose, a fake snake wrapped around his neck and a long fur coat. The guy who Jay stopped to ask for directions was also black. Jay asks him where the road to I-95 North was, and the man just stares at Jay, speechless. Jay yells to him, "What's wrong with you, boy, didn't you ever see a nigger before?"

They finally end up on I-95 North but were so tired that Mike turned the car in to a service stop so everyone could get coffee. There was no place to park except for handicapped parking. Jay says to park there, but Mike was hesitant, not wanting to get a ticket. Eventually, Mike caved to Jay's demands and parked. Mike is 5-foot-6 and Jay over six feet, so they looked a little strange when Jay draped himself over Mike, pretending to be handicapped.

In 1974, Mike had just gotten out of the Armed Services and formed his own jazz band. Soon after, he got the call from Robert Cutarella. Mike goes up to Jay's apartment for an interview. By this time, Jay was now living on the 27th floor of a mid-rise building on the east side of New York. Mike introduces himself, plays and gets hired.

For his first rehearsal with the band, Mike heads to Jay's apartment along with the new drummer, Mike's brother-in-law, August

Fesler. As luck would have it, just outside Jay's building, someone slams into August's car. Jay leans out his window and yells down, "Check the car for damage, check the car for damage!" Finally, Mike gets to the apartment where he is introduced to Mario, the sax player, who had just gotten out of jail for murder.

The band would practice in Jay's apartment, which didn't always go well with the neighbors. One time, the band was practicing, and the neighbor in the adjoining property kept banging and banging and banging on the wall. The band didn't stop, but the banging on the wall did. The band paused. The next thing everyone heard was someone thumping on the door. Jay opens the door. The neighbor yells, "I'm tired of hearing your music, I don't like your music! Stop it. I can't take the noise." The neighbor steps forward with his toe just past the base of the door. Jay warns the man, "If you take one more step, I'll floor you." Not realizing Jay had been a boxer in his youth, the neighbor takes the extra step and Jay quickly unleashes a punch to the man's face so powerful it knocks him flat to the floor. The neighbor was out cold in the hallway. When he comes to, the neighbor returns to his apartment where he calls the police who arrive soon afterward. Jay explained he was just defending himself and the police left without charging him with assault.

Then there was the story of Jay's cat. One time it was in heat, and Jay didn't want the cat to be with any male cat, so he would stick his finger into the cat's feminine parts, saying "no one is touching that cat but me." "The cat was in heat," recalls Mike, "and Jay decided to relieve it himself. The band was too stunned; no one knew what to say."

Jay's otherworldly relationship with his cat didn't stop there. He would allow the cat outside for what he called "exercise." One day, as the band was practicing, Jay says he needs to put the cat out. Jay lives on the 27th floor and Mike says, "You're putting the cat out? You have no yard here." Jay says, "I don't need no yard."

He opens his window and places the cat on a ledge no wider than 12 inches. It's a cold, windy day and the cat is 27 stories up. After about an hour, the cat had walked around the whole building and made it back into the house.

All good things come to a finale, and with the end of the 1970s came the breakup of Jay's band. "We were in New York, in Jay's apartment. It was 1979," says Mike. "Jay's manager and his booking agency didn't have any work for Jay for the next three months. The band could not keep going because they all needed money to support their families. The band split."

Sometime later, Mike finds out Jay was going to be opening for the Rolling Stones at its November 12, 1981 Madison Square Garden concert. Keith Richards requested Jay as a last-minute replacement. "I was shocked and mad at myself for leaving," Mike says in retrospect. "But who knew the future?"

Actually, the end of the band was a slow death spiral. Until Jay was bailed out by the Rolling Stones, gigs were getting scarcer, and so were his living conditions.

In 1973, Roni Hoffman was an art major at Hunter College in Manhattan, and an aspiring photographer. Her boyfriend at the time was Richard Meltzer, who is considered to be the first author to write an analysis of rock 'n' roll, and who would in turn become the inventor of rock 'n' roll criticism. Because of her relationship with Meltzer, Roni was hanging with a lot of writers and artists, taking pictures all the while. Through Richard, she met Nick Tosches, who had a misanthropic personality, but liked Roni, and when on assignment, would ask her to come along and photograph. At the time, Nick was writing columns about rock 'n' rollers for male-oriented publications like *Penthouse* and *Oui*. One of those visits was with Screamin' Jay Hawkins.

At the time, she says, he and Ginny were living in an SRO (single-room occupancy) hotel near Times Square. This was when

Times Square had not been Disneyfied and was a rough place filled with prostitutes and porn palaces. "The room was small but neat," Roni remembers. "Ginny's purses hung on a nail on the wall and her personal cosmetics and oils were on the one dresser. They had a cat, which they took turns holding. Ginny was a tiny Asian woman, with very long, dark hair. She didn't say a lot. They were friendly, and humble, and not concerned about their appearance. I felt awkward about taking photographs because I was in someone's bedroom. Nick was sitting on the bed. I was walking around, and then with nowhere else to sit, I plunked myself on the bed. Maybe there was a straight-backed chair in the room and a mirror. Their whole life was in there, personal stuff, and they were acting as if we were just coming over for a chat. There was barely room for all of us."

Nick wrote about the place this way: "He was living at the Hotel Bryant, in a shabby room nine floors above Broadway in Times Square. With him were his wife, Ginny, and an obnoxious, four-month-old Siamese cat named Cookie. A *Jet* calendar hung on one wall, variously weird hats from nails on another. The television was on, but without sound. Hawkins sat on the edge of the bed in a wool hat, Hawaiian-style sport shirt, and horn-rimmed glasses, taping a Frank Sinatra album from his stereo onto his reel-to-reel recorder. Beside him was a little ceramic foot-shaped ashtray in which he snuffed his Lucky Strikes."

For most of Mike's tenure with Jay, he remembers the eastside apartment on the 27th floor. However, when Seth Greenky, who would become Jay's manager, first met him in 1978, he and Ginny were living in an apartment back on the West Side midtown area of Manhattan and things were in dire straits.

Seth's story begins this way. In 1976, he was at the offices of Buddah Records, a New York record label that had a strong string of successes in the late 1960s and early 1970s with such varied records as Brooklyn Bridge's "The Worst That Could Happen," The

Five Stairsteps' "O-o-h Child" and Brewer and Shipley's "One Toke Over the Line."

"I had a demo for a group I was pitching; and I was friends with Bob Reno, head of A&R there," Seth says. "I was sitting in the lobby by the receptionist desk and in comes this well-dressed, hulking gentleman who walks over to the receptionist and in a low voice says, 'Please tell Mr. Reno that Jay Hawkins is here.'" Jay's voice, even in a whisper, made the walls rumble. He was trying to get an advance on some royalties, which was standard practice for him. He was always trying to get advances from record companies and BMI, primarily for "I Put a Spell on You."

Jay sits down on the chair next to Seth, who asks, "Did you say Jay Hawkins, as in Screamin' Jay Hawkins?" He said, "Yes, that's right." The two get to talking and after their various appointments, Jay asks Seth to walk home with him.

"When we walked in, the place was illuminated by candles. His wife, Ginny, was there. It turns out his electricity had been shut off. I looked in the cupboards; there may have been two cans of vegetables. There was almost nothing in the refrigerator. He couldn't have gotten much broker. I said, 'This is not right,' and marched the two of us over to the Con Ed office. I paid his electric bill and got his electricity back on. On the way home, we stopped at the grocery store, and we brought back all the groceries our four arms could carry. We re-stocked the shelves and the refrigerator." That started their relationship.

"He didn't have anything going. I thought, how is this possible? He was in deep poverty and I just wanted to turn on his lights. You can't think about show business or entertainment; this was about life or death. For the person who had had the success he had, I just saw this as a terrible tragedy. He was charming as hell. He could ingratiate you; he was a lovable character. He could charm the pants off you, but more often than not, a lot of his problems were due to him stepping on his own dick. He went to Hawaii and then came back; it was a whole new generation and people didn't know who he was, people younger than myself, and I was about 28 at that time. He wasn't womanizing then. He said he stopped drinking. At the time I was a staff producer and sales manager at the Bell Sound Studios, which used to be 237 West 64th Street. Jay could really sing his ass off. We people just thought he could scream, which he could do on pitch. The guy loved opera and he could sing opera. He had this magnificent low baritone, almost like a basso profundo, but maybe just a little higher with a huge range. He sang opera to me, but he didn't have a classic opera voice. This could have been an R&B version of the *The Barber of Seville*. He had the notes, the range and the power. I used to joke with him, when we went to the studio, we didn't need to roll tape, we just needed to hold the tape up to him.

"I met with his attorney. I started to manage him and was going to produce him, because I wanted people to hear that this guy could actually sing. He was a great R&B singer and he could play the piano, saxophone and melodica. His natural talent was off the charts. I found him an agent, Steven Amiel, who had a small agency located on West 55th Street and Broadway. He thought he could get Jay some steady work."

A lot of people didn't know Screamin' Jay Hawkins, and he didn't have a big following at the time. Seth and Steven's strategy was to slowly rebuild his credibility as a reliable performer. The agent felt he could get him work in and around the tri-state area, three or four nights a week, at about $800 a show. It wasn't terrible money. The idea was that if they could start building back Jay's credibility, then he could start asking for more money and get record companies interested again. "For God's sake," Seth and Steven said to Jay, "make some money and get out from under this deep hole you are in."

It was a good strategy, if Jay cooperated. He wouldn't. Jay refused to work for less than $1,500 a night, and consequently, he would only work two nights a year, New Year's Eve and Halloween. Seth points out to Jay, "If you are working four nights at $800, you're getting $3,200 a week. Some of that would go to commission, some to other musicians, but you are going to start to re-establish yourself."

Jay responds, "Seth, I got a name." Seth answers, "Yeah, but nobody knows it." This was the problem for Jay; he had too much pride based on his early success. He wouldn't work for less than $1,500 a night, which made it nearly impossible for an agent to find him gigs. There was an occasional gig, but not enough to sustain himself.

In 1977, Steven Amiel and Seth got Jay a gig at the newly revived Peppermint Lounge. The gig was for $1,500 and Jay was paying his sidemen about $100 a musician. Jay wanted to get paid before he played. The club owner kept saying we have to wait for more people to come in because "we don't have the money to pay you yet." Then the place started to fill up—it was jammed.

"We couldn't find the club owner and it was time for Jay to go on stage," says Seth. "Jay does the show and it was well received. Everyone is waiting to get paid and the club owner, we were told, had left. The agent and I were ticked off and managed to catch a glimpse of him leaving in his car. I had my car parked outside. Steven and I jumped in and it was like a scene out of the *French Connection* movie. It's two in the morning and we are screaming down Lexington Avenue because we don't know where he lived. The club owner pulls into some building and we are pounding on his door. He said, 'I'll pay you tomorrow' and I said, 'We are not leaving until you pay us.' Eventually, he paid the money, we went back to the club and Jay paid his musicians."

Going out on a limb for Jay didn't win you any favors, especially when the issue was money. In September 1977, Seth gets Jay booked into CBGB for three nights. CBGB was the hottest club in New York at the time. The idea was to get record companies to hear and see him performing in a hip venue. Jay was booked for Thursday, Friday and Saturday nights, and he would be reimbursed based on the money coming in the door.

"We get down there and the keyboard player did not have a keyboard; so I got in my car, drove all the way uptown and crosstown to my place on West 89th Street, picked up my Wurlitzer piano and drove it back downtown to the Lower East Side, scrambling for parking. I carry the piano inside, set it up and get the band ready. People are starting to come in. I'm keeping an eye out for record execs. The gig has started and I start making sure everyone is well lubricated. I'm going from table to table. Jay always put on a great show; he was a great performer. Hilly Kristal, who owned CBGB, was an honest man. No one ever accused him of stealing a penny. He had his usual guy working the door. We were getting $3, or $4, out of the $7 at the door, and made somewhere between $800 and $1,100 that first night. The only thing that Jay was worried about was that I was not sitting at the door counting the money coming in. I said I was with the A&R guys because this was about getting you a new record contract, and they are not going to be cheating you at the door. All he was fixated on was the money coming in the door. He looked at the small picture, not the big picture, and he busted my chops about this mercilessly. The money seemed right to me based upon the crowd. He only wanted to work for a certain minimum, and he only cared about what came through the door."

If Greenky found him difficult, Amiel remembers him as a charmer—although a difficult act to book.

"As an agent, I represented him for a period of time," Amiel says. "I did a couple of shows with him. It was delightful working with Jay. I really liked him and thought him a great guy. He was very passionate, and also very angry at not having the type of career and recognition that he thought he should have had. That was really no different from any other black artist from that time period that I ended up working with. They all got their asses kicked."

Besides organizing oldies shows and representing '50s and '60s singers, Amiel also booked for a west Manhattan club called the Red Parrot, on 57th Street, between 11th and 12th Avenues. The venue was once called the High Rollers, because it had a skating rink. In the era of Studio 54 and Xenon, the Red Parrot was a welcome antidote for those coked-up celebrity-obsessed clubs. It boasted the Red Parrot orchestra, who after 40 minutes of play would perform another 20 minutes of Big Band swing. Amiel started booking "unannounced acts who were 20 minutes from Broadway." This was so successful, he shifted to booking regular oldies acts on the nights the place was dark. Many did extremely well there, including performers such as James Brown. Jay, however, would remain locked outside of its pearly gates. Even with Amiel's weighty insider pull at the venue, he was never able to book Screamin' Jay Hawkins there.

"He was just barely getting by," says Amiel. "He wasn't a big enough draw where I could get him a gig as a single, headline performer. I could not keep him busy. And he always wanted more money than he could get."

There was one gig Amiel got for him—reluctantly.

"He was a great performer and a gracious man, so much so, he really wanted to perform at my wedding; my nice Jewish wedding with 250 guests at Temple Shalom on Long Island," Amiel fondly remembers. "As an agent for musicians, I had a great band. Rupert Holmes, who wrote 'Escape (The Piña Colada Song),' which was a Number 1 hit record in 1979, was a client of mine at the time and he performed and sang."

Jay would not take no for an answer; so he was invited to sing at the wedding, and did very nicely, working through three songs, and ending with "I Put a Spell on You."

The response was mixed. "You can just imagine some of my older Jewish relatives just ripping up the $36 check. [Jewish folk often give gifts in multiples of 18 as the letters that spell the word *chaim*, meaning life, also mean the number 18.] Everyone was very nice but 'I Put a Spell on You' was a lead balloon at my own wedding," Amiel laughs.

As a manager, or an agent, one could get only so many wins for Jay before he turned on you, as he did with almost everyone.

"I was managing him when the movie *American Hot Wax* was in production," says Greenky. The movie, loosely based on the Alan Freed story, had contracted with three performers who were original to the Freed shows at the old Paramount Theater in New York: Chuck Berry, Jerry Lee Lewis and Screamin' Jay Hawkins.

"I helped coordinate it, and make it happen for Jay, including taking Jay to the screen test with singer Kenny Vance," Greenky continues. "Jay brought his coffin and set it up. We were playing 'I Put a Spell on You' with the camera rolling. The coffin opened, Jay stood straight up and says 'hi' to the producer. I helped Jay with travel and schedule. I even got him a *Live At Five* interview with Cousin Bruce Morrow. They let him keep all his costumes from the movie."

After it was all done, Jay refused to pay Seth a commission. Eventually, Seth and Jay met with Jay's attorney, who said, "Jay, you have to pay the man."

Seth notes, "Jay reluctantly paid me my manager's fee but it was like pulling teeth."

With the '70s coming to a close, so was Seth's relationship with Jay. "I just couldn't do it anymore," he says. "He was reluctant to pay me; he was always trying to find a reason not to pay me. He was reluctant to follow directions. He was impossible to work with. Whenever we had a gig, he was overly concerned about getting paid. I would shake my head and just say, 'Jay, I'm doing this for you. No one wanted to handle you. What's your problem?' He was so used to in the 1950s and 1960s getting screwed over by the man; he trusted no one. Ginny would often take my side in arguments. She would say, 'Look what the man is doing for you. Why are you treating him like that?' One time, he misused a demo that was strictly for demo purposes and it could have gotten him in legal troubles. He threatened to get me in trouble for things I did for him. He would try to use this or that against me for leverage. I quit him."

Then the phone calls would come. This was in the days of answering machines. Jay would leave messages, "I'm a changed man. I changed my spots." He also tried other managers, sometimes working two managers at the same time.

Says Seth: "He finally convinced me that he changed and I went back to managing him, but within a few months it was back to the same shit, and he was also putting me in legal jeopardy. I took him into the studio, recording him doing some really good stuff. These recordings were meant for the ears of A&R people and no one else. Jay ended up going through that whole thing where people would make albums just as a tax shelter. He took the unauthorized tracks and sold it to someone for $2,000 or $3,000. Those tracks did not belong to him. I turned 32 and just walked away from him. He didn't change. He was ungrateful and tried to screw me, often threatening me. That was Jay. The last message I got from Jay was, "Seth. Seth get on the phone. I know you are there. Oh, come on Seth, pick up the phone. It's about money. You like money, don't you, Seth? Get our money. Pick up the phone."

Years later, while on the West Coast, Seth ran into musician/actor Robert "Smokey" Miles, who had worked with Jay. The two got to talking and realized they both knew Jay. Robert told Seth, "Jay regretted screwing you over all those times. He said you were the only honest manager he ever had."

CHAPTER

toWARd

the end of the 1970s, Jay was not only scrounging for gigs, but looking to record again to drum up hard cash. While this did lead to what Seth Greenky called "tax shelter recordings," Jay also managed to release two actual albums (and almost a third one) over the next few years. Two of the three enterprises were a long time in gestation, and like all of Jay's business dealings, were difficult and laced with animus.

First, the easy deal. In 1979, a Hendersonville, Tennessee, record producer with the friendly name of Koala Record Co. released a Jay album called *Lawdy Miss Clawdy,* the name of a hit record by a young Lloyd Price back in 1952. Jay reworked the song for this album along with nine other tunes, most of which were written by Jay. There's another version of "I Put a Spell on You," plus such songs as "Half Past Me," "Ashes," "Don't Deceive Me," and "Guess Who."

The little-known Koala Record Co. was mostly active from 1979 through 1981, issuing what looked to be compilation albums of unissued and rare tracks by such disparate performers as Gordon Lightfoot, Duke Ellington, Buddy Greco, Brook Benton, Jefferson Airplane, Johnny Paycheck and Bing Crosby. There was something a little suspicious about Koala, because the same year they issued *Lawdy Miss Clawdy* by Screamin' Jay Hawkins, the company also issued an album named after another old song, *Itty Bitty Pretty One* (a 1957 hit by Thurston Harris), by singer Jay Hawkins.

The smell of oldies wafted in the air at the end of the 1970s as a handful of small record companies were looking for unissued, rare, little-known and sometimes unauthorized recordings by older stars. Jay, too, was on the hunt, dealing with two European producers. The cross-border communications took place via old-world correspondence: long, handwritten, or typed letters that sailed between the United States and Europe.

Despite Jay's demonic stage act and juvenile outbursts, he was smart, erudite and well-read; an exceptional letter writer, with a steady, neat hand, every paragraph perfectly aligned on blank white paper.

Bill Millar, who exchanged letters with Jay from the 1960s to the 1970s, says that when Jay's relationship with Ginny ended, so did the letters, from which he concluded it was Ginny's perfect handwriting that everyone reads in Jay's correspondence. The same was true for Jay's correspondence with record producer Jonas Bernholm. As the 1970s turned into the 1980s, which was around the end of Jay's marriage to Ginny, eventually the handwritten letters ended and typed written letters became the norm.

The English record company Red Lightnin' Records was formed in 1968 to produce rhythm and blues records. Today, it boasts over 1,500 masters of blues songs that can be licensed for compilations, advertising and promotions. Peter Shertser has been associated with the company since it began in the mid-

1960s. Around the end of 1976, Jay discussed doing a reissue of old material for a European record company with Norbert Hess, a friend in Germany. By early the next year, Norbert had contacted Peter Shertser, who was interested in the project. At first, discussions moved along smoothly, so by June 1977, as Peter told *Blues & Rhythm* magazine, "Norbert confirmed track suggestions for the reissue of Jay's rare 45s and/or other material Jay may have." There were problems. Jay couldn't locate the master tapes for his Grand, Atlantic and Mercury releases. Still, by the end of 1977, Jay agreed to an album release "in principle," but as could be expected with Jay, he required more money.

"The problem was that all the discussions were going through this guy in Germany and things weren't getting done quickly," says Peter. "Then in 1978 Jay started writing to me directly because he was pissed off at Norbert. Jay wanted everything done immediately. We offered an idea for the project and he expected the project to be done yesterday. He would get very excited because he was in constant need of funds due to extenuating circumstances."

In the spring of 1978, Peter finally received the final tapes from Norbert with a letter that read "Jay wants to get it out soon," which was interesting, because Jay had not yet signed a contract. That didn't happen until August 20 of that year. With that small business concluded, according to the contract, Jay was to receive $1,500 in payment. "That was a big number for something so iffy," says Peter "He didn't own the rights to the songs. We just put it out as we had Jay's signature and the right copyright information."

In September, Jay wrote to Peter:

> I wish to express the dire importance … in settling the matter of the $1,500 quickly if not sooner. As I am in the midst, this very minute, of tapping all my present financial resources from publishers here I work with; from Paramount Motion Pictures

for American Hot Wax; from various booking agents that I work with throughout here and in Honolulu; and from banks here in New York that I do business with, because I am facing the funeral and burial costs of a son who was killed in a gang war in Philadelphia, September 4, 1978, and another son who is in jail and is in dire need of bail, plus his attorney fees, in or out of jail, including the bail until his case has been settled one way or another ... I wish this to remain in strict confidence between you and myself. But I did want to stress the point—the need for the fifteen hundred dollars ($1,500).

Later in this densely packed, four-page letter, Jay strongly sells himself to Peter:

First of all, back in the days before the word Rock 'n' Roll was ever heard, our type of music was referred to as Rhythm and blues. When I started, I wore tuxedos, tails, hat, gloves, cane and all. All colors including zebra stripes and leopard stripes or spots. Elvis Presley stole that act on the Ed Sullivan show singing Hound Dog. Chuck Willis and I worked together, he stole the act by wearing turbans. I started wearing capes, so did Little Richard. Then another feller came along named himself "Screamin' Lord Sutch" ... since then different bits and pieces of my act have been stolen by David Bowie, James Brown, Alice Cooper, Rod Stewart, the Funkadelics, the Isley Brothers, Arthur Brown, Earth, Wind & Fire just to name a few. My theatrical and bizarre visual effects eventually found its way to Star Wars and Close Encounters of the Third Kind. None of these imitators never once gave honest credit as to how they obtained these ideas.

In the colorful liner notes of his life's history, Jay not only invented rock 'n' roll, but science fiction as well!

Peter, who was moving his company during 1978 from London to the town of Diss in Norfolk, had his own cash-flow problems. Nevertheless, he quickly sent Jay a check for $750 as it appeared Jay had severe money woes involving family. The question is, what sons died or were arrested? Jay doesn't say, but there is a partial explanation in the next letter, where Jay thanks Peter for rapidly sending the money.

Jay wrote back:

> They have an indictment against him (my son) for breaking and entering … assault and battery and conspiring to commit murder. He has his mother's maiden name. Not mine! So therefore, there is no connection publicity-wise to me. So far, the lawyer has done a good job keeping it out of the newspapers. I know you can understand my point and help me keep this in the strictness of confidence. This is his first time in trouble. So since there's no previous record and since the lawyer knows the judge, we have good reason to believe he will get off as light as possible. Perhaps some probation in my custody, even if he is illegitimate.

Of course, further correspondence concerned the second check for $750, which was duly sent. However, with 1978 slipping away and the album not yet completed, Jay turned on Norbert Hess, complaining to Peter that he and Norbert had been talking about the album since the summer of 1977. Jay wrote, "as far as I'm concerned this is no way to do business," adding, "I have enough unreleased tapes here to make at least 10 more albums and they are all finished product. He [Norbert] has the gall to write me a letter asking me to send these tapes."

1979 rolled around, and with the album still in flux, Jay turned some of his ire toward Peter as there were always issues such as preview albums.

In the spring of 1979, Jay wrote, in his usual poetic language:

> *Where you and I are concerned, I'll try to be brief as possible. Love is love. Hate is hate. A lie is a lie. Time is money. Phone calls are money. Business is business. This album you're putting out on me, I promised a lot of people in 1978, when I was doing a great deal of T.V. shows that they would get copies of Red Lightnin' albums of me before I was Screamin' Jay Hawkins. After "you" gave me your word, by way of telephone, before you moved, that I would have a box containing 25 albums to pass out in California. That would have done me as well as Red Lightnin' Records some good ... you were not there. You did not feel the eyes staring dead in yours like I did ...*

Peter told *Blues & Rhythm* magazine, "In June 1979 Jay complained about myself and Norbert and abusive mail continued."

The album was finally released late 1979. Titled *Screamin' the Blues*, on the front cover it sported a colorful dash of Jay eclipsed by Henry, his longtime companion, and the personification of his stage magic. The liner notes were by an old friend from England, Cliff White, and the whole album was "mastered by" Norbert Hess. In spite of all the difficulties, *Screamin' the Blues* is a very interesting album as it showcased some of Jay's earliest recordings, including those done with Tiny Grimes and Red Prysock (tenor sax), such as "Not Anymore," "Please Try to Understand" and "Baptize Me in Wine." There were also four cuts where he was backed by the Leroy Kirkland Band, including "This Is All," "Talk About Me" and the fabulous "(She Put the) Wamee (On Me)." Sixteen cuts in all fill out the package, with some of Jay's recent recordings such as "Monkberry Moon Delight" and "Sweet Ginny."

About the album, Peter says: "The album was not going to go mainstream, which isn't what Jay wanted. He used to ring at five or six in the morning not realizing what time it was in Great Britain. He would say, 'My other son is in trouble, I need more money.' In 1983, there was a serious issue with another son. I sent him money because he was in such trouble. I had no problem with Jay, he was very funny. He was a crazy person. He wanted money. He always wanted money."

In his interview with *Blues & Rhythm,* Peter did add one note. "If Jay had 10 albums' worth of unissued material, at some point he would have made great strides to sell some of it to me, as he was frequently in need of urgent money, and knew he could rely on me for payment. I ended up giving him advances for future unearned royalties years after the original advance and royalties were paid regularly on sales."

None of this prevented Jay from hard-selling more unreleased records to another European record producer who also focused on original rhythm and blues: Jonas Bernholm of the Swedish label Route 66 Records. This entailed another series of lengthy correspondence, all of which began innocently enough when Bill Millar put Jay in touch with Jonas. Millar was just trying to help Jay out. He wouldn't know until years later that Jay was trying to take advantage of Jonas, "flogging" poor recordings that Jonas couldn't use.

The relationship between Jay and Jonas began on an upbeat note with Jay writing, "and I shall write Bill Millar, who I consider a very dear friend, and thank him also, for giving you my address."

Jay then addresses the question of his contract with Red Lightnin' Records, adding that at some point he had in his possession an anthology's worth of previously unissued material, which he kept on tapes.

Jay writes:

> Yes, I did make a deal with Red Lightnin' records with the help of Norbert Hess. Which began over 2½ years go. Since then, for extreme personal reasons—I do not consider myself a

friend of Norbert Hess. And I did write him and informed him of that consideration and decision. And I sincerely hope that I never, ever hear from Norbert Hess again. The deal between Red Lightnin' Records has been negotiated and completed. And I still cannot tell you to this very day, why they have not released that record as of yet ... I have in my possession enough "finished product" material to make at least ten more albums. Songs that nobody has ever heard me sing, songs that I would like to put out and on the market ...

Jonas was intrigued, and optimistically wrote back to Jay. Jay's next letter was typewritten on stationery from Glitter Management at 401 West 56th Street in New York.

First of all, there are songs that I have taken a band into the studio, with a full-size band, recorded stereo and I have "MASTER'S" here in my home. At the time I was recording a great deal of material for the purpose of selling to people involved in "tax shelter releases" for x-amount of dollars up front, with a royalty clause (foreign & domestic) and also, a mechanical clause for my compositions. And of course, artist royalties, and of course, publishing royalties. Which I do have my own publishing company. Which of course I would be willing to work a deal with you so you could sub-publish from your end there in Sweden.

Jay then lists some of the recordings he would like to use:

My Heart Tells Me—a ballad
You Keep Me Hanging On—rock
I Put a Spell on You—"laughing" version
Bathroom Window—rock
Looking Back—swing

The Thrill Is Gone—blues
Twelve Bar Blues—blues
For Your Love—ballad
Unforgettable—swing
A Sunday Father—reggae
A Folded Flag—reggae and rock
I Don't Want to Leave You—blues
In My Dream—blues
We Love—a ballad [Jay and Ginny singing]
Game of Love—a blues ballad with strong and vocal group
Your Kind of Love—rock 'n' roll
No Son of Mine—folk
The Cleaning Lady—folk
Alligator Wine—weird
Angel of Hell—rock

Jonas had also been putting together tours of R&B singers throughout Scandinavia and broached the subject with Jay, who wrote back:

> *I like the idea about a [7- to 14-day] tour in Scandinavia. I have the band to give you the sound you want. I am enclosing the name and address of an agency in England who wants me there this year. They have just written me a letter asking me my terms and requirements for a 10-day tour which would be a minimum of 8 shows. I told them, for me by myself, I would require $1,000 a day, 2 round trip airline tickets for me and my wife on any kind of airline except the DC-10 or a 727.*

Jay was expensive, too expensive for Jonas. The Route 66 record label was only three years old in 1979 and not yet financially sound. In addition, Jonas had already committed to an R&B tour in 1980 with Ruth Brown, Charles Brown, Floyd Dixon,

Chuck Norris and Preston Love. It wasn't successful, as the venues proved too small for that many artists on the bill. Jonas adds, "In Stockholm we were forced to accept money collected at the door while the club owner sold beer. That same night Bob Marley had a concert at the fairgrounds that broke all-time attendance records in Stockholm. We had a very small crowd that night."

At the same time, Jonas launched a gospel label called Clanka Lanka, which was another disaster. Jonas estimated that 5,000 people would show up for a big concert that the label was putting on in Birmingham, Alabama, and that the ensuing buzz would cause record sales to hit 1,000 copies. Only 150 people attended and just 25 copies of the deluxe double album were sold.

Jonas did have one success under his belt. In 1978 he underwrote a tour by blues singer Roy Brown that did well. Roy Brown was a known singer with a strong history of hit records. He sang one of the earliest pre-rock 'n' roll songs, "Good Rockin' Tonight," and from the late 1940s through the early 1950s had many Top 5 R&B hits: "Long About Midnight," "Rainy Weather Blues," "Rockin' at Midnight," "Boogie at Midnight," "Hard Luck Blues" and "Love Don't Love Nobody." For all those classic sounds, Jonas could only pay Roy Brown $1,000 plus expenses for a one-week tour. Jay was asking for $1,000 a night.

The correspondence continues with Jonas reiterating that he really wants to do an album of very weird Screamin' Jay Hawkins music. As a friendly gesture, he sends Jay some recent Route 66 albums.

In the next letter, Jay still pushes for a tour and says he has the music Jonas seeks for an album.

I had hoped that you and your promoters there in Sweden could work with the England agency and that would help on the expenses and all the money concerned … That is why I informed you about the English agency who wants me there this

*year, and that is why I informed the English agency about you,
who also wants me there this year. So that you both could work
together and share the expense and still have 2 tours with one
trip to Europe. This way, the $1,000 I am asking per night, can
be shared between your office and the English office.*

More importantly, Jay commits to sending a tape of the
kind of music Jonas has been expecting. Jay always refocuses
on the money.

*Again, let me say, I will make a tape for you and put songs
on there for you to hear. Different from the songs I wrote you
and told you I also have. The tape I am about to send you will
be that of a tenor sax and combo and piano. The type of music
your last letter just asked for. After you hear the tape then we
can discuss by mail, or, if you would like me (when I come to
Sweden to do the tour for you) to record the same songs "live"
and make an album that way. We can also discuss how I am
to be paid $2,500 and when. And we can also discuss monies
for the tours.*

Jay doesn't send a tape. He sends a fourth letter to Jonas, with
the same "Jay bargain": you give me the cash sight unseen, and
I'll send you the tape.

The tape finally arrives. Jonas listens and is not impressed.
The songs with his comments at the time follow:

I've Had It All (An uptempo number about food: Monkey toes
and string beans; roast baboon salad smothered with bubble-
gum; barbequed [sic] gorilla ribs; mosquito pie; I've had it all!)
An unnamed ballad with echo effects
You Put the Spell on Me (slow)
Voodoo (An up-tempo number: I met this chick; she real-

ly was exciting; she had a real dog face; asked me to her place; Voodoo!)
Unnamed ballad (The first time that I saw her. Bass/baritone)

Then a bunch of cuts from the old 1965 album *The Night and Day of Screamin' Jay Hawkins*:

Unnamed R&B tune (weirdie mid-tempo, very poor sound)
But It Is (R&B slow rocker)
Take Me Back Pretty Baby (mid-tempo R&B rocker)
My Heart is Crying (My soul is dying; I've been lying. R&B ballad with organ)
I Go Crazy (up-tempo with banjo)
I'm Tired I'm So Weak (I'm lonely with a *I Put a Spell on You* accompaniment)

In *Blues & Rhythm* magazine, Jonas wrote: "Jay sent me a strange tape. Six or seven songs were from the Planet album released in the U.K. in 1967. I didn't want to use those. Plus the quality of a couple more were too poor. And I really needed more weird numbers in order for it to sell. Jay also mentioned several other titles, but he had not included those on the cassette. I was disappointed."

After hearing from Jonas, who explained that the tape just didn't work for him, Jay quickly responded with one more letter filled with promises and gusto.

If you stop and think about the first correspondence I sent you, you will remember, I gave you a whole lot of song titles I have finished product on that no one has ever heard. Except me and the band, the vocal group who recorded them. True, on the tape cassette I have sent you tunes that have been out before, but, I still own them and I have the right to re-release them … I gave Peter Shertser the rights to re-release some of my old stuff … yes … I do have some original tapes from the Planet session. Some are also Blues Ballads. In other words Jonas, I have in a closet in my apartment as big as any full size engineer studio, all types of finished product, never been released to the world before.

Jonas ended the correspondence, noting, "I was disappointed as he could not send samples of the weird stuff I was looking for. There was a discrepancy between the content of the letters and the musical cassette Jay sent me. Some songs mentioned in the letters were missing and sound quality was not acceptable on others. That's one reason our contact didn't continue after 1979–1980 … I had not continued writing as he wanted much more money for stage performances than I could afford."

In one of the letters from Jay, he attempted to do right by Jonas, telling Jonas that he had gone to a nightclub to see a show by Nappy Brown, and that Nappy would be interested in touring Scandinavia. Born in 1929, Napoleon Brown Goodson Culp hit success with a string of R&B hits in the mid-1950s recording as Nappy Brown. Jay sent Jonas the contact information for Nappy. At first, Jay wasn't sure Nappy was going to follow through, so he sent a short follow-up letter to Jonas, offering to help book singers Rosco Gordon or Larry Darnell in his place. It appears that Jonas did team up with Nappy. In 1983, Nappy had a successful tour of Scandinavia which was followed by a new album, his first in 14 years.

Not all associations were so positive. Jay called Jonas from the apartment of singer Varetta Dillard attempting rapprochement. It ended badly. Jonas noted, "I understood why Johnny Otis had to erase Jay out of his address book." Otis was a major force in

R&B music as a singer, musician, composer, bandleader, record producer and in later years, a radio and television personality. When Jonas was talking about Johnny Otis, he says he was quoting Otis' best friend, Preston Love, who was working as the editor of the *Omaha Star*, a black newspaper. "When I told Preston about my contact with Jay, he didn't encourage it," says Jonas. "For two reasons: the first was that Preston felt songs like 'Constipation Blues' were not helpful to Black Pride. Secondly, as always with Jay, there were financial problems." Jonas adds, "Jay had proved to be unreliable."

Jay had called Jonas from Varetta Dillard's apartment because he had been thrown out of his previous place. He called offering a set of tapes that would be perfectly aligned to what Jonas had needed several years before. Varetta and Jonas knew each other as well. "She called me about various things," says Jonas. "She had inherited a piece of land and wanted my advice and financial help to turn it into a trailer park. She was not well known then but had since become a favorite among the fans of black rock 'n' roll. I wrote to her saying that I had hopes that the *Mr. R&B* LP would make everybody understand that she had been too long in the shadows of Ruth Brown. Unfortunately, she showed that letter to Ruth Brown. (They were friends.) And Ruth took it personally and probably thought I felt that Varetta was better than her, which I didn't."

Sometime later, Jonas gets a call from Varetta. She tells him that Jay was no longer staying with her, and that she was glad he had left. Jay made a lot of phone calls from her place, which he didn't pay for, and it cost her a lot of money. They didn't part as friends. As Jonas told *Blues & Rhythm*, "It almost sounded as if Varetta, who has been a rehabilitated alcoholic, had started drinking again."

If Varetta Dillard needed a drink, Jonas would later need a bottle. Perhaps he did have a few drinks before speaking with Jay, because when Jay rang him from Dillard's apartment to say he had the tapes that Jonas had always requested, Jonas bit hook, line and sinker. He told Jay that he was interested. "LP [album] sales in general were good and my financial situation had improved. I took a chance," says Jonas. He sent Jay a check for the original, agreed-upon price of $2,500 and sat back and waited for the tapes to be sent. The songs, tapes, cassettes, whatever they were, never arrived. Jay took Jonas' money and gave him a big Screamin' middle finger.

A few years later, Jonas noticed Screamin' Jay Hawkins was going to appear in Sweden for the first time, playing at Stockholm's Ritz Rock Club. Jonas decided to go so he could ask Jay for his money or the cassette. Jonas disliked the show. From his perspective, it looked like Jay had tossed together some Halloween items to shake at the audience. The show was as desultory as the props, Jonas recalled, "a low-budget performance."

"His backing group seemed like a typical English pub rocker band, rough-looking and just average musicians. They looked more like bouncers and fighters than musicians," says Jonas. "They were tough guys."

What happened next came as a shock to Jonas. He described the experience to *Blues & Rhythm* magazine.

When Jonas tried to see Jay after the performance, the pub rockers lined up in front of him creating a "Great Wall of Jay." If Jonas tried to go any farther, they promised to beat the shit out of him. After a long discussion, Jonas finally convinced the knuckle-dragging miscreants to let him in to talk to Jay.

"Jay looked very distinguished, dressed in an elegant smoking jacket," Jonas recalled. "His wife [probably Cassie] also greeted me and then left the room. He made lengthy excuses; and what seemed like a 14-minute monologue about our friendship; and what made the shipment of the tapes impossible." Jonas could finally see Jay's lies in the flesh.

It was all a big mistake, Jay continued. He had been "trying to contact Jonas" because he wanted to meet with him. The story didn't stop there. Jay even had the temerity to tell Jonas that the mythical tapes were with him in Stockholm. He asked Jonas if it was convenient for him to meet outside the club in one hour. Jonas said sure, and came back in an hour. He waited, and waited and waited. Jay never showed up.

"Of course I understood the chances were slim that he was to appear at all," says Jonas. "That was the last I heard or saw of him." Jay put a "spell" on Jonas Bernholm.

While Jay had spent so much time shaking Jonas Bernholm down for money, he had been back in the studio with one of his biggest breaks in decades, which is easier to follow in the press sightings.

A gossip note in *Cash Box* on December 22, 1979 reads: "NAMES IN THE NEWS. Keith Richards stopped by at Blue Rock Studios in Soho to lay down a guitar track for Screamin' Jay Hawkins' new version of his classic 'I Put a Spell on You.' Allan Schwartzberg is producing, and Hawkins is label shopping."

An article in the *New York Daily News* of December 23, 1979 reports: "KEITH PAYS DUES: New York session drummer Allan Schwartzberg was producing a new Screamin' Jay Hawkins record at Blue Rock Studios recently when someone suggested the tune they'd just cut would be greatly enhanced by some hot guitar—namely Rolling Stones Keith Richards' guitar. Schwartzberg didn't know Keith personally but Screamin' Jay did and he invited the Glimmer Twin down to Blue Rock. Keith came, and played, and indeed the record did sound hot. When Schwartzberg apologized to Keith for not being able to repay him, the Stone told him to forget it. 'Consider it payment for my education,'" said Keith.

Billboard caught up with the news on January 5, 1980, writing, "Screaming (Screamin'?) Jay Hawkins got a little help on the overdubs from Keith Richards when he was recording his '50s hit 'I Put a Spell on You' at Blue Rock studio in New York."

Allan Schwartzberg was a well-known musician, session player and producer. He played with the rock group Mountain and with Peter Gabriel's band, among others. In the studio he was the drummer on such hits as Gloria Gaynor's "Never Can Say Goodbye," Harry Chapin's "Cat's in the Cradle," Tony Orlando and Dawn's "Tie a Yellow Ribbon" and the *Star Wars* theme. He may not have personally known Keith Richards but in the 1970s and 1980s he knew, played with or produced almost everyone else. He did his job well, but by 1980 he disappeared from the Screamin' Jay project.

In May 1980, Jay wrote Peter Shertser another letter on Glitter Management stationery. It contained this paragraph:

> *Yes, I did record with Keith Richards. I am now with Mark Fenwick [a London-based talent manager]. He has had Polydor Records in England send me exclusive contracts to record only for them. My first record with Polydor will be "I Put a Spell on You" b/w Armpit #6 the very one I did with Keith Richards. They have already promised me a 3 million seller. The record will be out the first of July. Lots of exposure, 100% distributing and 100% airplay. Don't forget Mark Fenwick started with The Beatles. And, he has a very good man in the music industry.*

The Polydor/EG record was released on October 24, 1980 in the United Kingdom and elsewhere in Europe. Allan Schwartzberg was listed as producer. Then it disappeared without a trace. Keith Richards didn't forget about Screamin' Jay. The next year when the Rolling Stones needed an opening act for their three-night stint at Madison Square Garden in New York, Richards brought in Screamin' Jay Hawkins.

CHAPTER

in 1980,

Cliff White, an old friend of Jay's from the days of his tours to the UK in the early 1960s, came to visit Screamin' Jay in New York City. Jay was living in Manhattan over on 9th Street and 57th Street "or thereabouts," Cliff said. The apartment was crammed with books on the occult and all manner of exotic bits and bobs, draperies, crawling hands, mojo hands, a shrunken head and more mystical set pieces from Jay's stage act. Cliff called this new apartment "Jay's bachelor pad."

Ginny, who was born in the Philippines, "married" Jay in 1964. (The reader will recall that Jay was still married to his first wife, Anna Mae, when he and Ginny supposedly tied the knot.) They had been residing in Hawaii at the time and wherever Jay went after that, Ginny followed.

James Marshall first interviewed Jay for the alternative publication *East Village Eye* in 1979. The two met at a nightclub called the Lone Star Café, where a lot of old-time rock 'n' rollers would play including The Midnighters, Jerry Lee Lewis and even James Brown. Keith Richards used to hang out there when he lived in New York. James became friendly with Jay and his wife there.

"I never saw him when she wasn't right there," he says. "She never let him out of his sight. My friend Nick Tosches interviewed him and asked about 'Game of Love,' which Nick thought was the 1965 Wayne Fontana and The Mindbenders hit. It wasn't. It was about a love triangle and Ginny was really angry about the subject of the song. When I met Jay three or four years later, he was still mad at Nick for writing about the song. Ginny liked to smoke pot. Jay didn't except every once in a while. I would always bring some pot for Ginny, and the couple of times Jay smoked, he would just drift off and become quiet."

Ginny was the love of his life, says John C. Lange, an animator, and longtime friend of Jay from his days in Los Angeles. "They didn't have any kids together."

So why did she leave him after being right by his side for so long? There were some reports of physical abuse. Seth Greenky, Jay's manager in the 1970s, says "he was with Ginny for almost 20 years. She just got fed up."

Jay married four more times after he and Ginny split up, but he never got his hands busy with divorce paperwork if it wasn't forced on him. Divorces were seemingly "for other people." His divorce from his first wife Anna Mae was all done by her. When his fifth wife, Colette, filed for divorce, she said, "It took a lot of time and I had to do it from here [in France]." Jay never regarded an existing marriage as something that would limit him from affairs, engagements or subsequent marriage. He just proceeded as if the existing marriage didn't exist.

He did the same thing to his longtime paramour Audrey Sherbourne, who became "Lee Angel" when she stepped on stage. She said, "I stayed in his house in Los Angeles when he went to Japan and Australia, which was in the 1990s just before he went to France. He was engaged to marry me. When he came back from France he was married to Colette. I said, 'OK Jay, so long.' He bought four or five trunks, packed everything in the house and shipped it all to France."

These weren't even his first engagements.

A photo in *Ebony* magazine of May 1957 reveals Jay chatting up a beautiful woman. The headline read, "Spellmaker Screamin' Jay" and the photo caption noted, "Resting after show." The cutline underneath the picture said, "Jay chats with fiancée Barbara Blassingame of Philadelphia. Couple plan a June wedding. 'I don't like him to be gone all the time, but he likes it and I'll let him stay for a while.' Hawkins adds, 'I'm not henpecked.'"

No one ever heard from Barbara Blassingame again. Of course, he was still married to Anna Mae.

Jay continued to marry, or propose marriage to, young women because he didn't like to be alone. According to Colette, his fifth wife, "Jay was an insomniac, he didn't sleep much. He was afraid of the dark and would sleep with the television on with no sound. The lights stayed on. I started to be an insomniac like him but my body said no."

In an interesting interview in the *UK Observer* from April 18, 1999, the reporter writes, "We had talked for more than two hours when, after consulting his watches, Screamin' Jay somehow deduces that it was time to leave. He had a lot going on, he explained, what with all the wedding preparations. The plucky girl, Colette (Lebars), a former printer, became the fourth [actually, fifth] Mrs. Hawkins five days after our meeting."

In that *UK Observer* interview, Jay adds, "We're going to sail around in one of those boats with a glass top they got near the

Louvre. I told Colette, we can have a marriage that really works, so long as we respect each other. That means no physical violence."

In modern times, such a statement would sink a career. Back then, Jay was allowed to pontificate on marriage with reckless abandon. The reason he spoke so freely about physical violence in a marriage was likely because it was a way of life for him, as if cooking eggs in the morning. Reports of abuse to wives started with Ginny and continued with his third wife, Cassie.

When Cassie married Jay, she told him, "You just made the biggest mistake of your life." As it turned out, she was the one who made the biggest mistake.

When Jonas Bernholm met Jay in Stockholm to confront him about the $2,500 that was owed, Jonas brought along a buddy who stayed outside the dressing room. Jonas said, "A friend of mine, who was there, remarked afterward that Jay's wife had a bruise on her face—not a black eye, but something similar. I didn't see it; but he was sitting at another table at another angle."

Robert "Smokey" Miles, who became acquainted with Jay in the early 1980s and invited him to record one of his songs, met Jay at a friend's apartment in New York. As always, Jay's wife had to be with him at all times. Smokey recalls, "Cassie, his poor girlfriend [wife] was suffering. You could tell. Jay would yell, 'Cassie!' and she would jump; the question was always how high she would jump after hearing Jay's voice. I think she had a black eye every time we saw her. She was scared of him. During the long day, she would sit quiet as a mouse. When the day got long and night was about to fall, she said, 'Jay, let's go,' and he would go 'Cassie!' and she would jump back. She was terrified of him."

Not much is known about Cassie. John Lange met her and said she was a very pretty African American woman. Interviewed in a documentary, Jay explained, "My second marriage was to a Filipino from the Philippines. That didn't work. The third marriage was a black girl from Guadalupe. The next time I married, it was a Japanese girl from Tokyo. The next time I married, it was a French girl."

Smokey's interaction with Jay and Cassie was probably around 1983. She was with Jay as early as 1980 or 1981. During that same time, Rudi Protrudi of The Fuzztones remembers seeing a performance of Screamin' Jay Hawkins at the Mudd Club, a Manhattan nightspot popular with the punk and artsy crowd (artist Jean-Michel Basquiat was there that night). "He had a wife who would dress in a leopard leotard outfit," says Protrudi. "She would stand at the edge of the stage, and then at one point, would sneak behind the piano and turn on the flash explosions." Cassie passed the test, for now.

As Gerri Hirshey explains in her book *Nowhere to Run: The Story of Soul Music*, she first encountered Cassie from a distance. Gerri was in the audience watching Jay open for the Rolling Stones.

She writes:

> *Screamin' Jay vamps and shakes through the number, waving the skull at bewildered teenies in the front row. About to wrap it up, he signals to the woman who has been sitting beside the drums. She puts down her soda and ambles toward center stage, where she sets down a small black box in front of the singer. He has ground the song down to spasmodic growls and yelps … yo' miiiiiiine, mine, mi-i-i-i-ine … Unrolling the attached wire, the woman walks back to the drums, and at the agreed-upon cue, she throws a switch. The black box releases a flash and a wheezy puff of smoke … Aaaeeeeeeyowwwwww … The last of the scream whangs off the Garden scoreboard as the artist and his rubber totems exit through the smoke, stage right*

... Afterward ... as Mick Jagger bounds onstage ... Screamin' Jay tucks his skull under his arm, collects his snake and his woman, and heads uptown to his West Side apartment.

Cassie had taken over Ginny's role as Jay's roadie, nurse and servant.

Gerri added, "Cassie, the woman who set off his smoke box onstage, places a steaming mug of tea on the folding snack table beside him, along with two of the government-issue pill vials he gets from the Veterans Hospital down on Twenty-fourth Street."

In 1987, Rudi Protrudi and Jay were both living in the Los Angeles area. Rudi contacts Jay to let him know he had a video of some of their old gigs in New York. Jay invites Rudi to his house, which "was in a white suburb," says Rudi. "Possibly, it was Glendale. You would think Screamin' Jay Hawkins lived somewhere differently. He lived in a white-bread suburb and the inside of his house was normal. The only thing strange was in the garage; he had a white hearse with a white coffin that he sometimes used for gigs." Had Jay suddenly turned "square," with financial responsibility at the top of his mind? His actions at the time said otherwise.

Jay was living alone, and as he explained to Rudi, he had just broken up with his wife who lived nearby.

"After a night of cooking fried chicken for me and watching nothing but Screamin' Jay Hawkins videos that he put on, I told him I had to go," Rudi says. "He said, 'hold on a minute, would you give me a ride in my car just around the block?' I did. Eventually, he said, 'Stop here,' and we stopped in front of someone else's house. He had a remote and he just started pressing it again and again and again. I could see the garage door at that house going up and down and up and down. I asked, 'What are you doing?' Jay answered, 'My wife lives there and I just want to annoy her.' That was the last time I saw Screamin' Jay Hawkins."

Cassie and Jay separated. She left Los Angeles and left Jay for good. A few years later he learned that she had been killed in a shooting. According to John C. Lange, Jay was very upset about it.

Afterward, Jay married for the fourth time to a Japanese woman. This marriage was even more of a mystery, as few people even remember it, and those who do can't recall her name. It had the makings of a surreal Hollywood marriage one might see on the cover of a celebrity gossip magazine while waiting in line to purchase groceries. We can glean some information from an article in the *Albuquerque Journal* on September 22, 1990, where Associated Press writer Christopher Burns writes, "Hawkins has been riding high lately. After appearing in last year's Jim Jarmusch film *Mystery Train,* he came out with a new greatest hits album this year. In June, he and his band began another tour and he married a young woman from Japan, where he is a celebrity in Sony commercials."

The reason it is so difficult for anyone to conjure a memory of the Japanese bride is because people who knew Jay so well, like Audrey Sherbourne, say that the marriage was short-lived. As Smokey Miles said, "Jay tried to keep his Japanese bride sequestered, subservient and there when he needed her." The Japanese bride was not going to be the stereotypical Asian kept girl that he so desired. She freaked out, and her parents came to the United States to rescue her. Jay's role as authoritarian stage manager and head of household was quashed.

Other than changing the scenery of his home front with a new marriage or two, the 1980s were turbulent years for Jay; there were many low points followed by rocket-like highs in his music career. His hard work to stay relevant paid the bills, and finally brought him a younger audience and newfound fame outside of the rock 'n' roll sophisticates crowd.

In 1981, MTV debuted, which changed the equation for the current rock acts. On the music front, disco was dying down while post-punk and new wave were amping up. It was the latter genre, with its inherent rebelliousness, and even a big dose of outlandishness, that created space for an older performer such as Screamin' Jay Hawkins. While performing at the Mudd Club, where Rudi Protrudi first saw him, doesn't seem like much now, the nightspot was an urbane hipster hangout in the early 1980s, hosting some of the biggest names in the arts. Art, music and literary icons like Andy Warhol, Allen Ginsberg, Keith Richards and William Burroughs would frequent the small club in the Tribeca area of New York. It was also big with the emerging punk/new wave crowd; performers such as Lou Reed, Debbie Harry, David Byrne, Madonna and the B-52s were frequent guests if not performing themselves. The club was somewhat anti-establishment, so it was a perfect venue for someone as wild and unconventional as Screamin' Jay Hawkins.

Jay was also getting gigs at some of the older Manhattan clubs. Robert "Smokey" Miles first saw him at Gerde's Folk City in Greenwich Village around 1983. "He used to perform there with his band. He had an amazing show," says Smokey, who was a struggling musician at the time. Soon after seeing Jay's show, Smokey traveled to Haiti, where he experienced a whole new world of voodoo and zombies. He was so impressed with the Haitian subculture, he wrote a song called "Zombie" specifically for Jay. Smokey gets back to New York, calls Jay, plays the song and Jay says, "Bob, I get the same feeling from 'Zombie' as I get from 'I Put a Spell on You.' I got to record that song."

Smokey was going through a divorce and renting a room from another struggling but up-and-coming musician named Hilly Michaels, an interesting young man of the times. Hilly got his start playing in a band called Joy, which featured another hungry-for-the-limelight musician, Michael Bolton. Then he moved on to the band Sparks before releasing two solo albums in 1980 and 1981, *Calling All Girls* and *Lumia*. Hilly was doing well enough at the time to be living in a duplex in Greenwich Village. Jay, on the other hand, was living in a broken-down hotel in New Jersey with his wife Cassie.

"Hilly had a studio in mind for the recording of the song so I thought I would bring him on as co-producer," says Smokey. "Jay would come into the city for discussions. There were a couple of problems. Jay wanted to do the song backed by a real band; Hilly had a different idea, something more modern, more electronic. Plus Jay wanted $500 to sing 'Zombie.' That was his fee. We didn't have it."

Then things got sketchy: Jay literally had no money. "He was broke all the time," says Smokey. "He would hold us hostage for hours to get $5 to pay the tolls to get back to New Jersey. He would say, 'Boys, I gots to get back to Jersey. I need $5 to get through the tunnel.' We were looking at each other thinking what the heck; we had maybe $10 in cash between us. Eventually, we had to pay him the $5 to get our lives back."

Smokey would eventually record the song himself.

The failed attempt to record Jay didn't mean that Jay was through with Smokey and Hilly. He was as charming as ever, and the two up-and-comers liked the association with a legend like Jay.

One time Hilly and Smokey were heading over to their friend Danny's house. Danny was a gourmet chef by day and aspiring musician by night, the perfect person to host a gathering of music minds. Hilly and Smokey invited Jay along. Danny crafted a delicious fish meal to set the tone for the night. After the plates left and the libations took their place, Jay sat down at the piano and played "Constipation Blues"—the perfect musical aperitif to follow a great meal. "I loved it," says Smokey, but Danny's wife was not happy to hear such a song after the dinner. It was as if "Constipation Blues" was a toy gun that Jay could pull out of his pant leg and fire at a gracious audience whenever he pleased.

Danny owned this big Cadillac, which he kept in Greenwich Village. One day, Jay asks Danny if he could just borrow the car and bring it back at night. About a month later, Smokey gets a call from a distraught Danny, "I never heard back from Jay and I never got my car back." Smokey tracked down the car. Jay's charm was nearly serial; Danny, like many others before him, let Jay slide. Danny and his band even backed Jay on some local gigs.

Car problems led to one of Smokey's most memorable days of dealing with Jay's one-man circus. "Jay had this big brown Buick," he says. "We would drive around Manhattan and the car would die at every stoplight. He would say, 'It's something with the radiator. I gots to put pepper in the radiator.' He would pop the hood at every stoplight in Manhattan. He had a giant can of pepper and he would pour a bunch into the radiator, slam the hood, jump in the car and it would start right up again and we would be good until we made the next light. It was a harrowing ride, but I could see the pepper did work." Jay had a magician's set of tools at this side, ready to fix any earth-shattering problems the music gods would throw his way. He had seen it all, and had only adapted by then.

The days of the Mudd Club and Lone Star Café had slipped away from Jay. While he was still working, the quality of the clubs degenerated. By the mid-1980s, his career was hanging by a thread, and time was slipping past him quicker than a three-minute music video on MTV.

About a year after seeing Jay at the Lone Star Café, around 1981 or 1982, James Marshall runs into him again. James was living in the East Village section of Manhattan, which was a dodgy area of the city. One day, he was strolling by "a fucked-up little bar and tranny hangout on Bowery between St. Marks and Ninth streets. There was always some tranny sitting on a barstool in the doorway trying to lure you in with a five-dollar blowjob." James looks again and sees that the bar was displaced and a straight-looking rib joint had opened in its place. This was still the Bowery, home to transients, low-end prostitutes and punk rock kids. James does a double take when he sees a sign in the window that reads, "Every Wednesday night Screamin' Jay Hawkins." "I said to myself, 'that's the damnedest thing' and I started going every Wednesday night," he says. "At first he was just playing by himself, just him and the piano. Then he got a drummer and a bass player. Eventually a guitar player joined him."

Jay was over 50 years of age, but James remembers he could have been 30 years old or he could have been 60 years old; he looked great. "His skin was beautiful. He didn't have wrinkles, gray hair and never lost any teeth," James observed. "He was really a strongly built guy."

After that meeting at the rib joint, James would hang out with Jay on Wednesday nights and imbibe with him at the bar. "He would drink whole glasses full of Black & White Scotch," James says. "Although Jay would drink five of those in a row I never saw him remotely look like he was drunk. Little by little, the crowd started building for him after he had been there four or five weeks."

A few years later, around 1984, Rudi Protrudi met Jay for the first time at that same spot.

"I was walking around St. Marks Place on the Lower East Side, which is where I lived," Rudi recalls. "I came across a flyer attached to a telephone pole that said Screamin' Jay Hawkins was playing at this little dump called Jack The Ribber, which was formerly Slugger Annie's, which was a bar owned by the mother of Jackie Curtis, an Andy Warhol protégé and drag queen. Prior to that, the place was a transvestite bar called Little Peters. I found it really hard to believe Screamin' Jay Hawkins would be playing this place, so I went in."

Rudi looked around and saw 30 to 40 yuppies drinking beer and eating ribs. "Screamin' Jay was sitting alone at the piano.

There was no band. Jay was dressed in a suit, playing the oldies but still doing his shtick." The owner, "an old guy," kept coming up to him mid-song and saying why don't you play this or play that. Sometimes Jay would announce a beer special, "stuff you couldn't imagine Screamin' Jay would put up with." Rudi realized Jay was really down on his luck playing a joint like this.

"He was playing three nights in a row," says Rudi. "I hung out with him all night long and whenever he would take a break I would sit and talk to him. At first, when I introduced myself, the very first thing he said to me was, 'I don't like white people.' So, I said, 'I don't like any people.' He thought that was funny and it broke the ice and got us talking. We developed quite a rapport."

About the third night of rapping with Jay, Rudi tells him that he is in a group called The Fuzztones, a garage band Rudi formed in 1980 that was getting some buzz in the indie music scene. More importantly for Jay's ears, the band was on a label called Midnight Records, an independent record producer in the East Village. Rudi told Jay that it was just an indie label, but he could get Jay a record deal, which could lead to him to playing decent venues again.

Rudi hooks Jay up with J.D. Martignon, who ran Midnight Records. Immediately, Jay starts making outrageous demands that J.D. couldn't possibly fulfill on an indie label. Jay and J.D. went round and round but never could settle on anything.

J.D. was rather a cunning guy and he arranged for Screamin' Jay Hawkins to guest with The Fuzztones at a Christmas gig at Irving Plaza, a concert venue in lower Manhattan. The Fuzztones were going to be the backup band. The Fuzztones took the gig seriously and did two rehearsals, learning "Alligator Wine" and "I Put a Spell on You." Jay did not attend either rehearsal. Rudi rented an electric piano for Jay and had it conveyed to the show stage. Jay doesn't show up for the sound check. Getting worried, J.D. has some of his people call the telephone number Jay left. It turned out that Jay had been living in a trailer court in Newark and had just skipped out on his rent the night before—in the middle of the night! The landlord was extremely angry and wanted J.D. to pay his rent. At that point Rudi figures Jay was never going to make the gig, so The Fuzztones play on. After the first set, Rudi looks to the side of the stage and sees Screamin' Jay in full regalia. Rudi announces him and Jay comes to the front of the stage. The band buzzes through "Alligator Wine" and "I Put a Spell on You," and afterward, figuring the show is over, Rudi gets ready to depart the stage with the rest of the band. Jay has other ideas. He grabs the mic and tells the audience that he is not done yet. The audience is revved up and cheering with thunderous applause.

"The audience is going crazy," says Rudi. "We had no idea what he had planned, so we just ad-libbed it. We did two more songs, 'Constipation Blues' and 'It's That Time Again,' a Christmas song. We just followed him, improvising, and it came off really well; we sounded as if we had rehearsed all the music with Screamin' Jay, but we hadn't."

Jay was so impressed with the band that when he had a gig in Harlem a few nights later, he asked The Fuzztones' rhythm section to back him up for a few nights. They did.

Not everyone was impressed. "There was a garage band revival going on at the time in New York and the clubs started filling up with people who liked that rough music," says James. "This band called The Fuzztones started backing Screamin' Jay. The lead singer of The Fuzztones was one of the worst douches in the history of New York and his band was really trying hard to be The Cramps [a garage punk band led by singer Lux Interior]. It was a bad fit. The Fuzztones couldn't play well enough to play with Jay. This guy J.D. at Midnight Records decided they should all make a record together. Jay put up with it for a while."

The Fuzztones/Hawkins story doesn't end there. On the first night of their gig at Irving Plaza, Rudi brings along a blank cassette tape and gives it to the soundman, asking him to record the concert through the soundboard.

"It turned out to be a very good recording and when Screamin' Jay and J.D. couldn't come to terms about a record deal, I gave J.D. the cassette and with Screamin' Jay's approval, we released it as a four-song live EP," says Rudi. "It did very well, got really good reviews."

The EP's cover featured Screamin' Jay eclipsed by his long-time associate, Henry, atop the cane. A gold-and-black checkered cape floats softly over his shoulders, and covers the face of a guitarist in the lower right corner of the background—possibly one of The Fuzztones. The whole photo including the type is awash in blood crimson.

According to Rudi, J.D. was penurious when it came to royalties or advances. "I think Screamin' Jay and me were the only ones who ever got a penny out of him. Screamin' Jay went into J.D.'s store and chased him around the desk until J.D. gave in and handed over the money Jay felt was owed him. I tricked J.D. into giving me my due."

James Marshall may not have appreciated the mash-up of Screamin' Jay Hawkins and The Fuzztones, but his old publication did. A review by Henry Beck of the *East Village Eye* for the December/January 1986 issue read:

> Screamin' Jay Hawkins, the man who can scream, bellow, and holler longest and loudest, with nary a polyp or wheeze to show for it, has recruited G-meisters The Fuzztones to assist him. Alligator Wine, It's That Time Again (a Christmas song), the unsurpassed I Put a Spell on You, and the slightly tired Constipation Blues add up to about 21 heart-stopping minutes on this beautifully illustrated low-cost disc. Buy this or you'll have no one but yourself to blame if Screamin' Jay "Blows the moonlight clean through you[r] bald head."

Other reviews were equally positive.

Jenny White at an alternative publication called *Tasty World* magazine, which featured bands and musicians from the Athens and Atlanta, Georgia, clubs in the 1980s, wrote:

> If you're a Screamin' Jay Hawkins fan, you'll like this EP, and you'll probably like it even if you're not. Screamin' Jay is backed by The Fuzztones and it works out just fine. His gruff, grating vocals stand up to the pounding keyboards of Deb O'Nair on Alligator Wine, It's That Time Again and the classic I Put a Spell on You. The final song on the live EP is called Constipation Blues. It is in this song that Screamin' Jay is at his rudest, crudest, and best as he grunts, groans and snorts his way through, while a harmonica wails in the background.

Jay's time in New York was almost over, so he had the chance to leave the city on a high note after his performance with The Fuzztones. The problem was that Jay barely left his apartment on a high note. There is one more story that is forever etched into the minds of everyone who knew him in New York in the 1980s. This story involves perhaps the wildest of early rock 'n' roll singers, Esquerita, whose path continued to cross with that of Jay's since the early 1950s. According to Little Richard, Eskew Reeder, the man who changed his name to Esquerita, taught him how to play the piano sometime around 1953. Esquerita recorded on numerous labels in the 1950s, but never crossed into the mainstream.

Jay Halsey, who is an Esquerita historian, says, "I'm led to believe that Jay and Esquerita knew each other in an early period, from around the late 1950s. That's difficult to confirm although I believe Esquerita stated at some point they had known each other and possibly worked the same shows. Esquerita didn't cross-dress, but wore as close to what you would say is feminine T-shirts or big baggy shirts. He didn't gig as a cross-dresser in the 1950s and 1960s. However, that changed in the late 1970s and early 1980s when he was working the gay bars in New York City, where he was living at the time; he was going under the name FabuLash Drag Act. He did spend time in prison, probably for drugs."

Billy Miller, who founded Norton Records in New York, issued some Esquerita albums, Jay Halsey continues, "and he knew Screamin' Jay and Esquerita had a love/hate relationship. They admired each other for what they were able to do musically, but when it came down to working together or being in the same room for a long enough period, hackles were raised. At some point they were having a feud."

In the mid-1980s, Esquerita had a regular Monday night gig at Tramps, a funky blues bar in lower Manhattan. It's here where Jay Halsey and Esquerita became friends.

"One night Esquerita stopped by my apartment when I was living on Avenue B," says Jay Halsey. "Esquerita started copping on my block because the coke was cheaper than in Midtown. So he comes by and I said, 'I'm going to see Screamin' Jay Hawkins at a club on Third Avenue.' Esquerita goes, 'Oh, let me come with you. He's an old friend of mine and I would like to catch up with him for old times' sake.' As soon we get through the door of the club I realized it was a big mistake. Screamin' Jay looks at me as if to say, 'Why did you bring this asshole?' He pulls me aside, 'You know that guy?' I say, 'Yeah, that's Esquerita, man, he taught Little Richard how to play rock 'n' roll. I know who he is …' Jay answers, 'That man will steal the fillings out of your teeth.' Sure enough, by the end of the night they were having an argument about money. Apparently, Esquerita still owed Jay hard cash from the 1950s and they ended up in the middle of Third Avenue. Jay had a knife, Esquerita held a broken bottle, and they were slashing at each other. Blood was spilled. Screamin' Jay had a funny, expressive face and he gets this weird look in his eyes. Suddenly, he just up and clocks

Esquerita with a left hook to the side of his head; knocked him out cold. End of fight."

Rudi Protrudi was also a big Esquerita fan and would go down to Tramps to see him gig. This was after the big fight. "I told Screamin' Jay that I had just seen Esquerita's show and Jay tells me they used to hang out together and at one time even shared a jail cell," says Rudi. "According to Jay, he had to beat the shit out of Esquerita because he was fucking queer."

That was Jay's opinion after beating up Esquerita on Third Avenue. It wasn't always that way. "Esquerita and Jay used to hang out at clubs together," Rudi continues. "They would jam together with Esquerita on the piano and Jay on sax. They used to dress to see who could be the most outrageous and from what I understand these jam sessions used to be at real underground clubs in upper Manhattan. They also had lots of fights."

The Fuzztones broke up in 1986 and Rudi moved to Los Angeles where he re-formed his band. The next year, The Fuzztones got a gig opening for Screamin' Jay Hawkins at the Palomino Club in North Hollywood, California. The nightspot opened in 1949 and throughout most of its history was country music's most important West Coast club; everyone from Johnny Cash to Patsy Cline to Merle Haggard and Willie Nelson played there. In the 1980s, the club began to feature more rock acts.

"As usual, Jay wasn't there when we arrived at the club," says Rudi. "And then he arrives, and in typical Jay fashion he pulls up a chair right in front of the stage and sat down in front to intimidate us, which didn't work at all because the band was cocky."

Jay was so impressed with the re-formed Fuzztones that he offered to find them gigs through a new booking agency that he was going to launch. Rudi arranged a meeting and then forgot about it. "We didn't follow through because The Fuzztones were really big in Los Angeles and we got so busy we forgot about the meeting," says Rudi.

Jay had moved to Los Angeles in the mid-1980s, part of a migration of other New York–based musicians such as Rudi Protrudi and Robert "Smokey" Miles. The latter proceeded to California having taken a stage job playing Bob Dylan in a rock bio that was put together in San Francisco.

"Jay apparently had gotten a new lease on life, a new career, and he would sell out at the Palomino Club on New Year's Eve," says Smokey. "I was in the recording studio when they were doing some overdubbing on the song 'Is You Is or Is You Ain't My Baby,' the Louis Jordan classic from 1943. I went to see him at the Palomino Club. After his show, I came forward to say hello. He snubbed me, just ignored me. That was the last time I saw him."

According to Audrey Sherbourne, he didn't marry his longtime girlfriend Cassie until he moved to California. "That marriage lasted about a year or two," she says. "After that he married a Japanese woman because he wanted to go to Japan, which he did, even after that marriage ended quickly. He toured Japan and Australia."

There were problems on that tour.

An Australian reviewer recalling Jay's visit to Australia wrote: "The vintage R&B screamer expressed outrage that on a 1985 tour, he was called on to support [Nick] Cave: [Jay] said, 'Just a minute, back up, my records were sold here before Nick Cave was born. Before his daddy knew how to get an erection!'"

More disconcerting was the scam. Audrey reports, "Jay would get to the concert venue and he wouldn't play, claiming that he was never paid, although money had already been sent to him. In effect, he would want to get paid twice." Being very kind, Audrey says, "he would forget he was paid already," although by the time Jay got to California he had stopped drinking and his memory was very much intact. Actually, it was a hustle he continued to pull even in later years.

206

Audrey always had an abiding affection for Jay. They became lovers again as soon as the Japanese wife was back in Tokyo. She eventually moved in with him.

The move to the West Coast gave Jay a whole new lease on life. He had been played out in New York, but in Southern California he was something new. Younger music aficionados who might have heard of him and his wild stage antics or listened to "I Put a Spell on You" were coming out to see him—most for the very first time. Jay had a new audience and much bigger exposure. In the 1980s, he was up and down the West Coast. Michael Jack Kirby caught him at the Pine Street Theater in Portland, Oregon, where he emerged from his "fancy but well-worn coffin" decked out in his voodoo-jungle garb, doing two shows, opening and closing both with "I Put a Spell on You."

In the 1980s, one of the hottest nightspots in Los Angeles was the legendary Club Lingerie, which hosted booming new bands such as the Red Hot Chili Peppers, Jane's Addiction and Nirvana. Not all bands that played Club Lingerie made the big time, although anyone who played there found it memorable. Pleasant Gehman of the Screamin' Sirens recalls a gig there that featured Screamin' Jay Hawkins, Tex and The Horseheads, and her band. "It wasn't unusual for true rock and blues legends to play at or just hang out at local clubs that were featuring punk and alternative bands. Screamin' Jay Hawkins was getting stoned in the kitchen at Raji's, while Iggy Pop, Sky Saxon from The Seeds and the Legendary Stardust Cowboys were around all the time."

When Jay lived in Los Angeles, one of his close friends was animator John C. Lange. "He lived here for a number of years and played the clubs regularly. You put him on the stage for an hour or two and you loved everything you were hearing," says John. "He played the Palomino Club for six New Year's Eves in a row—those were the best New Year's Eves I ever had."

In November 1985, music writer Richard Guilliatt caught up with Screamin' Jay for a lengthy interview ahead of an Australian tour:

> On a warm Los Angeles afternoon, 56-year-old Jalacy Hawkins is at home in his small apartment. He has nothing on but his bathrobe and the television. Grey tinges in his fuzzy hair, thick-rimmed spectacles and slight paunch give him the appearance of a school teacher taking it easy at the weekend … But after years of controversy, followed by years of obscurity, Screamin' Jay Hawkins is feeling pretty expansive these days. A whole new audience of white punks is discovering him via Jim Jarmusch's offbeat film Stranger Than Paradise, which uses "I Put a Spell on You" repetitively in its soundtrack, and his Australian club tour this month with Nick Cave is testament to the new-found popularity … "I get packed houses everywhere I play, and every time I get a packed house my money goes up."

Besides moving to the West Coast, the other major thing that boosted Jay's career in the 1980s was a sudden resurgence as a motion picture performer. It all began in 1984, when director Jim Jarmusch wove "I Put a Spell on You" throughout the soundtrack of his movie Stranger Than Paradise. The small, independent film became a cult favorite of cinephiles and has since become what Criterion calls a "minimalist masterpiece" that has "forever transformed the landscape of American independent cinema." The plot is bare-bones, about a rootless Hungarian émigré and his pal visiting a 16-year-old cousin. In 1984, the film was shown at the Cannes Film Festival, where it won the Caméra d'Or award for a debut film. It has since been selected for preservation in the United States National Film Registry by the Library of Congress. In 2003, Entertainment Weekly ranked it Number 26 on its list of the Top 50 Cult Films.

According to Jarmusch, the first time he heard "I Put a Spell on You," it was on a really small transistor radio. The song, he recalled, had a waltz tempo, and yet it had a strange, snarling, R&B and blues side. He said, "putting those two together made it interesting for me for the character in the film who comes from Hungary, who has some knowledge of American culture, which is through Screamin' Jay Hawkins."

In the *I Put a Spell on Me* documentary, Jim Jarmusch said about Jay that "he could fuck with other people but he got hurt if you did it back." That Jay was kind of contradictory, but that was because he was such a sensitive man.

Jarmusch had nothing but praise for Jay. He said that Jay was a strong man to go through all the shit he went through: dealing with racism, his troubled childhood, and the theft he experienced at the hands of charlatans in the music industry. He thought Jay was incredibly talented but did not get the dignity he truly deserved. To Jarmusch, Jay was a national treasure. Jarmusch commented: "He was getting some respect in the U.S., but he was always more popular in Europe. Even before I made *Stranger Than Paradise* I was in a band for a while and this one guy Felipe was a bass player in our band. He was French and he knew everything by Screamin' Jay Hawkins. But others in the band, in the punk scene in New York, were not that familiar with Screamin' Jay Hawkins. He was more appreciated there [in France], but that's true of most of the non-mainstream culture in America. The real shit is appreciated elsewhere."

Although Jay's association with Jarmusch was a huge break for him and meant much greater paychecks, Jay couldn't help himself. He told Jim Jarmusch the same old lies about his life and his war years. Jay was so affable and forthcoming, so charming and smart, Jim bought into Jay's fabrications lock, "film stock," and barrel.

When Jay did a movie with Jarmusch a few years later called *Mystery Train*, Jay gave him his best performance off-camera as the wounded war veteran. Jarmusch believed it, as he recalled in the documentary *I Put a Spell on Me*.

> *When he was captured by the Japanese, he was tortured. He had a big problem with Asian people because of this memory. He had to act with these two young Japanese people. He took me aside and said, 'I have a problem, I have too much bad memory. I'm trying to get over it, it's not rational, I don't dislike these two people, I'm afraid of them, they make me nervous.' It was good and he was very open about it. I made sure they understood. I talked to them separately about his life and they were in awe of him, they really loved him and then I made them spend time together and once he spent time with them he changed, he got more relaxed around them even to the point that later he had a Japanese wife. I don't think that would have happened before* Mystery Train.

No matter how much you did for Jay, he never played you straight. That was also part of his personality.

In 1986, Jay appeared in an even smaller movie called *Joey*. The plot runs something like this: Joey Sr. was in a successful band in the 1950s, but now works at a gas station. Meanwhile Joey Jr. starts a rock band, which makes his father jealous, so Joey Sr. reorganizes his old band. At the end of the movie, both groups play the same show and accept each other. A few oldies acts appear in the movie such as the The Ad Libs, The Silhouettes and Screamin' Jay Hawkins.

With recognition from *Stranger Than Paradise*—less so from *Joey*, which came and went in the blink of an eye—came television appearances and a second movie in 1988, *Two Moon Junction*, directed by Zalman King.

While not the most famous of American film directors, Jim Jarmusch is well-esteemed for having a singular vision throughout his long career directing independent films. His oeuvre is consistently respected, but outside of the mainstream, with such other movies as *Coffee and Cigarettes, Ghost Dog: The Way of the Samurai,* and *Down by Law.* The same cannot be said for Zalman King, who is most known, if at all, for his erotically charged films including *Wild Orchid* and *Wild Orchid II: Two Shades of Blue.*

Two Moon Junction starred Sherilyn Fenn, Richard Tyson and Louise Fletcher, and it was basically about a young Southern debutante who rebels against her lifestyle and upcoming marriage by having an uninhibited affair with a handsome drifter. In the movie, Screamin' Jay Hawkins plays a singer at a blues club; he performs a song called "Dig."

With Screamin' Jay's star rising thanks to Jim Jarmusch, Jay's old acquaintances from the music business started to take notice. Midnight Records in New York, which released the EP with The Fuzztones, got hold of Screamin' Jay Hawkins' live recordings when he played at the Jack The Ribber eatery back in September 1984, and had the tapes remastered at Saxon Recording in Rochester, New York. The result was the 1988 release of the live album *At Home With Jay in the Wee Wee Hours.* The poorly drawn cover art featured a character that was supposed to be Screamin' Jay Hawkins dressed in a pink shirt and G-string, but it could have been anyone's cousin Fred. Since the figure is holding a skull on a cane one assumes it is Henry. In the background is a woman sitting on a bench showing a lot of leg. The art was done by the owner of Midnight Records, J.D. Martignon, thus avoiding paying anyone for the rights to an actual photograph. If J.D. still held a grudge with Jay for having to pay him after being chased around his record shop, it showed in the cover art. Twelve cuts appeared on the album, many of which were the usual Jay standards: "Hong Kong," "Constipation Blues," "Feast of the Mau Mau," "Bite It" and "I Put a Spell on You."

In the 1980s, Jay recorded two albums in France. The first, *Real Life*, was a studio album recorded in 1983 at Anagramme Studio, Paris. This was a rare album in that it is one of the few without some version of "I Put a Spell on You." Better are the less recognizable Screamin' Jay songs such as "Serving Time," "Poor Folks," "Mountain Jive" and "Your Kind of Love." The cover art is just a strange, ultra-close-up photo of Jay's head, where he makes the googly-eye face of his comic performances.

On a tour of France in the spring of 1988, Jay played the Hotel Le Méridien Paris Etoile, and that performance was recorded. The result was the album *Screamin' Jay Hawkins: Live and Crazy*. The cover art looks to be a photograph of Jay performing at the Hotel Méridien. He's wearing a wild jacket of African print against an equally busy backdrop. There is one backup musician in the lower right, half cut out of the picture, eerily similar to the cover art for the Screamin' Jay Hawkins and The Fuzztones live album. Jay is surrounded by a sharp maroon rhombus, encased in a hot pink background that can only be described in the most positive sense as "art deco." The font was ripped straight from the title cards of an '80s teen film. The album was released in 1989 and it has an interesting mix of Jay standards and reinterpretations of rock classics such as "Lawdy Miss Clawdy," "Ain't That a Shame," "Itty Bitty Pretty One," "Goodnight Sweetheart" and "Tutti Frutti."

In 1989, Jay turned 60 years old, and he was back in the United Kingdom again, appearing in July at the Town and Country Club on Highgate Road in London. His career hadn't yet peaked that second time around.

CHAPTER
10

in 1980, JiM

Jarmusch directed a small, independent movie called *Permanent Vacation*. Just 75 minutes in length, it was a non-linear film about a man wandering the streets of Manhattan meeting and greeting an assortment of people. Each encounter is a separate incident unrelated to any other encounter. The success of the movie was not in its reception, but in its execution and completion. *Permanent Vacation* boasted a minimalist style that audiences were not used to at the time. It was the beginning of Jim Jarmusch's very long career of producing, screenwriting, directing and even acting in movies. If there was a golden age of Jim Jarmusch movies, critics might say it was at the very start of his journey, when he wrote and directed some of the best independent features of the last 40 years including *Stranger Than Paradise* in 1984, *Down by Law* in 1986, *Mystery Train* in 1989 and *Night on Earth* in 1991.

To be an independent director and producer means operating outside of the Hollywood machine, in day-to-day function, outlook and revenue. Jarmusch's stories are often of a small journey or episodic engagements. Being an old punk musician, Jarmusch likes to weave specific musical themes through his movies. In his early releases, he would utilize musicians who had the same sort of maverick ideals and offbeat view of the world. So one might see The Clash's Joe Strummer or husky-voiced singer-songwriter Tom Waits, Memphis survivor Rufus Thomas, or Screamin' Jay Hawkins.

Jarmusch's affection for Screamin' Jay and his music almost single-handedly resurrected him from the ungrateful dead, that netherworld of old-timey musicians barely eking out a living. This was decades before the proliferation of Indian casinos and small city arts and performance centers that now keep such musicians afloat. In *Stranger Than Paradise,* the song "I Put a Spell on You" was as important to the movie as the actors. The irony was that no one before Jarmusch thought to use the song for a movie or television show, but after *Stranger Than Paradise,* "I Put a Spell on You" was used in more than 50 television shows and movies, from *Hocus Pocus* in 1993 to *Kinky Boots* in 2005 to *Fifty Shades of Grey* in 2015.

Jarmusch had such an abiding affection for Screamin' Jay that he employed him in his movie *Mystery Train* as a hotel clerk, and not in the usual consideration as a performer in a blues band or as a nightclub singer. In Jarmusch's alternative cinematic vision, Screamin' Jay was the perfect actor to play a specific comedic role—and Jay didn't disappoint. He was wonderfully subtle and funny.

Jarmusch hadn't met Jay until after making *Stranger Than Paradise.* While in post-production on the film, Jarmusch realized Jay had no rights to the song "I Put a Spell on You" and he had to pay a licensing fee to other entities. As Jarmusch said, "I knew the money would never get to Screamin' Jay Hawkins." Employing Jay in *Mystery Train* was a way to ensure that Jay would make some money from Jarmusch's cinematic endeavors, a kindly payback to the importance of "I Put a Spell on You" to the success of *Stranger Than Paradise.*

Besides Screamin' Jay, Jarmusch employed other musicians in the movie: Joe Strummer as Johnny (a.k.a. Elvis), Tom Waits as a radio DJ and Rufus Thomas as a man in a train station.

Like many of Jarmusch's films, the concept for *Mystery Train* is episodic with three separate stories linked together to form the plot. The action takes place in downtown Memphis at a seedy accommodation called the Arcade Hotel. All stories happen on the same night. Working from back to front, the last story, "Lost in Space," is the most complicated involving Johnny (Joe Strummer), Charlie (Steve Buscemi) and Will Robinson (Rick Aviles). After a liquor store hold-up, the three crooks hide out in the hotel, where Charlie realizes that Will Robinson shares the same name as the character from the television show *Lost in Space.* They soon realize that they are lost in space after the events of the night. The second story, "A Ghost," concerns two women stranded in Memphis and forced to share a hotel room. One of the women sees the ghost of Elvis Presley. The first story is "Far From Yokohama," about a Japanese teenage couple who are making a pilgrimage to Memphis.

The Arcade Hotel is a flophouse managed by the night clerk, played by Screamin' Jay, and the bellboy, played by Cinqué Lee, younger brother of filmmaker Spike Lee. Jay looks sumptuous wearing a deep red jacket and matching tie against a black shirt. He looks strong and handsome, with his full head of hair sheened and curly. The weirdest scene in the film is with the bellboy and Screamin' Jay observing and discussing a plum, which sits on the front desk. Jay scrutinizes it and says, "I don't think you should eat that thing." The bellboy answers, "You are probably right." Jay continues, "Are you going to eat that thing?" The bellboy responds, "I ain't going to eat that thing." Jay grabs the plum and puts the whole thing in his mouth. Jay never moves from the desk.

In his 1989 review of the movie, Roger Ebert wrote:

> *A thread from the beginning has involved the deadpan interplay between the desk clerk and the bellboy, with a little Philip Morris hat worn at a rakish angle. They're sleepy and bored. The clerk has seen everything. The bellboy seems to be experiencing everything for the first time. Elvis sings Blue Moon on the radio. It's heard during all three stories, which are possibly happening at the same time. The bellboy observes, "At the time of his death, if he were on Jupiter, Elvis would've weighted six hundred and forty-eight pounds." The clerk says, "Damn!" Screamin' Jay Hawkins has the innate authority to make this, and everything else he says, sound like the final word on the subject.*

The movie premiered at the New York Film Festival and was shown in Cannes, where Jim Jarmusch won the Best Artistic Achievement Award. It was the first American independent film financed by a Japanese company. Critical assessments were mixed. A review by David Denby in *The New Yorker* summed up all the critical analysis: "One feels Jarmusch has pushed hipsterism and cool about as far as they can go, and that isn't nearly far enough."

For Jay, the performance earned him a small role in the 1991 mainstream film *A Rage in Harlem* starring a terrific cast of African American actors: Forest Whitaker, Gregory Hines, Robin Givens and Danny Glover. Screamin' Jay Hawkins makes an appearance as himself.

One very small film that most people have passed over, because they don't know about it, but nevertheless should be commented on because it's a beautiful little enterprise, is the animated short *Joshua's Harvest* by Jay's friend John C. Lange. The two met at the time of *American Hot Wax* when John wanted to do an animation of "Constipation Blues." The project got "flushed," but the two remained friends for decades. "Screamin' Jay Hawkins brought a lot of color to my life; he was larger than life," says John. "He was one heck of a talent and a real original." Anyway, for *Joshua's Harvest,* Jay let John Lange use the instrumental track of "Sweet Ginny," one of the most unheralded but better songs in the Screamin' Jay canon. To see the animated character of Joshua bop to the blues is a perfect marriage of animation to song.

The *Los Angeles Times* caught up with Jay in August 1991, noting that he was living in Pasadena and still headlining at the Palomino. The writer observes, "Hawkins, despite being 62, looks so good he could pass for a 40-year-old man." Hawkins told the writer, "Movies are my ace in the hole. If things stop working for me in the record business again, I can always turn to movies."

Fortunately for Jay, the record business once again swung in his direction.

Still riding high on his numerous screen appearances, a slew of Screamin' Jay albums appeared the same year as *A Rage in Harlem.* The best of the lot is *Screamin' Jay Hawkins: Black Music for White People.* The cover is the played-out vision of Jay, dressed in wild African print clothes, bone through the nose, crazy stuff hanging on a chain from the neck and of course, Henry in the foreground. The major difference is the extra luridness: in his left hand he holds a slumped white woman, blonde and dressed in white, as if she had just fainted. It has the look of Fay Wray in

King Kong's palm. Jay still sings the classics, "Is You Is or Is You Ain't My Baby" and "I Hear You Knockin'" and, as always, there is another version of "I Put a Spell on You." This one comes with a bit of discourse between Jay and his engineer. "What is all that echo?" "Your imagination, Jay." "Oh, OK."

He does, however, add a few unusual Jay songs such as "Ig-nant and Shit," "I Want Your Body" and "Swamp Gas." The latter is a lively, bayou-type cut with obligatory tribal chants and Jay screaming "swamp gas." Or, as the lyrics note, "something smells bad, it's called swamp gas."

What's more interesting is that Jay crosses paths with sing-er Tom Waits, cutting two of his songs, "Ice Cream Man" and "Heartattack and Vine." The latter rendition was purloined by Levi's to sell denim jeans. Waits sued in European court over the use of his music. He won and Levi's issued an apology and a statement: "This commercial featured Tom Waits' song 'Heart-attack and Vine' performed by Screamin' Jay Hawkins. We ob-tained the rights in good faith and were unaware of Mr. Waits' objections to such usage of his composition." A 1994 news report on the lawsuit stated Tom Waits was awarded a six-figure sum in damages from his former publishing company, Third Story Music, for licensing the material for commercial use without his consent.

British writer Fred Dellar in 1993 noted the Hawkins–Waits re-lationship including the Waits songs on the album *Black Music for White People*, adding, "Now if the single of 'Heartattack' takes off, then maybe Screaming Jay will, at last, achieve the modicum of fame that has always eluded him on this side of the Atlantic. He may even become as famous as he is in Japan, where his 'Consti-pation Blues' made him the pride of the Tokyo loo trade …" It was a prescient call by Dellar as "Heartattack and Vine" became Jay's only Old World hit, reaching Number 42 on the UK singles chart.

Also to appear in 1991 was the album *I Shake My Stick at You,* which was recorded in Sydney, Australia, during Jay's tour of the continent. The record was issued on the Aim label. Probably feeling very Aussie at the moment of the recording, Screamin' Jay wrote a couple of "Down Under" tunes for this album including "Bushman Tucker" and "Rock Australia Rock." Screamin' Jay penned all the songs on the album; he was still an R&B maestro even into the '90s.

Then there was a live album release of *Screamin' Jay Hawkins and The Chickenhawks—Dr. Macabre* with numerous Jay standards plus covers of rock 'n' roll classics such as "Wooly Bully," "Ain't That a Shame," "Goodnight Sweetheart" and "Shout." The Chickenhawks (sometimes Chicken Hawks) is an elusive backup band for Jay. In 1989, Jay toured the United Kingdom under the group heading Screamin' Jay Hawkins and His Chicken Hawks.

Jay kept at it in the 1990s. A couple singles emerged including "The Art of Screamin' Jay" on the Spivey label in 1990 and "Heartattack and Vine" with "I Put a Spell on You" and "On the Job" released by Columbia in 1993. More importantly were the albums. Bizarre/Straight/Planet Records, which released *Black Music for White People,* was a production company originally formed to release Frank Zappa and Mothers of Invention albums in the late 1960s. The 1993 Screamin' Jay Hawkins album *Stone Crazy* is listed on the label Bizarre/Straight/Planet Records although other sources list this as a Rhino album. The title song "Stone Crazy" first appeared on the 1969 album *What That Is.* The backup band was the Chickenhawks.

The one unusual song on the *Stone Crazy* album is "Sherilyn Fenn," the name of the actress from the *Twin Peaks* television show and movie. The song sports a jazz intro and bluesy beat with the added bonus of Jay throwing in a reference to *Two Moon Junction.* Lyrics include:

The whole time that movie played, I kept thinking how good it would be to get laid.

And even though the movie was about him, it was [for] me Sherilyn Fenn …

Two Moon Junction, a railroad function, [for] me Sherilyn Fenn.

This album was followed by *Somethin' Funny Goin' On* in 1994, again on the Bizarre/Straight/Planet label. The only interesting cut on the album was another Tom Waits song, "Whistling Past the Graveyard."

He did one last studio album, called *At Last,* on the French label Last Call. The songs were mostly penned by Screamin' Jay and they were played straight, except for "Shut Your Mouth When You Sneeze." He also sings Bob Marley's "I Shot the Sheriff." Last Call also recorded Jay's last album, *Live at the Olympia, Paris* in 1999. In the 1990s, there was one other Screamin' Jay Hawkins live recording, *Rated X,* which was produced in the Czech Republic.

Starting with *Stranger Than Paradise,* and then straight on through to *Mystery Train* and into the 1990s, Screamin' Jay entered what was probably the busiest time in his 40-year career. He appeared in commercials, his songs were all over television and movies, he recorded new albums, had a new band backing him, made a couple more movies and toured incessantly all over the world. His fifth wife, Colette, remembers there were some years he was touring more than three hundred days a year. He was in Australia for five months, Japan for two months, in North America and then everywhere in Europe. "He was on tour for a whole year," she recalls.

In the early 1980s, Jay was starving in New York with barely a can of soup in his apartment. By the end of the 1980s, he owned a house in sunny Los Angeles. He went from that infamous junker car, requiring pepper in the radiator at every stoplight, to owning two brand new cars free and clear by the end of the decade. Jay could look at all that was in front of him and know that his music was finally getting the financial recognition it has always deserved. He could curse the music gods no more.

In 1991, *Los Angeles Times* reporter Mike Boehm caught up with Jay at his home. He wrote, "Sitting Tuesday in the kitchen of his San Fernando Valley home, a modest house that looks like all the others in its tract...the master of the house is a tall goateed man with a chiseled face, a still-muscular body...a youthful look for his 61 years. Watch out for his handshake. Among the large silver rings that adorn his fingers is a potential killer on the right pinky. It's shaped like a helmeted skull, with sharp prongs shooting from its head."

Two years later Jay would move to France.

In the remarkable resurgence of Jay's career, starting in the mid-1980s, he began to tour Europe as if it was the 1960s all over again. If anything, the Europeans' deep appreciation for American rhythm and blues pioneers was even more profound than ever before. Indeed, many early American R&B and soul artists found such enlightenment and remuneration in Europe. They either toured exclusively on the continent or relocated to Germany or France. It was no different from the way Europeans continued to idolize American jazz singers and musicians long after Americans shifted their musical appreciation to rock 'n' roll.

For Jay, one of the countries where he remained extremely popular was France. This affection for Screamin' Jay Hawkins goes back to the 1970s when he was befriended by one of France's most popular singers of the day, Serge Gainsbourg. The two men took to each other, drinking and partying their way through French nightspots and public spaces. Appearing on a French television station, the two inebriated singers marched through the scheduled program and then launched into a rendition of "Constipation Blues"— producing one of the most soulful takes on this song Jay has ever done, with Serge, cigarette clenched between his lips, providing a wonderful bluesy backbeat on the piano. As Jay howls "let it go, let it go" in English, Serge raps in French. The two could just as easily be in a small, dark jazz bar in Montmartre instead of on dueling pianos, under the bright lights of a television set.

At the start of the 1980s Colette Lebars was working at a pirate radio station in Paris, where she not only played R&B but also interviewed guest singers. She knew a lot about the American music scene so when she was visiting friends on the outskirts of Paris in 1984 and met Jay there, she knew exactly who he was. By the next year, they became lovers. She was 30 years younger than Jay. "We had become very good friends and he would call me day and night everywhere he went." At the time, back in the United States, Jay was married to Cassie, and he had a black girlfriend in Germany. "He had more than one woman in his life at that time," Colette says. "We didn't talk much about his wife, who was named Cassie—and he wasn't giving too many details. We would see each other when he was coming to France."

He didn't come to France often enough, because after Cassie, Jay married the Japanese girl. But that ended quickly and when it was over, Jay turned his attention back to Colette. Jay married not out of love, but out of need. His life was too difficult for him to manage on his own. He didn't like to be alone, he didn't like to sleep alone and he sure didn't like to travel alone. His personal life and his stage act both required the constant nurturing and attention of another person. If he was lucky, he could find a submissive woman like a Ginny or Colette, who could be in love with him. If not, it was like being married to a Cassie, who stayed out of terror and left in hatred, or the Japanese girl, who just didn't understand that the requirements of the job were much greater than just sleeping with Jay. That was only the side benefit. As Colette says, Jay was a good lover and if that weren't the case she would have said no when he asked her to be his wife.

"He didn't want to have a woman in his life without being married, so he asked me many times to get married," Colette recalls. When Jay told her that the divorce with the Japanese girl was finalized around 1988, Colette said she would move to Los Angeles. "We decided to have a common-law life. I left everything I had in France. I didn't know what would happen." Colette and Jay would eventually marry in France in 1992. The marriage lasted until the end of 1995.

"I began to follow him all over the world," she says. "They were an amazing three years of marriage. It was a love story. In explaining the life we had together, I made a joke about it. I would tell my friends, the only time we are not together is when one of us goes to the toilet. When he was on stage, he always asked that he be able to see me. It was an intense few years. When you are living like this, 24 hours a day, 365 days a year, you know the person very well."

Being in love is often like living in a kind of fog, but when applied to a relationship with someone like Jay, it could be like living in an alternate universe. The most interesting comment Colette says about her time with Jay was, "He never lied to me; Jay was not a liar."

Colette was naïve and didn't want to see the truth. Their relationship began with a lie—the usual one, about his war years. Jay might have quit drinking a decade before, but he still had addictive habits like smoking and taking codeine. In fact, he was doing so much codeine he was often confused. "When I met Jay, because of his war years, he was taking medication that was pushing him to be somebody else," says Colette. "He was talking languages I did not understand. He didn't know where he was anymore," Colette continues. The reason for the codeine, he explained to Colette, was when he was a prisoner during the Korean War he had been wounded. Doctors put a metal plate in his head, which over the years continually caused him pain, therefore he took the codeine. It is obvious now that Jay was never a prisoner of war, didn't fight in the Korean War, and if he had a plate in his head he would have been ushered out of the service with a medical discharge. Jay took the codeine for the pleasure of codeine. Nevertheless, Colette probably saved his sanity—and maybe his life. She took him to French doctors, who, as Colette says, "were able to purify his body from the American medicine. When he was on the French medication, he never went back to doing these kinds of things."

He also told Colette he was straight about the law and maintaining and collecting important documents (he kept a suitcase full of papers) because he had an image to keep and "didn't want to be fucked up by any kind of thing I have done." Those "things that he actually did" included a jail sentence for statutory rape, numerous instances of non-payment for child support, and two marriages at the same time. No matter how far across the world Jay moved, his demons followed him with each footstep as if sewn into his travel bags.

Journalist James Marshall says that when Jay got that role in the Jim Jarmusch movie *Mystery Train,* he received what was a huge paycheck for Jay at that time, but management and publishing took a piece. He also had to pay back debts. After that, nothing was left when the tax bill came. "The last I heard he was in Paris and because of the tax bill he couldn't come home again," James reports.

Colette says she never heard Jay had a tax problem, but just that there was a mortgage situation. "The reasons Jay decided to move to France was, first, that we were a mixed couple in the United States and that meant trouble in the United States," she says. "He was tired of the racism."

The second reason was Jay's house, which had a large mortgage left to pay. When Jay traveled, he arranged for his bills to be paid, says Colette, "but people were taking Jay's money and not doing the right thing about the house. He had a young man helping him who stole money and the two had a big argument." Jay, in a flash decision, decided the two of them would move to France and just "let go" of the house. Just walk away. "He didn't try and sell it," says Colette. He also walked away from two cars he either owned or leased.

Jay's friend John C. Lange witnessed the departure. "It's true, he owned a house and then just walked away from it. I'm not sure if it was financial. This was the first house he ever owned, the mortgage was a little steep and he got behind in his payments. I was at the house the day the limo pulled up and Jay got in." He said goodbye to John and the house.

Although Colette truly loved Jay, their marriage only lasted three years. From Colette's perspective, she just couldn't take the nomadic life anymore. Jay was an insomniac, and Colette realized she was becoming one as well and her body was rebelling. "I didn't want to follow him on tour all over the world more than three hundred days a year because my body was not capable of it," she says. "I had to tell him, 'I can't follow you anymore.' I had to stop."

Jay had his own reason for separation, which Colette was aware of, and that was taxes. "One of the reasons we got married in France was so Jay could become a French resident," Colette explains. "However, French taxes took 75% of his income. After the divorce he asked to be an American citizen again."

The divorce wasn't as smooth as Colette expected. "In the last weeks of the marriage Jay was disagreeable, getting angry all the time," she says. Colette interpreted the anger as Jay thinking she was out to get him; that she would ask for his money in a divorce settlement; that she would do what the other women in his life had done. She told him, "I don't ask for anything. I didn't marry you for your money and I'm not going to ask you for any." With that settled Jay told her, "Colette, you would be the only one to have the right to keep my name." The divorced couple parted from each other as friends, and Colette is known as Colette Hawkins to this day.

When Jay and Colette went their separate ways, he was 66 years old. The fears that plagued him throughout his life still haunted him, and he still needed someone to care for him at all times. It was obvious that another marriage would not be out of the question. "I wasn't surprised to hear he was married again," says Colette.

For a while, he still continued to meet with Colette although they were no longer married. Then, by random chance, he met the woman who would become his sixth wife. With 70 years of age just ahead of him, Jay was no longer the force of nature he once was when marriages were on his terms and women were subservient. He could no longer physically dominate, and he was not well enough to emotionally dominate. His last marriage was just one marriage too far for Screamin' Jay Hawkins.

In 1999, when Demetra Madzouka was co-producing the documentary *I Put a Spell on Me,* she had the chance to communicate with his sixth wife, Monique Hawkins, and then saw her again at Jay's funeral. "Monique was about my age at the time, in her early 30s [in the year 2000, Monique was 31]. I think she really loved him," says Demetra. "When they met, she didn't know who he was. She fell in love with this crazy guy who was driving around Paris in a car that had black snakes and fake skulls. He picked her up when she was hitchhiking. She had a break in her workday and was getting her nails done. It was late, and she was hitchhiking so she was trying to get back to work without being late. She was confident and looked like a very strong person."

That's a similar story to the one Monique tells in the documentary. On film, she's a pretty, young woman with short, straight hair and she speaks English with an accent. She wears a purple suit and sits in a room with no wall adornments. It could be a bedroom or a waiting room at the doctor's office. She tells the camera, "I was hitchhiking, coming from the beauty parlor, doing my fingernails and going to work. I see this car with a black guy, I say 'OK, here's a black guy, it could be safe.' Jay opens his door and says, 'Hello, where are you going? Can I help you?' In his car, he had all things like [rubber] snakes. I look around and say to myself, 'What is all that?'" Then she comes to the conclusion, "he's a witch doctor."

Monique was from Africa and the thought "witch doctor" came immediately into her head. According to Colette, Monique was from the Republic of Cameroon. Colette says the couple was married in Las Vegas and that they never attempted to get marriage credentials in France. "The marriage was not legal in France," says Colette.

While Jay still looked like he was 10 years younger than he actually was, by the time of the documentary, he was frail and his health was failing. "He was old, but he didn't look old. He looked like a man in his 50s," says Demetra. "When in Athens, we went to the Acropolis and he could not walk all the way to the ruins. He said to me, 'I can't do it' and I realized this was an old man. It was midday, the sun was up, and I said to him, 'Let's go have lunch.'"

Having heard about Screamin' Jay's interest in opera, the documentary crew took him for a tour of the Athens Opera House. "While he sat dreaming, Nicholas [Triandafyllidis] and I came up with the idea to have Jay eventually perform at the Opera House. We said, 'Now listen Jay, we know these people and we know the orchestra, why don't we set up something special, just for Greece, do a concert with you singing opera. You can pick and choose a set list and we'll arrange everything.' He asked if he could use my phone and he called his wife Monique saying, 'Hey Monique, this is my new office. Meet Demetra. We are going to do an opera.' Monique was very excited, very enthusiastic."

Jay had his own take on opera. Backed by the Chickenhawks, in one of his last concerts he mimics, in his deep baritone, lyrics from the opera *The Barber of Seville,* "Figaro, Figaro, Figaro, Figaro. Let me finger her ho(le). Let me touch it some mo(re)."

In the documentary, Monique, in a very contemplative mood, says, "Opera was the dream of his life. He always wanted to do opera, but nobody was interested in signing a contract for opera. [She smiles.] So when he went to Greece, he called me and said he was going to do opera. I said that's great. When he came back, he was so happy. I never saw him so happy about a project like that. He was like a little boy."

She seems like a wonderful wife.

She wasn't.

Even Demetra noted, "He was afraid of her." And Amanda Livanou, also a co-producer on the documentary, adds, "I don't know what the deal with Monique was. She seemed a bit dodgy. Jay seemed to be scared of her. When he was here in Athens, he kept saying, 'I got to call Monique. I got to call Monique.' You felt the money was Monique's thing. That he had to make money."

John C. Lange would get calls from Jay in Europe and he often complained that Monique would physically beat on him, that she was physically abusive. After a while, John says, Jay had an apartment on one floor and she had an apartment on another floor. The tables had finally been turned on Jay. At the end of his life, when he was at his weakest point, he came face to face with his abusive behavior in the form of his new wife Monique.

John wasn't the only person getting frantic missives from Jay. Colette was getting slammed with phone calls, letters, even faxes from Jay, saying that marrying Monique was the biggest mistake he ever made in his life. "He was not happy with her," John said. Colette noted, "he had lots of regrets and was trying to get out of the marriage when he died. Her family, they were all from Cameroon and were crazy people living in a bad way in Paris. The last time I saw him, he was playing the Olympia in Paris. He asked me to come by. I met him in the dressing room before the show. He was not eating anything and he had lost a lot of weight. I almost didn't recognize him. He just didn't look good. I didn't see Monique, but while I was there about 10 men from her family burst in. The dressing room fridge had a lot of food in it for Jay and the band. The family came in and took everything, the food, the bottles anything they could get their hands on. In a few seconds everything was gone. I looked at Jay and he didn't say anything. He had a desperate look in his eyes and gestured with his hands as if to say he could do nothing about it. It was very hard for me to see."

During his marriage to Monique, Jay kept a small apartment for many of the things he had accumulated over the years. Colette also kept some of the things from her life with Jay in that apartment. She also had a key to it. "Monique took the key away from Jay because she was completely crazy," says Colette. "She was so bad to him that sometimes he would be walking in the street and she would be jumping on him. It was like she wanted to kill him."

Jay died in 2000.

On Tuesday, February 15, 2000, *The Guardian* reported, "Screamin' Jay Hawkins, who had died of an aneurism, aged 70, may have been the wildest of rock 'n' roll men."

Dick Houff writing for *Blues on Stage,* wrote, "On Sunday morning, at 2:30 A.M. I received a call from Paris, France, from Noel Genet who politely informed me that Jay had died on Saturday during surgery for an intestinal blockage. This came as a shock to me, after having had several conversations in the last few months with Jay. I assumed everything was okay. He never once hinted that there was a medical problem."

Jay died suddenly and unexpectedly.

After Jay's death, Monique's family changed the locks on the door to that other apartment and Colette never again saw the clothes, paintings (of Jay) and papers she had kept there. Monique even tried to keep her away from the funeral, but Colette found out about it because the band members were friends of hers and called to tell her what was happening.

Rudi Protrudi of The Fuzztones said, "I do know that one person in his band insinuated that Monique killed him."

Asked about the allegations of murder, Colette responded, "Jay was sometimes calling me, telling me that every time she cooked for him, he was sick. Did she kill him? That's what Jay thought was happening. The day before he went into the hospital he asked me to meet him. When I arrived at the hospital, the girl there told me he was dead."

Sometime after the funeral, Colette received a call from Monique, who had discovered, while ransacking that other apartment, that Jay had sent Colette faxes and letters asking for her help in getting rid of Monique and her family. She also found a lot of Colette's things. Monique made the call because she wanted to trade. Monique would give back to Colette all of her things if Colette would give Monique all the letters that Jay had written about her. Colette said no.

In 2017, Graham Knight, an old friend of Jay's from England, stumbled upon an earlier auction of Jay's personal items: clothes, capes, jewelry, tapes, records, scrapbooks, photos, just about anything you can think of. The auction information was in French and from the year 2013. Jay's outfits were listed at € 1,000 to €$1,200; cane and white gloves from €80 to €300; album of personal photographs at €300 to €400; various pendants and pins at €500 to €600; various tapes at €E300 to €400; and a group of photographs including one with Serge Gainsbourg from €100 to €150 among many, many other items. Graham wrote to friends and this author: "This is quite amazing. I knew nothing about this sale or I would have bid on the old photographs and all the tapes. I do recognize the tape collection as being Jay's I have seen it over the years and although it contains some newer items it is mostly very old stuff including some out-takes. I would like to know where Henry is. I would especially like to know where Jay's three large scrapbooks are now. I presume all these items were sold back in 2013. They must have been put on sale by Monique ... presumably these items are spread all over. What a shame."

Monique had put the final spell on Jay, years after his death.

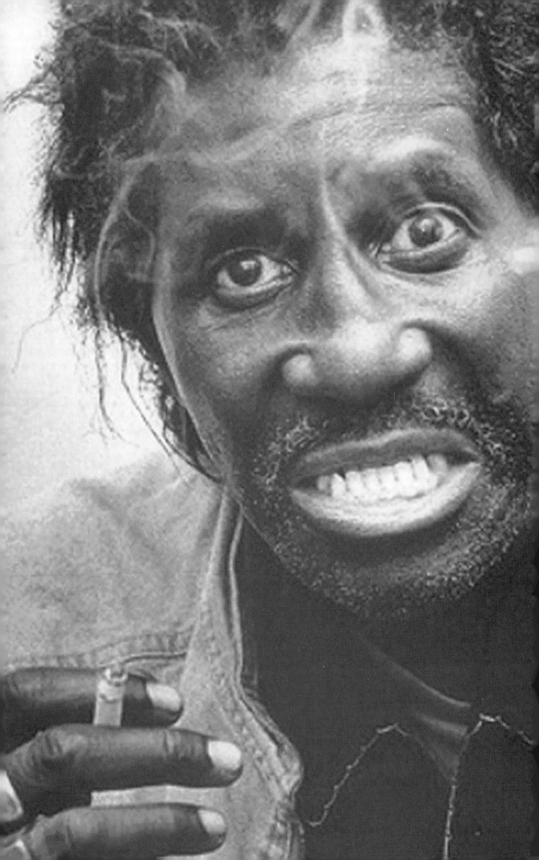

CHAPTER 11

i put a SpeLL On Me

was the last major production of Jay's career, and like everything Jay did, it came about sideways, not directly.

In 1999, Demetra Madzouka, a concert promoter, was in a serious relationship with Nicholas Triandafyllidis, who had directed a number of films and documentaries in Greece. One day Demetra gets a fax from the agent of Screamin' Jay Hawkins, informing her that Jay would like to perform in Greece, and listing his availabilities. "He had performed in Greece in the past, working with another promoter," says Demetra. "It wasn't successful, but I was confident that I could make it a success. I faxed him back. The agent turned down my offer because he thought the pay was too low and wanted more money." As always, Jay wanted more money.

Demetra realized she couldn't squeeze any more money out of her budget, but she really wanted to bring Screamin' Jay Hawkins back to Greece. In a stroke of brilliant creativity, Demetra thought they could produce a documentary about the visit for Greek television. "At first Nicholas didn't think much of the idea, but I really wanted to make it happen," says Demetra. "It turned out to be good for everyone. I faxed a new offer including the documentary idea to the agent and we drew up a contract for the documentary and two live shows in Athens. The first was to be in Salonika (Thessaloniki) at the Mylos Club on December 10, 1999, and the second show, which turned out to be his last show ever, was at the Rodon Club in Athens on December 11, 1999.

Amanda Livanou, who co-produced the documentary, got involved when Nicholas called her saying, "Screamin' Jay Hawkins is coming for a gig in Athens, and for something that wasn't a lot of money we could get the rights to film the gig." Then he asked, "Do you want to split the cost?"

"We had to pay his manager some money, which was about 1 million in drachma, some cost for renting the equipment and Jay would give us the entire next day for interview," she says. "We would spend the day with him in Athens. Nicholas did some research with Alex, who also prepared questions for us to ask. I remember very well there would be a limo ride where he would talk and then we would go to a funeral parlor and he would do hokey stuff with the coffins like he did when he was younger— but that part didn't come off. We went to the Acropolis and Jay couldn't walk up the hill—he was old and his legs seemed quite weak. He had requested that we not walk up to the Acropolis, so we sat down and had a cold drink. He got a Coca-Cola. He kept talking all day. He was lovely. He was smoking Marlboros. We went for a late lunch. He ordered spaghetti and shrimp and he didn't touch anything. He was just smoking and talking."

Since this was a Screamin' Jay project, it was not without surprises.

"Screamin' Jay Hawkins arrived in Greece the day before the show in Salonika," says Demetra. "We all went to the airport to pick him up. We had all the cameras with us since this was to be a documentary. Screamin' Jay was annoyed, really annoyed, when he saw us. He had this horrified look as if to say, 'What are you doing here?' I was shocked and turned to the agent and said, 'What's going on here? We are here to film a documentary and two large shows.' The agent said, 'Jay just needs to rest.' Then I realized Jay knew nothing about the documentary."

Everyone goes to Jay's hotel suite where he is left to talk to his agent. Eventually, Demetra intercedes. "I said to the agent, we have signed contracts, we have a crew waiting. Then I knocked on Jay's door and walked inside. I said, 'This is a big mess, but we have to make it work.' I pointed out what was his fee for the concert and what was his fee for the documentary. I said, 'I don't know what your agent has told you and or what he didn't tell you or that you simply can't remember. But, I'm a nice person and we are going to have fun. I'm not afraid of you so let's do it.' Something clicked and we became friends."

In the documentary, Jay looks relaxed and as conversational as always, telling stories with his usual gusto. In real time, Jay wasn't so congenial and calm.

"The Rodon is sold out for this gig and we have a van outside with five cameras," says Amanda. "Right before the gig and everybody is waiting for Screamin' Jay Hawkins to come out, there is a problem. Nobody really understands because Screamin' Jay is not very communicative. He's freaking out because he doesn't know where he is other than being in Athens. He doesn't know when he's flying back to Paris, he doesn't know where his plane ticket is, and [most importantly] he hasn't received any money. Jay wouldn't come out. Nicholas and Demetra go backstage to calm him down. Maybe even give him some money right there."

Demetra explains what happened. "We were about to do the second Screamin' Jay Hawkins show, the major one at the Rodon, where we had a bigger crew, a crane, boom and all this stuff you have when you want to film something properly. During the sound check, the agent disappeared with Jay's money. We had paid the agent in cash. He booked himself a flight and took off. We had a sold-out venue and Screamin' Jay Hawkins was refusing to perform [until he got his fee in advance]. We had a contract with the national television, we had the crew ready, we had 1,500 people in the venue screaming for Screamin' Jay Hawkins. We ended up paying his fee twice."

It all sounds so familiar. At the very end of his life, for his very last performance, did Screamin' Jay Hawkins pull one last scam?

Demetra doesn't think so, but the incident was the most common form of Jay's chicanery. He was always so charming and fun to be around. He was everyone's new best friend, and just when you were loving the dude, you got blindsided by the usual Jay deception. At the last possible minute, before a show was to begin, he would claim he never received his advance payment. He would not, come hell or high water, go on the stage without being paid on the spot. Panicked promoters usually gave in, thus insuring he would be paid all over again. Jay had put a spell on everyone—and got his money twice.

Jay used so much kitsch, and silly-scary stuff in his performances—a walking hand, Henry the smoking skull, charms and amulets—it was hard to take all the voodoo jive, groans, gurgles, and evocative lyrics seriously. Some people, however, truly believed Screamin' Jay Hawkins had a touch of the otherworld, the dark side, about him.

Demetra Madzouka, who was captivated by the performer, says one of the spookiest stories of her life involved Screamin' Jay Hawkins. "In February 2000, Nicholas [Triandafyllidis] was hospitalized for about 10 days because of health problems," she relates. "I was seeing him in the hospital and spending less time in the office. Business was left behind, and one of the things left undone was the Screamin' Jay Hawkins opera project, which I really hoped would happen. EMI Greece wanted to do this and we had a producer, orchestra and venue booked. Everything was ready. One night I fell asleep on my couch and I had this dream where the couch was floating and I was still sleeping. Then this huge white limo approached and Screamin' Jay Hawkins came out wearing white and holding on the stick. I couldn't understand what he was saying because Jay was doing all his Screamin' Jay Hawkins noises. I woke up screaming. It was horrifying. The next day I went into the office and said to the people who were working for me that I had this dream where Screamin' Jay Hawkins started cursing me because I had neglected him."

Feeling guilty, Demetra calls Jay's apartment in Paris. She only gets the answering machine, so she begins to leave a message, "Hello, Jay, this is your office, sorry I haven't called ..." and before she could say another word Monique picks up the phone and starts screaming that Jay had died the night before. "The people in the office couldn't believe it," says Demetra. "They kept saying Screamin' Jay Hawkins had come to tell me goodbye in my dream."

Rudi Protrudi claims that after Jay died he made himself known to Rudi on numerous occasions. "When my current girlfriend and I had our first romantic encounter in a hotel room, I was talking to her about Screamin' Jay Hawkins and, as I was talking, the lights, which were off, suddenly came on, flickering back and forth like the lights of the garage when Jay was tormenting his ex-wife in Los Angeles. When I came off the tour and I was driving across a bridge at night, all of a sudden my headlights went out and then started blinking, again just like in the hotel room. It scared me. The next night the same thing happened."

The coincidences kept piling up for Rudi. When he and his girlfriend moved to Germany, they went to a local club. As soon as Rudi started talking about Screamin' Jay Hawkins, the band played "I Put a Spell on You."

The weirdest incident happened when The Fuzztones were

playing a festival in Orange County, California. After The Fuzz-tones' set, Rudi and his wife went to the airport to catch the next plane so they could make a connection to go home. Rudi's story: "The ticket agent leaves the counter for five minutes. When she comes back she had a piece of paper in her hand. She says to me, 'Do you know this person?' I look down at the paper and it says Screamin' Jay Hawkins. I said yes and she put us on the plane and we went home. He's my guardian angel."

Before he died, Jay told Colette, "When I'll be gone, you'll see signs that will tell you I'm around." Strange things happened just as Jay foretold.

"It is not one day I don't think about him," says Colette. "The 'spell' did work on me so well that a big part of me died with him and it made my life miserable. There were material signs [for many years, noises, things moving or falling in the house], our dogs howling like wolves, which they never did before, and hearing him talking in the next room. His songs and movies played on radios or televisions getting me back to him every time I was in a forgetful mood and so many other little things it made me cry so many times. Honestly, I can't tell if it is his spirit or mine that plays tricks on me. Whatever, the difference is today and for years now, when it happens I say hello to him and smile."

Besides phantasmagoria, Jay left something else behind— a will.

The odd thing about the will was that it was written in the 1970s when Jay was married to Ginny, and then it was forgotten about. If there was a copy of the will in Jay's belongings at the end of his life, it disappeared when Monique took control of all of the things that Jay left behind. It would have evaporated into thin air for good reason: the will was written two decades before he met Monique and there would have been no mention of her name. Only one person had knowledge of the will: his old manager from the 1970s, Seth Greenky.

"I had a copy of his will," Seth explains. "All these progenies of Jay were coming out of the woodwork thinking there was millions of dollars." There wasn't. What there was included a decent annuity and about $100,000 in accrued royalties.

Seth took the will to an attorney, who was able to shut down all claims to Jay's estate except for the only two people mentioned in the will: Ginny and a niece. Well, there was one other claim. When Jay and Seth stopped doing business many years before, Jay owed Seth $8,000. He wanted his money.

"The only will was the one I had," says Seth. "Ginny's suffering could be mitigated and alleviated by getting this small annuity. In order to operate on her behalf, I signed Ginny to a management contract so I could deal with the documents. I told her the only thing I wanted was the $8,000 Jay owed me. After I got my check, I released Ginny from my management contract."

The question of what happened to the rights to "I Put a Spell on You" is still in doubt. In one of Jay's many stories, he said he sold the rights to the song back in the 1950s for peanuts. Jim Jarmusch noted when he used the song in the movie *Stranger Than Paradise,* he had to pay a licensing fee to someone else other than Screamin' Jay. Seth says that a year or two before he died, Jay sold whatever rights he had left to the song for a mere $25,000.

"What that did was damage the amount of money that his estate would generate, because the only way the estate gets money from 'I Put a Spell on You' is if the leased version embodies his performance," says Seth. "So, he retained performance rights, but no songwriter royalties." That really cut into the annuity Ginny and the niece would be sharing.

As for his three legitimate children by Anna Mae, he left them each $1.

Sookie is still waiting to get it. "When he died, Jay left me and my siblings $1," Sookie spits. "I never got it. The $1 went to my cousin in Washington, D.C. She never gave it to me. My father thought he was all that, but not to me.

"Screamin' Jay Hawkins didn't treat people right," Sookie says, reiterating for emphasis, "He was a performer, but he didn't treat people right." There is no inheritance and no spell to relieve the pain of a child abandoned by a parent. Unfortunately, emotional distress was the only thing Screamin' Jay Hawkins shared with his children and the one thing he left them when he died.

As for the song, it keeps on giving—to someone. "I Put a Spell on You" was selected as one of the Rock and Roll Hall of Fame's 500 Songs That Shaped Rock and Roll. It was also ranked by *Rolling Stone* magazine as one of the 500 Greatest Songs of All Time. There are several hundred versions of the song available for download in online stores. In 1998, the Rhythm and Blues Foundation honored Screamin' Jay Hawkins with a Pioneer Award. While Jay left the world in 2000, "I Put a Spell on You" is still alive and will only get better with age.

OTHER SOURCES
(NOT FROM INTERVIEWS)

CHAPTER 1

Triandafyllidis, Nicholas, *Screamin' Jay Hawkins: I Put a Spell on Me*, documentary 2001; www.rollingstone.com/music/music-lists/500-greatest-songs-of-all-time, #320

Liner notes to album Screamin' Jay Hawkins, *The Planet Sessions*, Ace Records, 2017

Hirshey, Gerri, *Nowhere to Run: The Story of Soul Music*, Times Books, 1984

Tosches, Nick, *Unsung Heroes of Rock 'n' Roll: The Birth of Rock in the Wild Years Before Elvis*, Da Capo Press, 1984

Schoemer, Karen, "Pop/Jazz; Screamin' Jay Hawkins as Pitchman and Actor," *New York Times*, 1991

The Blindman's Blues Forum, "Screamin' Jay Hawkins: War Hero?", May 12, 2013

CHAPTER 2

"Just Call Me Screamin,'" *Observer Sunday*, April 18, 1993

Tosches, Nick, *Unsung Heroes of Rock 'n' Roll*, 1984

Liner notes to album *At Home With Screamin' Jay Hawkins*, Epic Records, 1958

Millar, Bill, liner notes to album *Screamin' Jay Rocks*, Bear Family Records, 2008

Schoemer, Karen, "Pop/Jazz; Screamin' Jay Hawkins as Pitchman and Actor," *New York Times*, 1991

Guilliatt, Richard, "At Home With the Real Black Prince," *The Age* (Melbourne, Australia), 1985

"Screamin' Jay Hawkins: Granddaddy of Shock 'n' Roll," *Albuquerque Journal*, September 22, 1990

Hunt, Dennis, "The Return of Legendary Screamer," *Los Angeles Times*, August 2, 1991

BIBLIOGRAPHY

Liner notes to album Screamin' Jay Hawkins, *Spellbound 1955–1974*, Bear Family Records, 1990

Hirshey, Gerri, *Nowhere to Run*, 1984

Theiss, Evelyn, "In Cleveland's 'second downtown,' jazz once filled the air: Elegant Cleveland," *The Cleveland Plain Dealer*, February 5, 2012

Joe Mosbrook, Jazzed In Cleveland: Part 138—Lindsay's Sky Bar, www.cleveland.oh.us/wmv_news/jazz138.htm

"Screamin' Jay Hawkins: Jay Rock," *Rock n Roll Stars*, 1957

Obit: Billy McCann, *Peninsula Clarion*, January 26, 2001

Billy McCann, BoxRec.com/en/boxer/151577

Sarrouh, Adonees, "Gleason's Musical Bar," www.clevelandhistorical.org

Adoption No. 1197, *Honolulu Advertiser*, November 11, 1970

Jalacy J. Hawkins, Ohio Divorce Index, 1962–1963, 1967–1971, 1973–2007

CHAPTER 3

List of *Billboard* Number-one rhythm and blues hits, revolvy.com

Collis, John, *Ike Turner: King of Rhythm*, The Do Not Press, 2004

Rocket 88, Wikipedia.org

Tiny Grimes, *The Daily Squid*, 2000–2001

Liner notes to album *Screamin' Jay Rocks*, Bear Family Records, 2008

Jackson, John A., *The Big Heat: Alan Freed and the Early Years of Rock & Roll*, Schirmer Books, 1991

Hirshey, Gerri, *Nowhere to Run*, 1984

Ruth Brown, discography, wikipedia.org

The Blindman's Blues Forum, "Screamin' Jay Hawkins: War Hero?", May 12, 2013

Triandafyllidis, Nicholas, *I Put a Spell on Me*, 2001

Top Songs 1953, www.musicoutfitters.com

Screamin' Jay Hawkins live with Johnny Otis on Being Locked in Coffin, www.youtube.com

Marion, JC, "Johnny Sparrow and His Bows and Arrows," 2004

Marion, JC, "Song of the Wanderer: Lynn Hope," 2004

Bernholm, Jones, The Screamin' Jay Letters: "Unadulterated, funky, rot-gut blues," *Blues & Rhythm*, March 2017

"Hy Siegel Back in Biz; Forms Timely Records," *Cash Box*, September 5, 1963

"Timely Records Formed by Hy Siegel," *Cash Box*, September 12, 1953

Marion, JC, Philadelphia's Grand Records

Koda, Cub, *The Golden Era of Doo-Wops: Relic Records Vol. 1*, Allmusic.com

Jerry Osborne and Bruce Hamilton, *Original Record Collectors Price Guide: Blues, Rhythm and blues, Soul*, O'Sullivan, Woodside & Co, 1980

Coleman, Stuart, Repeating Echoes, *Now Dig This*, February 2000

CHAPTER 4

Jackson, L.A., "OKeh Records," *Musicology 2101: A Quick Start Guide to Music Biz History*, MKM Publishing, 2012

Sylvia Robinson, Wikipedia.org

Shaw, Arnold, *Honkers and Shouters*, Macmillan Publishing Company, 1978

Ennis, Philip, *The Seventh Stream: The Emergence of Rocknroll in American Popular Music*, Wesleyan University Press, 1992

Elvis Australia, Otis Blackwell & Elvis Presley, www.elvis.com.au

1956, Wikipedia.org

Billboard Year-End Top 50 Singles of 1956, Wikipedia.org

Billboard Year-End Top 50 Singles of 1953, Wikipedia.org

Billboard Year-End Top 50 Singles of 1950, Wikipedia.org

Tosches, Nick, *Unsung Heroes of Rock 'n' Roll*, 1984

www.atlanticcity experience.org

Herman's Bar, New Jersey Trade Name, bizapedia LLC

Hirshey, Gerri, *Nowhere to Run*, 1984

Coleman, Stuart, Repeating Echoes, *Now Dig This*, February 2000

"XXX" (Version Two)

"XXX" (Version Three)

"The Flying Saucer" (parts 1 and 2), www.45cat.com/record/101us17

Billboard, November 14

Ward, Ed, *Rock of Ages: The Rolling Stone History of Rock & Roll*, Rolling Stone Press, 1986

Marsh, Dave, *The Heart of Rock & Roll: The 1001 Greatest Singles Ever Made*, New American Library, 1989

rateyourmusic/list/goldwax217/the_top_100randb_singles_of_1956

List of best-selling albums by year in the United States, Wikipedia.org

Jerry Osborne and Bruce Hamilton, *Original Record Collectors Price Guide: Blues, Rhythm and blues, Soul*, O'Sullivan, Woodside & Co, 1980

www.alanfreed.com

Alan Freed and his "Rock 'n' Roll" Easter Jubilee program

Cleveland Ohio Press (UPI), "Boston Bans "Rock" Rallies," May 5, 1958

Woburn Times, "After The Brawl Was Over," May 5, 1958

Liner notes to album *Screamin' Jay Rocks*, Bear Family Records, 2008

Guilliatt, Richard, "At Home With the Real Black Prince," *The Age* (Melbourne, Australia), 1985

White, Cliff, "He Put A Spell On Me," *Now Dig This* #180, March 1998

CHAPTER 5

Jackson, John A., *Big Beat Heat, Alan Freed and the Early Years of Rock & Roll*, Schirmer Books, 1991

Ward, Ed, *Rock of Ages*, 1986

"Alan Freed Pacted For Six Week Tour," *Cash Box*, November 16, 1957

"Big Beat Show Features Top Hits," *Philadelphia Inquirer*, March 23, 1958

Akron Beacon, August 16, 1957

Minneapolis Star Tribune, April 15, 1958

Tosches, Nick, *Unsung Heroes of Rock 'n' Roll*, 1984

Buddy Holly, Wikipedia.
org

Delaware County Times
(Pennsylvania), May
27, 1955

Philadelphia Inquirer,
October 16, 1957

"Screamin' Jay
Hawkins: Jay Rock,"
Rock n Roll Stars, 1957

"Apollo Theater
Presents A Speedy
Variety Show," *New
York Age*, March 23,
1957

Triandafyllidis,
Nicholas, *I Put a Spell
on Me*, 2001

Billboard Number One
Rhythm and Blues
Hits, Wikipedia.org

Enrica, discogs.com

Millar, Bill, Liner notes
to album *Screamin'
Jay Rocks*, Bear Family
Records, 2008

"Singer Jay Hawkins
Admits To Rape
Charge," *Jet*,
September 25, 1958

Delaware County Times
(Pennsylvania), May
5, 1961

Guilliatt, Richard, "At
Home With the Real
Black Prince," *The
Age* (Melbourne,
Australia), 1985

Philadelphia News, June
15, 1962

Johnny Carroll,
allmusic.com

James, Gary,
Bob Marcucci
Interview, www.
famousinterview.
com

Globaldogproductions.
info/c/chancellor.
html

"Screamin' Jay
Hawkins, You Put A
Spell on Me," *Blues &
Soul #158*, April 15,
1975

Pittsburgh Courier,
December 8, 1962

Philadelphia Daily News,
January 23, 1963

Doganis, Dimitri, 57
Screamin' Kids, BBC
Cutting Edge, 2001

Triandafyllidis,
Nicholas, *I Put a Spell
on Me*, 2001

Honolulu Advertiser, May
3, 1964

Murrells, Joseph, *The
Book of Golden Discs*,
Barrie & Jenkins Ltd,
1978

Harada, Wayne, "Hilton
Hotelier Will be
Honored," *Honolulu
Advertiser*, November
12, 2001

A Night at Forbidden
City, www.allmusic.
com

CHAPTER 6

Liner notes to album
Screamin' Jay
Hawkins, *Spellbound
1955–1974*, Bear
Family Records, 1990

Millar, Bill, Diary

Watkins, Jack, "Spell
or Curse?" *Record
Collector #446*,
November 2015

Eagle, Roger, *RnB Scene*,
August 1964

Eagle, Roger, *RnB Scene*,
December 1964

Knoedelseder,
William K., Jr.,
"Morris Levy Gets
10-Year Sentence,"
Los Angeles Times,
October 29, 1988

Edwards, David, and
Mike Callahan,
Roulette Album
Discography Parts
1–3, www.bsnpubs.
com

Liner notes to album
Screamin' Jay
Hawkins, *The Planet
Sessions*, Ace Records,
2017

Eagle, Roger, *RnB Scene*,
April 1965

Liner notes, *The Night
and Day of Screamin'
Jay Hawkins*

Millar, Bill, "3.9
Screamin' Jay
Hawkins: A Most
Singular Man," *Now
Dig This*, April 2000

The Best Worst Album Ever—The Story of "Lord Sutch and Heavy Friends," www.wearecultrocks.com

The Crazy World of Arthur Brown, www.discogs.com

Smith, Steve, and The Diagram Group, *Rock Day By Day*, Guinness Books, 1987

No Living Without Loving, www.discogs.com

The Animals—Animalisms, www.discogs.com

Marsh, Dave, *The Heart of Rock & Roll*, 1989

Simone, Nina, with Stephen Cleary, *I Put a Spell on You*, Da Capo Press, 1991

CHAPTER 7

Nina Simone discography, Wikipedia.org

Whitburn, Joel, *Top Pop Singles 1955-2002*, Record Research Inc., 2003

Simone, Nina, with Stephen Cleary, *I Put a Spell on You*, 1991

Creedence Clearwater Revival, www.discogs.com

Philips, www.bsnpubs.com

Liner notes to album Screamin' Jay Hawkins, *Spellbound 1955–1974*, Bear Family Records, 1990

CHAPTER 8

Koala Record Co., www.discogs.com

Bernholm, Jonas, "The Screamin' Jay Letters: Unadulterated, Funky, Rot-Gut Blues," *Blues & Rhythm*, March 2017

Red Lightnin', www.redlightnin.com

Screamin' Jay Hawkins, *Screamin' the Blues*, www.discogs.com

Whitburn, Joel, Top Pop Singles 1955–2002, Record Research Inc., 2003

Whitburn, Joel, Top R&B/Hip-Hop Singles: 1942–1995, Record Research, 1996

Tomko, Gene, "The Right Time For Nappy Brown," *Charlotte Magazine*, March 2008

Biography, Johnnyotisworld.com

Varetta Dillard, biography, www.allmusic.com

Cioe, Crispin McCormick, "Trade Secrets," *Soho Weekly News*, August 2, 1979

"Names in the News," *Cash Box*, December 2, 1979

Hume, Martha, "A Stone To The Rescue," *New York Daily News*, December 23, 1979

"Talent Talk," *Billboard*, January 6, 1980

Allan Schwartzberg, www.allmusic.com

Screamin' Jay Hawkins, Polydor, www.45cat.com

CHAPTER 9

White, Cliff, "He Put a Spell on Me," *Now Dig This* #180, March 1998

"Spellmaker Screamin' Jay," *Ebony*, May 1957

"Just Call Me Screamin,'" *Observer Sunday*, April 18, 1993

Triandafyllidis, Nicholas, *I Put a Spell on Me*, 2001

Hirshey, Gerri, *Nowhere to Run*, 1984

Burns, Christopher, "Granddaddy of Shock n Roll," *Albuquerque Journal*, September 22, 1990

Hilly Michaels, Wikipedia.org

"Screamin' Jay Hawkins & The Fuzztones," *East Village Eye*, December/January 1986

White, Jenny, "Screamin' Jay Hawkins and The Fuzztones," *Tasty World Magazine*

Bordowitz, Hank, "Screamin' Jay Hawkins & The Fuzztones," *Island Ear*, December 23, 1985

Monnery, Pierre, with Jay Halsey, "The Magnificent Malochi: The Esquerita Story," *Blues & Rhythm*

Lecaro, Lina, "Tales of Debauchery from L.A. Scene Queen Pleasant Gehman," *LA Weekly*, September 26, 2013

Stranger Than Paradise, www.imdb.com

Maslin, Janet, "Joey, Rock Tale," *New York Times*, 1986

Joey (1986 Film), www.imdb.com

Two Moon Junction, www.imdb.com

Real Life—Screamin' Jay Hawkins, www.allmusic.com

Screamin' Jay Hawkins: Live and Crazy, www.allmusic.com

CHAPTER 10

IMDb.com, Screamin' Jay Hawkins

Triandafyllidis, Nicholas, *I Put a Spell on Me*, 2001

Mystery Train, movie

Ebert, Roger, *Mystery Train*, www.rogerebert.com

Boehm, Mike, "Screamin' and a Coffin: The Spell Still Works for Hawkins, Father of Shock 'n' Roll," *Los Angeles Times*, April 12, 1991

"An Apology to Tom Waits," *Mojo*, February 1996

Dellar, Fred, 1993

Boehm, Mike, "Screamin' Jay Hawkins: Sheer Madness in Motion," *Los Angeles Times*, April 15, 1991

Triandafyllidis, Nicholas, *I Put a Spell on Me*, 2001

"Screamin' Jay Hawkins," *The Guardian*, February 15, 2000

Houff, Dick, "R&B Legend Screamin' Jay Hawkins Dies at 70," *Blues on Stage*, 2000

Doganis, Dimitri, 57 *Screamin' Kids*, BBC Cutting Edge, 2001

Tosches, Nick, *Unsung Heroes of Rock 'n' Roll*, 1984

Burke, Cathy, "R&B Legend's 'Daughters' In Fight Over His Body," February 14, 2000

ACKNOWLEDGMENTS

I would never have considered writing a biography of the talented and outlandish rhythm and blues singer Screamin' Jay Hawkins if it weren't for jazz guitarist Mike Armando, who had played in Screamin' Jay's backup band during the 1970s. Mike strongly suggested there was a great story to be told in regard to Screamin' Jay and he was right. When I committed to the project he arranged the first interviews and gave me his notes about those years.

I would also like to thank my other interviewees, who not only gave me their time but also, in many cases, sent me oodles of information, data, photographs and recordings by, of, and about Screamin' Jay Hawkins: Jonas Bernholm, Jack Cione, Robert Cutarella, Roger Fairhurst, Seth Greenky, Jay Halsey, Colette Lebars Hawkins, Lee Anna "Sookie" Hawkins, Roni Hoffman, Alex Kalofolias, Graham Knight, Alan Lee, Amanda Livanou, Demetra Madzouka, James Marshall, Robert "Smokey" Miles, Bill Millar, Rudi Protrudi, Milton Russ, Audrey ("Lee Angel") Sherbourne, Peter Shertser, Brian Smith, Charlie Thomas, and Helen Vernon. Also, a nod to Carolyn Thomas for additional Internet research and Brian Smith for beautiful photos.

ABOUT THE AUTHOR

Steve Bergsman has contributed to a wide range of magazines, newspapers and wire services for more than 25 years, including the *New York Times, Wall Street Journal Sunday, Toronto's HomeFront, Black Enterprise, Oldies, Executive Decision, Chief Executive, The Australian, Phoenix Magazine*, and Reuters, Inman, Copley and Creator's Syndicate news services. He has been a regular contributor to the "Ground Floor" real estate column in *Barron's* and has written for all of the leading real estate industry publications, including *National Real Estate Investor, Institutional Real Estate Letter, Retail Traffic, Multifamily Trends, Real Estate Portfolio, Shopping Center World, Mortgage Banking* and *Urban Land*.

His books include: *The R&B Set—The Death of Johnny Ace, The Seduction of Mary Wells; The Friends of Billy Preston; Growing Up Levittown: In a Time of Conformity, Controversy and Cultural Crisis; After the Fall: Opportunities and Strategies for Real Estate Investing in the Coming Decade; Maverick Real Estate Financing: The Art of Raising Capital and Owning Properties Like Ross, Sanders and Carey; Maverick Real Estate Investing: The Art of Buying and Selling Properties Like Trump, Zell, Simon and the World's Greatest Land Owners; Passport to Exotic Real Estate: Buying U.S. And Foreign Property in Breath-Taking, Beautiful, Faraway Lands; and Transforming Dirt Into Gold: Land Investments, Finding Opportunities Where Others Fail To See It.*

FOR MORE INFORMATION, FOLLOW STEVE AT:

Facebook: @SteveBergsman

@The R&B Set: The Death of Johnny Ace & The Seduction of Mary Wells

@Growing Up Levittown

Twitter: @SBergsman

Instagram: @SteveBergsman

LinkedIn: @SteveBergsman